Saint Mary s College

Short sermons

Preached in the chapel of St. Mary's College, Oscott

Saint Mary s College

Short sermons
Preached in the chapel of St. Mary's College, Oscott

ISBN/EAN: 9783741190605

Manufactured in Europe, USA, Canada, Australia, Japa

Cover: Foto ©Andreas Hilbeck / pixelio.de

Manufactured and distributed by brebook publishing software (www.brebook.com)

Saint Mary s College

Short sermons

SHORT SERMONS.

PRINTED BY BALLANTYNE, HANSON AND CO.
EDINBURGH AND LONDON

SHORT SERMONS

PREACHED IN THE CHAPEL

OF

ST. MARY'S COLLEGE, OSCOTT.

COLLECTED AND EDITED

BY

THE PRESIDENT.

LONDON:
BURNS AND OATES,
17 & 18 PORTMAN STREET AND 63 PATERNOSTER ROW.
1876.

ADVERTISEMENT.

IT is now ten years since a volume of "Short Sermons, chiefly on Doctrinal Subjects, preached in the Chapel of St Mary's College, Oscott," was published by Dr Meynell, at that time Professor of Philosophy and Literature in the same College.

The Sermons in the present volume having been preached by several different persons, without reference to one another, and without any idea of publication, cannot lay claim to the same unity of design. It has not seemed necessary, therefore, to assign them to their several authors, nor to point out the sources whence the leading ideas of any of them may have been taken, *e.g.*, of Sermon III., from *La Vierge Marie et le Plan Divin* by Auguste Nicolas.

J. S. N.

ST MARY'S, OSCOTT,
  1876.

CONTENTS.

SERMON I. 1
    THE NATURAL VOICE OF CONSCIENCE THE PREPARA-
    TION FOR THE SUPERNATURAL PRESENCE OF
    CHRIST.
            (*Third Sunday in Advent.*)
                S. JOHN I. 23.
   "I am the Voice of one crying in the wilderness, Prepare ye
          the way of the Lord."

SERMON II. 13
    PERSONAL DEVOTION TO JESUS CHRIST.
            (*Third Sunday in Advent.*)
                S. JOHN I. 26.
 "There hath stood One in the midst of you Whom ye know not."

SERMON III. 22
    THE MEASURE OF CHRISTIAN OBEDIENCE.
               I COR. III. 22, 23.
 "All things are yours, and you are Christ's, and Christ is God's."

SERMON IV. 37
    WISDOM, NOT KNOWLEDGE, THE END OF EDUCATION.
           (*Third Sunday after Epiphany.*)
                WISDOM VIII. 2.
 "Wisdom have I loved, and have sought her from my youth,
    and have desired to take her for my spouse, and I be-
    came a lover of her beauty."

CONTENTS.

SERMON V. 48

THE CHRISTIAN STUDENT'S PRAYER.

PSALM CXVIII. 66.
"Teach me goodness, and discipline, and knowledge."

SERMON VI. 57

RELIGIOUS PRINCIPLES IN CONTACT WITH THE WORLD.

S. MARK VIII. 36.
"What shall it profit a man, if he gain the whole world, and suffer the loss of his soul?"

SERMON VII. 67

SANCTIFICATION OF DAILY WORK.

(*Fifth Sunday after Epiphany.*)

COL. III. 17.
"All whatsoever you do in word or in work, all things do ye in the name of the Lord Jesus Christ."

SERMON VIII. 76

THE RACE OF LIFE.

(*Septuagesima Sunday.*)

I COR. IX. 24.
"Know you not that they that run in the race, all run indeed, but one receiveth the prize? So run that you may obtain."

SERMON IX. 82

THE VICE OF SLOTH.

(*Septuagesima Sunday.*)

S. MATT. XX. 6.
"Why stand you here all the day idle?"

CONTENTS.

SERMON X. 90

SCANDAL.

GEN. IV. 8–10.

"And Cain said to Abel his brother: Let us go forth abroad. And when they were in the field, Cain rose up against his brother Abel, and slew him. And the Lord said to Cain, Where is thy brother Abel? And he answered: I know not. Am I my brother's keeper? And He said, What hast thou done? The voice of thy brother's blood crieth to Me from the earth."

SERMON XI. 99

THE CONFESSIONAL.

S. JOHN XX. 23.

"Whose sins you shall forgive, they are forgiven them."

SERMON XII. 108

REVERENCE, THE TEST AND MEASURE OF RELIGION.

(*Passion Sunday.*)

S. JOHN VIII. 49.

"I honour My Father."

SERMON XIII. 121

THE NATURE AND GROUNDS OF CHRISTIAN FAITH.

(*Low Sunday.*)

1 S. JOHN V. 4.

"This is the victory which overcometh the world, our faith."

S. JOHN XX. 29.

"Jesus saith to him, Because thou hast seen Me, Thomas, thou hast believed; blessed are they that have not seen and have believed."

CONTENTS.

SERMON XIV. 136
CHRIST TEACHING BY HIS SPIRIT IN THE CHURCH.
(Fourth Sunday after Easter, 1870.)
S. JOHN XVI. 12.
"I have yet many things to say to you; but you cannot bear them now. But when He, the Spirit of Truth, is come, He will guide you into all truth."

SERMON XV. 149
THE TRANSFORMING POWER OF THE LIFE OF GRACE.
ROMANS XII. 2.
"Be not conformed to this world; but be transformed in the newness of your mind, that you may prove what is the good, and acceptable, and perfect will of God."

SERMON XVI. 162
ENGLAND AND ROME.
(September 29, 1875.)
PSALM CXXVI. 1.
"When the Lord brought back the captivity of Zion, we became like men comforted."

SERMON XVII. 176
NATURE, THE SERVANT OF GOD.
(Fifth Sunday after Easter.)
PSALM CXVIII. 19.
"By Thy ordinance the day goeth on; for all things serve Thee."

SERMON XVIII. 189
THE VENTURES OF FAITH.
(Fourth Sunday after Pentecost.)
S. LUKE V. 5.
"Master, we have toiled all night, and taken nothing; but at Thy word, I will let down the net."

CONTENTS.   xi

                                              PAGE
SERMON XIX. 198

CHRIST WITH US IN THE DESERT.

(Sixth Sunday after Pentecost.)

S. MARK VIII. 2.

"I have compassion on the multitude; for behold, they have now been with Me three days and have nothing to eat."

SERMON XX. 204

THE BLESSED EUCHARIST.

(Sixth Sunday after Pentecost.)

S. MARK VIII. 2.

"I have compassion on the multitude; for behold, they have been with Me three days, and having nothing to eat, And if I send them away fasting to their home, they will faint in the way."

SERMON XXI. 216

ON THE CHOICE OF S. PETER.

(Feast of SS. Peter and Paul.)

S. MATT. XVI. 17.

"Blessed art thou, Simon Bar-jona: because flesh and blood hath not revealed it to thee, but My Father Who is in heaven."

SERMON XXII. 223

THE POPE.

(Feast of SS. Peter and Paul.)

S. MATT. XVI. 18.

"Thou art Peter, and upon this rock I will build My Church."

SERMON XXIII. 232
FEAST OF THE SACRED HEART.
S. LUKE XV. 2.
"This man receiveth sinners, and eateth with them."

SERMON XXIV. 242
FEAST OF THE PRECIOUS BLOOD.
APOC. I. 5.
"Jesus Christ hath loved us, and washed us from our sins in His own blood."

SERMON XXV. 256
HOW TO SAY THE ROSARY.
I COR. XIII. 15.
"I will pray with the spirit; I will pray also with the understanding."

SERMON XXVI. 265
GUARDIAN ANGELS.
PSALM XC. 10, 11.
"There shall no evil come to thee, nor shall the scourge come near to thy dwelling; for He hath given His angels charge over thee, to keep thee in all thy ways."

SERMON XXVII. 275
THE FEAST OF OUR LADY'S PATRONAGE.
"We fly to thy Patronage, O Holy Mother of God."

APPENDIX.

TWO FUNERAL SERMONS . 287

I.

THE NATURAL VOICE OF CONSCIENCE THE PREPARATION FOR THE SUPERNATURAL PRESENCE OF CHRIST.

"I am the Voice of one crying in the wilderness, Prepare ye the way of the Lord."—S. JOHN i. 23.

IT was the office of the holy and austere Baptist to be the Precursor of Christ, to prepare the way before Him; and this, not only or chiefly by announcing His Advent as the promised Messias, but by arousing the consciences of men, by bringing home to them their sin, by reminding them of judgment, and by insisting on obedience to conscience in the simple matters of their common daily duties.

He did not teach them any new truths. He would not take the name of Prophet or Teacher (though He was a Prophet, and the greatest among prophets). He called himself a "voice"—the voice of one crying in the wilderness—a stern arresting voice, speaking aloud to the hearts of men that which was already in their hearts, unsparingly enforcing claims which the inward voice had been ever whispering to them.

It mattered not who came to him; country

peasants or city artisans, rough soldiers or smooth lawyers, reckless publicans or precise Pharisees. He had the same word for all; for rich and poor; for the learned and the ignorant; for the disreputable and the outwardly moral. It was no word of comfort. "Why do you come to me?" he said; "Who hath warned you to flee from the wrath to come? It is your own conscience hath warned you. I speak nothing new to you; nothing but what your own conscience has spoken for years, and is now speaking. There is, you know it well, a judgment to come. Every day you live, this judgment is drawing nearer. The axe is even now laid to the root of the tree; and He who has laid it there is looking up for fruit, or the signs of fruit. Every tree which brings not forth good fruit shall be cut down and cast into the fire. Make no excuses. Trust not in your position as the children of Abraham. Say not in yourselves, We have Abraham for our father, for I say unto you that of these stones God can raise up children to Abraham. Your position as the children of Abraham, as God's chosen nation, will not screen you; it will expose you to a severer judgment; it will give you more to answer for. Delay not then. Do penance for the past, and now at once bring forth fruits worthy of penance."

And when the different classes of his hearers asked him for more particular directions how they were to do works worthy of penance, it was still to their conscience he appealed: "You ask me (he said) what you are to do. Do that which the voice within you tells you to do. Obey your conscience; and be faithful in the duties of your different callings. If you are publicans (that is, public collectors of the taxes), in a position where you can defraud with impunity, be honest. Demand nothing more than is appointed you. If you are soldiers, and apt on account of your arms and strength to be insolent and overbearing to your neighbours, then do violence to no man, calumniate no one, be content with your pay. And for all of you, follow the dictate of your heart in showing mercy and compassion to others. If you have two coats and your neighbour none, give him one. If you have food and your neighbour none, divide your food with him. Do that at this present moment which your conscience instructs you to do, and you will thereby be preparing yourself for the higher Instructor. Follow faithfully the light which is already in you, and it will lead you on to the noonday truth. But delay not; be not content with good resolutions; turn them at once into good actions. For One is coming who is mightier than I, and His winnowing-fan is in His hand, and He will thoroughly cleanse His floor and gather the wheat into the barn, but burn up the chaff with unquenchable fire."

Such was the voice in the wilderness. There was nothing cheering in it, nothing consoling, nothing in it of the forgiveness of sin or of the promise of grace. The very desert in which it resounded was the emblem of its own naked sternness. Reproaches for the past; Judgment for the future; Duty for the present: this was its sole burden.

And yet this voice it was which prepared the way for Christ. The preacher of Duty and Judgment was the Divinely-commissioned Precursor of the Gospel of Grace and Salvation. And it was not till he had aroused the conscience of his hearers, and taught them to respect it, that he was permitted to point them to the Redeemer, saying, "Behold the Lamb of God, who taketh away the sins of the world."

And the reason of this is very obvious. What would these men have cared for a Redeemer unless they had first been made to feel that there was a fearful power of evil within them from which they needed to be redeemed? What would they have cared for Christ's supernatural help and grace, unless they had first been made conscious of their own natural weakness? What obedience would they have rendered to the word of Christ without them, if they had not first learned to respect and obey His word of conscience within them? What credit would they have given to His warning of an unending punishment for sin, unless they had first experienced that a disobeyed conscience is even here, in this life, a tormentor and an avenger, the foretaste of the gnawing of the worm which dies not?

But not only for these men to whom Christ was coming was this stern voice of preparation needful; it is needful, too, for some of us, my brethren, to whom He has already come. And it is because Holy Church knows that many of her children need this voice of warning, that she sets before us this teaching of the Baptist on the two Sundays that precede the feast of our Lord's Nativity.

We are Christians, it is true. We have been baptized into the one threefold Name. We have received the gift of supernatural faith, and this faith, the germ of which was planted in our souls at our baptism, has been nourished and expanded by our education in the one true Home of faith, Christ's Holy Catholic Church. This is what God has done for us. It is a pledge to us that if we do not put an obstacle in the way, He will do yet more for us. For He has made us Catholics that we might save our souls, that we may pass at our appointed time from the Church on earth, and by means of it, to the Church triumphant in Heaven.

And yet, alas! the mere fact of our being Catholics is no proof that we are living as Catholics should live, and therefore no proof that we are actually in the way of salvation. If we are trusting to our outward privileges as members of the true Church, and looking to them as the evidences of our safety, rather than to the internal evidence of our own actual life, what are we doing but exactly that against which the holy Baptist warned the members of the ancient Church when they were inclined to feel secure as the children of Abraham? The faith and light we enjoy, the sacraments of the Church, and all the other means of grace we possess as Catholics, so far from being a ground of security, add immensely to our responsibility, and will, if we use them not aright, increase our final condemnation most fearfully and unspeakably; for "to whom much is given, of him much shall be required."

It is to your daily life and conduct, then, my brethren, that you must look, and to this alone, if you would know whether you are Christians indeed. A Christian is one who has received the gift of a supernatural life to enable him to live supernaturally, that is, to overcome the temptations to which his fallen nature is prone, and to live after a higher standard than that of the world. He may still have many great imperfections; he may from time to time be surprised into serious sins; but he is nevertheless a true servant of Christ, if he sets before himself the law of Christ and really aims at obedience to it, and denies his own lower inclinations in order to obey it, and goes on, striving to obey it more and more in spite of his daily shortcomings and frequent falls, and uses the necessary means of grace in order to obey, namely, prayer and the sacraments, looking for the power of obedience not to himself but to the continual influx of Divine grace.

Such is the life of a true Christian in the lowest possible conception of it. And I ask you, my dear brethren, to enter into yourselves for a moment, and to examine whether your own life comes up even to this. I do not ask you whether you are saints; not even whether you are aiming at perfection; but simply this, whether the main object for which you are living is to do the will of God, and to obey the law of Christ? whether you are offering a real decided resistance to temptation, and seeking the grace of

God to overcome it? Is your interior life in any considerable respect different now from what it would have been supposing you had not been brought up a Catholic? You would have had the same natural virtues which you have now, the same good nature, and easy temper, and honesty, and generosity, and truthfulness, which perhaps you now have. But has your religion done anything more for you? Has it enabled you to acquire supernatural virtues which were not born in you, such as the love of God, charity to those around you, humility, self-denial, gentleness, simplicity, and purity? Are you conscious of your besetting sin, your predominant temptation, and are you bringing to bear on it all the means of resistance you can, prayer, watchfulness, confession, communion? And so, if not wholly conquered, is it in the way to be conquered? Can you remember the time when you were proud and overbearing to others, and has the religion of Christ taught you by degrees to be more humble? more considerate to the feelings of those around you? Were you once in the habit of allowing your thoughts and imagination to rest on forbidden objects, and do you now carefully guard your mind and senses from all defilement? Is your temper more under control than it used to be? Are you less self-indulgent in eating and drinking? Have you overcome that indolence of mind that made religious duties burdensome to you, and have you become more regular and diligent in prayer and the other means of grace?

If you can, indeed, say an honest yes to these

questions, then truly you have great cause to be thankful that you have not received the grace of God in vain. Though far yet from what you might be, from what you desire to be, you are going forward in the right direction, bearing substantial fruits with you. You have been a Christian and Catholic to some purpose; for you are now what you never would have been but for Christ and His Church. The change for the better which you can see in yourself (so far as humility allows you to see it) is a pledge to you that under the same grace of God, and by the same fidelity to grace, you will go on improving year after year, mastering your faults of character more and more, growing more thoughtful, more patient, more bravely detached from the world, more gentle and charitable to those around you, more humble, devout, and loving towards your God. Within you there is a voice preparing the way for the Lord Christ, preparing the way, not for His first coming to you, but for His fuller and more perfect presence within you in this life, and for His eternal manifestation to you in the life to come. That voice is the still small voice of grace to which you are obedient. It is not the voice of one crying in the wilderness, for it is heard and it is obeyed in a soul which is no waste barren desert, but which is already a garden of the Lord, fenced in from temptation, fragrant with many virtues, bearing goodly fruits, and blossoming with the promise of fruit still more abundant.

But I fear we cannot all of us thus console ourselves. There are, perhaps, some amongst us who, as they look back to what they were a year ago, or two, five, ten years ago, as the case may be, and compare their state then with their present state, cannot discover in themselves anything of this spiritual progress. In them there have been no brave conquests of self, no determined wrestlings with temptation, no effort to root out their vices and faults of character, and to plant in their place holy Christian virtues. Perhaps, on the contrary, there has been a gradual deterioration of character. Perhaps they can remember the time when they were holding sin in check, and really trying to live a Christian life, when prayer was a reality to them, when the sacraments were their strength and consolation, when, during the trials and temptations of the day, they looked upwards for supernatural support and found it too. But now all is changed. Carelessness and indifference have succeeded to earnestness. The world and the spirit of the world, or self and the spirit of self, have taken the place in their hearts of Christ and His spirit. The sacraments, if not altogether neglected, are approached without fervour or contrition. Prayer has ceased, or become an empty form. Their soul, once carefully fenced in from temptation, is now open to the inroad of every proud, envious, uncharitable, or sensual thought. The little germs of virtue which once were beginning to show their head, are crushed down and trodden under foot. The blossoms of hope have been nipped and have fallen. All within them, so far as the fruits of a

Christian life are concerned, is the desolation and barrenness of the wilderness.

What, then, shall I say to you, my dear brethren, if, indeed, there be any of you to whom this applies, or in some measure applies? what shall I say to you but this,—that a wilderness as your soul has become, there is yet within that wilderness a voice, a voice which still cries and still seeks to prepare in you again the way for Christ.

You may not like to hear that voice. It has nothing in it of consolation. It is very stern and unsparing. You hear it, or rather it makes itself heard within you, from time to time, amidst the pauses of the noise of life, in the stillness of the night, or in the moaning of the wind, or when some word or token recalls to you the happier days that are gone. You hear it then, and it speaks to you of the past and of the future. It speaks to you of the past. It tells you of misspent years, of sins unrepented, of opportunities lost, of resolutions broken, of graces abused. It speaks to you of the future. It tells you that every day and week and year you delay repentance, repentance and amendment will become more difficult. It tells you that you, like those who have gone before you, will die as you have lived; and that after death will be the judgment, when your character and your destiny will be fixed for ever, even as you yourself are now shaping them in time.

But, oh! turn not away from that voice, unwelcome as it may be. Drown it not again in the noise and dissipation of this deluding world. It is true that it reproaches for the past, that it threatens you for the future; but yet it is a most merciful voice. It only reproaches, it only threatens, that it may save. Do you not know whose voice it is? You did not place it within you. It is greater than you. It is the voice of Him who is "the Light that enlighteneth every man born into this world." It is the voice of Christ speaking to you through the herald and precursor of His supernatural presence within the soul; speaking to you through conscience, that conscience, heard and obeyed, may prepare in you His way before Him.

Listen again then to that voice, and you will find that it not only speaks to you sometimes, in dreary tones, of the past and of the future, but that it speaks to you at all times, in commanding tones, as to the present moment. It says "Do this;" "Abstain from that;" "Fulfil at once this present duty honestly and punctually;" "Check at once that envious, revengeful, or impure thought;" "Overcome your sloth and kneel down to pray;" "Conquer your selfishness and give something to that poor suffering neighbour." There is not a day, there is not an hour in the day, in which this voice of conscience does not thus speak within you and enforce present duty. It matters little, at first, what the particular duties are which it commands, but it matters everything whether you obey or disobey that command. Every time you disobey, obedience for the future becomes more difficult; for resistance to it strengthens into a habit, and, at the same time, the voice within, which would break through that habit, becomes fainter and weaker. Every time you obey, obedience itself will strengthen into a habit. Temptation will lose its force. Duty will become plainer and clearer. Its light will fall on many objects which are now in darkness. You will be taught that you need a strength stronger than nature; a light brighter and more constant than the natural light of conscience.

And that supernatural strength, and that supernatural light, you will find in Him who is even now seeking, by the natural voice of conscience, to prepare in you a way for Himself, in order that the spirit of obedience and love may again take possession of your heart, in order that He Himself, through that Divine Spirit, may be reborn within you, and dwell within you, once more, full of grace and truth.

II.

PERSONAL DEVOTION TO JESUS CHRIST.

"There hath stood One in the midst of you, whom you know not."
S. JOHN i. 26.

MY DEAR BRETHREN,—During the holy season of Advent, the Church especially places before our minds the great mystery of the Incarnation, and the sacred Person of the God-Man, that great centre of the love and adoration of every Christian heart. Taking up, therefore, the spirit of the Church, let us endeavour to direct our thoughts to that noble Object of our worship, and to enkindle within our hearts some of those feelings of chivalrous love and devotion which the Saints have ever felt towards Jesus, at once our God and yet our fellow-man, our Creator and yet our brother, friend, and spouse.

There are two feelings or affections whereby we are drawn towards our fellow-beings—the affection of respect and that of love; and it is the union of these two, when happily reciprocated, which forms a true and lasting friendship—one of the richest treasures which a man can enjoy in this world. If these powerful affections of the human heart be directed in a proper channel, and restrained by the limitations of conscience and religion, they may become the foundation of the most heroic virtue ; whereas, if they be allowed to rest upon unworthy objects, and to gratify their unreasonable desires, they degenerate into passions of the fiercest nature.

What, then, is the principle which should guide us Christians in this all-important matter? What is the centre round which the affections of our hearts should be entwined? What is the friendship which will never fail us either in life or in death? What is the love which can never lead us astray, which will ever keep our young hearts pure and undefiled, which can alone guide us safely through the false attractions of the world, which will cherish us in adversity as well as in prosperity, which chastens and sanctifies the friendship of earth, which advances in time and is perfected in eternity? It is the love, it is the friendship of Jesus, the God-Man. Would to God it may be in my power to cast some few sparks of that sacred fire of charity into your hearts, while yet they are free and innocent, for that fire, when once enkindled, must grow and increase, unless it be extinguished by our own deliberate sin ; and there is nothing which could be more agreeable to the heart of our Divine Redeemer, Who has said, "I came to cast fire upon the earth, and what do I desire but that it be enkindled," and Who is particularly desirous of the affections of a heart that is young and undefiled. With this intention, therefore, let us consider a few of those relations which attract our love and respect towards our fellow-beings, and applying them to our dear Lord, strive to rouse within our souls similar feelings towards His most sacred Person.

The first and purest affection of the heart of man is the love and respect which the child bears towards his parents. Nature has implanted it in the human breast, the great Creator has commanded it, and the whole universe shrinks with horror from the wretch who violates its sacred law. But why do we entertain this love and respect for our earthly parents? They are the authors of our being, they have watched over us and protected us during the years of our helpless infancy, they have fed and clothed us, they have provided for our numberless wants, they have ever loved and cared for us, laboured and suffered for us. We know and feel that we are the centre of their warmest attachment, the objects of their ceaseless care and solicitude, that our wellbeing is their happiness, our misfortune their misery. But Jesus bears all these relations towards us in an infinitely higher degree; He is the real author of our being, our Omnipotent Creator. "He made us and not we ourselves," nor our parents, who were but the instruments in His hands. He again it was that infused into the breasts of our earthly parents that loving care and solicitude which they so profusely display, and He gave those parents the means whereby they have fed and clothed and protected us. Nay, more, He hath Himself watched over us, and tended us with more than a father's or a mother's love from the days of our childhood, before even we could lisp His sacred name, and has continued that tender solicitude even to the present day; "He hath, moreover, given His angels charge over us, to bear us up in their hands, lest we dash our foot against a stone." Never by night or day does He relax that affectionate providential care, but His loving eye is ever fixed upon us, unobtrusively, yet unceasingly, supplying our every need for soul and body, for "by Him alone we live, and move, and are." Lest, however, the idea of the majesty of an Omnipotent Creator should overpower us, and crush our love in the intensity of our respect and awe, for our sakes, and to gain our love, He has emptied Himself of that sublime majesty, and has entered into the more intimate connection of brother and fellow-man; "He has raised us to the adoption of sons" of His Eternal Father, that we might be enabled really to view Him in the close and familiar relationship of a brother. He has passed through all the different stages of infancy, childhood, youth, and manhood, that all might find One who could love and sympathise with them, One whom they could love, and in whom they could feel sympathy. Thus hath He fulfilled in His own Person all the near and dear relations which the opening of life presents; and if father, mother, brother, sister, and the close ties of nature earn and receive our love and respect, surely Jesus, who unites in His own sacred Person all these relations, deserves and claims our most devoted affection and love.

But let us pass on and notice other and different relations that engage men's affections as they advance in life. Men respect the representatives of moral and physical power; the loyal subject entertains the deepest respect and love for the person of his sovereign, the soldier for his general, the servant for his lord, and this feeling of loyalty has at times been displayed in the most heroic degree even for those who were unworthy representatives of those dignities. But when talent, generosity of character, and self-devotedness are united in the person of one who holds the position of a king, a general, or a lord, what can set bounds to the enthusiasm of men? In the cause of such a leader, life, property, the nearest and dearest ties have again and again been sacrificed without a moment's hesitation. But Jesus is the great King of kings and Lord of lords, He is our valiant General in the spiritual warfare of life, the mighty struggle for the kingdom of Heaven; He is our Lord and Master, who, by every right and title, can claim our very beings, can claim the ceaseless service of our every moment. His wisdom, too, is infinite. He is the uncreated Wisdom of the Father, the eternal "Word of God made flesh and dwelling amongst us." He is the very type of everything that is generous and self-devoted, as is abundantly displayed in that Divine history recorded by the Evangelists, which forms one uninterrupted series of scenes of the most devoted generosity and love that could possibly be even conceived. Can we then hesitate to bestow upon Him the loyalty of our hearts? Can we refuse Him that loving confidence which such relations fail not to produce even between man and man?

Again, happy is the man, who, as he passes on through life, finds that inestimable blessing, a true and faithful friend; not the flatterer who will fawn upon him in the day of prosperity and abandon him in adversity; not the chance acquaintance with whom he may while away an idle hour; but a faithful well-tried friend, one whose affection endures equally through good repute and evil repute, through the tempest no less than the sunshine; one who can sympathise with him under all circumstances, rejoice with his joy and weep with his sorrow; who is true to him in his absence no less than in his presence; who has the prudence to direct as well as the will to assist him in the great struggle of life. Such an one may each and all of us find in the person of Jesus, the God-Man. He hath truly loved us, loved us even from the long days of eternity, and He hath manifested that love by countless benefits. "Greater love than this no man hath that he lay down his life for his friend;" yet Jesus hath laid down His own most sacred life to ransom us from sin and death. The storm of adversity can never overcloud the bright sun of His friendship, nothing can separate us from His love except our own deliberate act. His power to aid us is omnipotent; His will, unlimited. He can and does sympathise with us in all the varied circumstances of life to which we, poor children of earth, are subjected. He can rejoice with us when we rejoice, as He did with the assembled guests at the marriage-feast at Cana; He can weep with us when we weep, as He did with the sisters of Lazarus over their brother's tomb; He can assist us, when contending with the difficulties of life, as He did the Apostles when struggling against the stormy sea; He, and He alone, can afford us real consolation amid the troubles and vexations of this valley of tears; He, and He alone, can preserve our hearts from the contamination of a wicked world; He, and He alone, can bring us safely to the haven of eternal rest.

What more do we require to engage our respect and love? If our hearts feel attracted by the beauty and comeliness of God's creatures, how completely does that beauty fade away before the majestic attractions of the God-Man! The beauty of earth, what is it but mere outline of form? Once change the mere outward form of that very matter we so much admire, and our admiration is at once turned into disgust. But how very different is the ineffable Beauty of that Divine Being whose sight ravishes the Angels, which is the object of the contemplation of God Himself, which forms the very essence of Infinite Beauty! If kindness and goodness of heart engage our affections, where else shall we look for the true standard of perfection in every amiable quality than in the Sacred Heart of Jesus, the good Shepherd, the charitable Samaritan, the Redeemer of mankind? If talent and wisdom claim our testimony of affectionate regard, surely none can compare with the infinite wisdom of the Incarnate God. In a word, if our imaginations build up for themselves an ideal of human perfection, if we unite together in that one creature every amiable and endearing quality which we know to be possessed by any one in the circle of our acquaintance, if we remove every fault and human frailty, if we exaggerate to the utmost every perfection that we may imagine, we must conclude at last, that as the slight ray of light which forces its way through the close bars of a dark and dismal dungeon may indeed afford some slight comfort to the wretched prisoner but sinks into insignificance before the brilliant splendours of the noon-day sun; even so would this creature of our imaginations, though exalted to the highest perfection that our thoughts could attain, become perfectly annihilated in the presence of the sublime but attractive loveliness of Jesus, the God-Man.

Still there is one more claim to our affection and respect which Jesus possesses, which no creature, be he ever so exalted, can even in the slightest degree share with Him, which is, however, first in importance and should be first in its influence over our hearts. He is our God, our first Beginning and our last End, the one supreme Good, who alone can satisfy the longings of our hearts which were made for Him, and which can never rest until they rest in Him.

This, then, is the Divine Being, who deigns to offer us His friendship. To constitute friendship, however, there is required a mutual gift and return of love and respect. Does Jesus possess the love and devotion of our young hearts? As Christians, we are bound to love Him, by the first commandment of the law, with a love which is at least appreciatively supreme, that is, to be prepared to sacrifice everything that is near and dear to us, nay, even our very lives, if it should be required of us, rather than offend His Infinite Majesty by wilful sin. This, at least, I trust we all fulfil; otherwise, we are Christians in name only. But there is a higher degree of love than this to which He is eminently entitled, and which no generous heart can refuse Him. There is the love of intensity, as theologians term it; that vehement, chivalrous feeling of love and attachment which we find in a more perfect form in the lives of God's saints, but which has been acquired and may be acquired even by those living in the world amid the distractions of life. Have we any of this love for Jesus? Let us apply the test given us by the saints who have practised it. Do we take pleasure in thinking of Jesus? Do we take pleasure in giving for Him? Do we take pleasure in suffering for Him? I leave the answer to your own hearts. This is, however, what we should aim at: "Oh, taste and see how sweet is the Lord;" think of Him more frequently, give for Him more generously, strive, at least, to be prepared to suffer for and with Him: that love, once acquired, will form your strength and happiness during life, your solace in death, your ecstatic bliss for eternity.

III.

THE MEASURE OF CHRISTIAN OBEDIENCE.

"All things are yours, and you are Christ's, and Christ is God's."
1 COR. iii. 22, 23.

FEW and simple words, my brethren, but they are the words of God, and therefore "more piercing than any two-edged sword" (Heb. iv. 12); a short and apparently easy text, like the grain of mustard seed, in outward appearance "the least of all seeds," but "when it is grown up," when having been received into "good ground," it is "kept in a good and perfect heart," brought to maturity by continual meditation, and suffered to bring forth its proper fruit, it "shooteth out great branches," which fill the whole world with their shadow. So these words rightly understood penetrate to the inmost depths of each individual heart, whilst in extent they reach from one end to the other of the world's history. Yes, my brethren, they give you a complete summary of the world's history; the history not of its outward and ever-shifting appearances, as seen by the eye of man, but of its inward, essential and eternal relations, as existing in the mind of God; the history not of its struggles and its triumphs, its sorrows and its joys, its labour and its rest, but of its beginning and its end, its purpose and its destiny.

For, what is the world's history? We read that "in the beginning God created heaven and earth." But why did He create them? For what end or purpose were they created? since we cannot suppose that God would have worked at random, as it were, and without a purpose. Moreover, we see that every created thing, and every part of every created thing, has its own especial end and object for which it was designed, and which it faithfully fulfils; and since it stands to reason that the whole cannot be less perfect than its parts, we know for certain that the whole work of creation—"Heaven and earth, and all things visible and invisible"— must also have been designed for some special end of its own, over and above the special ends for which the several parts were designed. Just as in the works of man, in a watch, for example, the end of the mainspring is to keep the works in motion, of the hands to point to the hour, and so on, whilst the end of the whole watch is to tell us the time; or as in our own bodies the end of the eye is to see, of the ear to hear, of the feet to walk, and so on, but the end of the whole man is something beyond and above all these; so, I say, of the whole work of God's creation there must be some one great universal end or object, whether or not we are able to discover what that end is.

Now, when we come to think of it, it is not difficult to see that, as God is the first beginning of creation, so is He also its last end; He is the "Alpha and Omega, the first and the last, the beginning and the end" (Apoc. xxii. 13). It must be so; it could not possibly be otherwise. We might indeed perhaps conceive of Almighty God as never creating at all; such at least was the dream of an ancient heathen school of philosophy. We might perhaps picture Him to our imagination as remaining always as He was from all eternity, Himself alone and nothing else but Him; but, if He condescends to change this state of silence and repose, if—to use the language of Holy Scripture—He begin to "work," then He must needs work according to the most perfect rule, Himself, and with a view to the most perfect end, which again could be no other than Himself. And what the voice of mere natural reason thus feebly whispers to us on this subject, the voice of Revelation distinctly proclaims: "I have created him for My glory," says the Lord by the mouth of the prophet Isaias (chap. xliii. 7); and in the Book of Proverbs (chap. xvi. 4), it is written still more plainly, "The Lord hath made all things for Himself;" and S. Paul also in our text refers everything at last to Him: "All things are yours, and you are Christ's, and Christ is God's." The end of all things then, *i.e.*, their last end, is God. But there is also, according to the Apostle, another end, subordinate to this last and general end of all creation, a second and particular end, Christ; and yet again, below Him, as the first and immediate or proximate end of all things, is man. So then, the whole economy of the Divine plan—if we may dare so to speak as though we fully comprehended what to us is at present incomprehensible—the whole economy of the Divine plan, consists of three several orders: the first or lowest, which ends in man, "all things are yours;" the second or intermediate order, whose end is Christ, "and you are Christ's;" and the last or highest order, whose end is God, "and Christ is God's." The first is the order of nature; the second, of grace; and the third, of glory: and these all are made one for the other, all enter and penetrate into one another; all depend one upon another, with a most close and intimate connection, yet without confusion.

Let us briefly consider each of these three truths, and the practical consequences which flow from them.

First, "all things are yours." In the order of nature, man is the end of creation. I need not use many words to convince you of this. You both see it for yourselves, when you consider the actual condition of the world in which you live; and it is clearly shown by the history of creation, as recorded in the Book of Genesis. Of the six days of creation, man was made on the last; the world was first made and furnished as the house, or palace, in which man was to live, and then he was brought into it, not as its occupant only, but also to be, in a certain real and true sense, its owner, its lord and master, of whom therefore the Psalmist says, "God set him over the works of His hands." The work of creation progressed from that which was less perfect to that which was more perfect, until at length on the sixth and last day was created man, containing in himself, as it were, the perfections of all the various classes of beings that had gone before, and so being, as the ancients delighted to call him, "a little world" in himself.

Man, then, is the end of creation viewed only in the order of nature; but then God's work did not stop here; the order of nature is not its own end; its end is to be found in the order of grace, for which it was created and to which it is subordinate. God might indeed, had He so willed, have ordained otherwise; He might have created the order of nature, and then stopped there, leaving His creature, man, always to remain at an infinite distance from Himself, the Creator. Nevertheless, of His great goodness, such was not His will; it was His gracious purpose, from the beginning, to add a second blessing that should far exceed the first blessing of creation, by giving to His work a personal communication of Himself in the gift of grace through the Incarnation of His Son; in other words, He made an order of grace to be the end of the order of nature. Man is the head of all things in the visible creation; but "the head of every man," or of all men, says the Apostle (1 Cor. xi. 3), "is Christ;" "all things are yours, and you are Christ's." The crowning work of God's hands was not the first Adam, but the second:

the first was but "a figure," the Apostle tells us (Rom. v. 14), "of Him who was to come;" "for *Him* are all things, and by Him are all things" (Heb. ii. 10); "Him hath God appointed heir of all things, by whom also He made the world" (Heb. i. 2). As the material world was but the house or palace in which man was to live, so men are but as the house—St Paul in his Epistle to the Hebrews uses the very word (chap. iii. 6)—the house over which Christ was to reign; the subjects over whom He should rule; the inheritance which He was to receive. In a word, as the world was made for man, so man for Christ: as the work of creation would have been unintelligible without man as its head, so man without Christ. "All things are yours, and you are Christ's."

"And Christ is God's." This is just what the Apostle says also in another place of this Epistle, already referred to; "the head of every man is Christ, and the head of Christ is God;" and again (1 Cor. xv. 24, 28), he says of the end, "when death shall be destroyed" and "all things shall be subdued unto Christ, that then the Son also Himself shall be subject unto Him that put all things under Him, that God may be all in all." Time will not allow us to enter upon the deep mysteries of Christian Theology which are contained in this last part of our text, neither indeed is it necessary for our present practical purpose. You all know as an article of the Faith, that Jesus Christ is true God and true Man; and that as to His Divinity, He is equal with the Father, but as to His Manhood, inferior to Him. You understand, therefore, how He could say of Himself at one time (S. John x. 30), "I and My Father are One," and at another, "the Father is greater than I" (S. John xiv. 28), and again, how in one and the same conversation with Thomas and Philip He could say (S. John xiv. 6-12), "I am the way, and no man cometh to the Father but by Me," and "I go to the Father," and yet, "he that seeth Me, seeth the Father also; I am in the Father, and the Father in Me." It is of Christ as Man then that the Apostle speaks, when he says of Him not that He is God, but God's, *i.e.*, belonging to God, as the world belongs to man. But then Christ was not Man only but God, God Incarnate; and it was only in and through Christ, as God Incarnate, that the Creator could receive that honour and glory which are His due. We have already seen that this is the ultimate end of all creation; and although of course in a certain sense it is quite true that the heavens and the earth, and every work of God's hands, "show forth His glory" (Psalm xviii. 1), and thereby do Him honour and service, yet they do this unconsciously, and only as the servile echo of God's own voice; faint and broken reflections, as in a mirror, of some rays of His Majesty; they have no consciousness of their own beauty, no sense of the benefit of their own existence, no knowledge of what they owe to God, and therefore they cannot offer Him "a reasonable service" (Rom. xii. 1). It is only in man that they find a thought, a heart, a voice; *he* sees their goodness and their beauty; and understanding by the things that are made the invisible things of Him who made them (Rom. i. 20), *he* can praise and worship Him and give Him thanks. But after all, how poor and weak and full of imperfections is even this, when compared with Him to whom it is paid. None can praise God worthily, but God Himself; and therefore it is only in and through Christ, God and Man, that the creation really attains its proper end and purpose as expressed in that passage of Holy Scripture already quoted, "The Lord hath made all things for Himself." It was only at the Birth of Jesus in the stable at Bethlehem, that the heavenly host could truly sing, "Glory to God in the highest." Henceforward, by means of the Incarnation, God could receive an honour and glory truly worthy of Him.

But we must not pursue further the doctrine contained in S. Paul's words. It concerns us more to see what practical consequences flow from it. And first, "All things are ours." How do men interpret this? What conclusion do they draw from it? Ah, my brethren, there needs no prophet to answer this inquiry; we need only look around and see. Are not men daily and hourly using God's creatures as though they were in very deed their masters, as if they had not only the use, but also the property and dominion of them? Is not man continually going forward, making new advances day by day in this use of the visible world around him? subjecting by the power of his genius even what seemed to be the most unruly elements of nature, and obliging them not only to minister to his wants and conveniences, but even to gratify his mere whims and caprices? Is not the very lightning of heaven, one might almost say, made now to express man's thoughts, speak his words, and execute his will? You know that it is the very boast of all the popular sciences of the day, that they are gradually discovering more and more the hidden properties of matter, as they speak; the laws and powers of nature, the uses to which everything can be put, the things which it can be made to do; and the moment they have discovered that a thing is possible, they conclude also that it is lawful, for "all things are ours," they say, "and may we not do what we will with our own?" This, in a few words and in popular language, is the practical commentary which all the world is daily making on the first proposition of our text, "All things are yours."

And now look for a moment at the third proposition, "Christ is God's," and consider the commentary supplied upon it by Christ's Life in the Gospels. "Christ is God's;" and therefore, as the prophet said, or rather, as He says of Himself by the mouth of the prophet, "I came to do Thy will, O God," and again, "My meat and My drink is to do the will of Him that sent Me;" and St Paul says, "He pleased not Himself;" and elsewhere, that though He was God's Son, "yet learned He obedience by the things which He suffered." Surely, if ever there was one among the sons of men who might allowably have taken his pleasure and done his own will here below, surely it was He who came down on earth from the bosom of His Father, and who was so pure and spotless in that human nature which He took on Him, that He could have no human wish or aim inconsistent with the will of His Father. But no! even He, the Son of God, the Eternal Word, came on earth, not to take His own pleasure or to follow His own natural inclination, but simply and in all things to glorify His Father and to do His will. "Christ is God's;" and therefore He lived and died for God.

But now with these thoughts fresh in our minds, having cast an eye on the material world below us, and on God our Saviour above us, let us next turn our eyes inwards; let us look well within ourselves, and see how far we are drawing the same practical conclusion from the truth that we are Christ's, as Christ drew from the truth that He was God's, or as we ourselves draw from the other truth, that all things are ours. The conclusion we ought to draw is quite obvious. It is so plain that he who runs may read. "It is the will of God, the order of service which He has established, that His Son, Jesus Christ, should serve and honour Him; that men should serve and honour His Son; that the whole world should be employed in the service of men. The Son of God did, and does, render to His Father an eternal and infinite honour; all the creatures of the world render us continually an infinity of services, and are consumed for our use. And such is the model and the measure of what we ought to do for our Lord. We ought in our degree to honour Him as He honours God. We ought to serve Him as all creatures serve us; and we ought to be consumed in His service as they are consumed in ours" (Lallemant's "Doctrine of the Spiritual Life").

Do we—I will not ask—do we faithfully fulfil this obligation? but do we even honestly and heartily recognise that it is an obligation? Do we even in theory fully concede to Jesus Christ the same absolute dominion over ourselves, our fortune, our talents, our time, our thoughts, our words and deeds, as we claim and continually seek to exercise over all created things? Do we seriously and steadfastly propose this standard to ourselves, that we should serve Christ with the same complete and continual faithfulness as we expect, and (so far as we can) insist, that the earth and the wind, fire and water, shall serve us? This is a plain practical question; let each man seek to answer it honestly in the light of his own conscience. Who is there among us, who, if he be not habitually living for himself, yet does not sometimes knowingly step aside to do his own will, seek his own pleasure, pursue his own ends, as if he were independent, his own master, and not "bought with a great price" (1 Cor. vi. 20)? How many thousands and tens of thousands are there who openly profess this doctrine, that man is his own end, that he was born for himself and nothing else, and that life is not worth having upon any other terms, except a man may have his own way, think what he will, believe what he will, do what he will! And how few are there, even among the better sort of people, who really act and live in strict accordance with their daily prayer, "Our Father, Thy will be done in earth, as it is in heaven!"

One great proof of the practical disbelief in the doctrine of our text may be seen in the language which even religious-minded men sometimes allow themselves to use about the religious life, as it is called—the life, I mean, of monks and nuns. What is that life but the simple carrying out into practice of the Apostle's words, "You are Christ's"? A man or woman who takes religious vows, does but proclaim that it is the one wish and desire of his heart that Christ may daily gain that increased dominion over him which man is striving to gain over the world; that he is willing and ready to be consumed in Christ's service even as creatures are daily consumed in the service of man. What is there in such a profession that should excite wonder, still less hatred or contempt, in the mind of any Christian man? Yet what is a more common subject of ridicule among many who call themselves Christians? or who are more bitterly hated and persecuted by the world? Sometimes, indeed, they will profess to base their objections against the religious life upon a part of the very text we are considering; "S. Paul," they say, "distinctly teaches that all things are ours; why then do monks and nuns deny themselves so strictly, abstain from this or that enjoyment, and renounce so much that is lawful?" The answer is obvious, and will reveal to us more fully what is contained in our text. The answer is this, that the connection between the two propositions is really a conditional one; all things are ours only on the condition of our being Christ's. If a man aims at securing the first without taking any heed to the second, most assuredly he will lose both: let him secure the second, and the first will follow of itself. "Seek ye first the kingdom of God and His justice," said our Lord, "and all these things shall be added unto you" (S. Matt. vi. 33). And it is one of the Christian paradoxes insisted on by S. Paul (2 Cor. vi. 19), that "they are needy, yet enriching many; as having nothing, and possessing all things." And the truth of this paradox is almost within the reach of common experience; it may be seen in daily life, that the secret of possessing all things consists in the most complete detachment from everything. We see indeed many rich and mighty and noble in this world, and we see the genius and industry of man continually at work, traversing the whole earth and ransacking it in all directions for the satisfaction of their desires, and striving still further to extend their dominion. But in the progress of this dominion over nature and the world which is so patent to all, who can fail to be struck with this other fact which is surely no less patent, viz., the progress of man's subjection to the world? the more he possesses, the more he is possessed; the more he has, the less he is master; his necessities increase with his enjoyments, and his own conquests devour him.

Two persons have died within the last few years,

whose histories very remarkably illustrate what I am saying. At an early period of their lives, they occupied dependent positions in the same house, and the position of the man was, perhaps, inferior to that of the woman. Years rolled by, and the man had amassed an enormous fortune, I forget whether of one, or two, or even three millions; but at any rate, when he died, the *Times* devoted a leading article to his memory. The woman took a vow of poverty and became a religious; in course of time she restored an ancient order in this country, gathered together under the mantle of S. Dominic, and the invocation of S. Catherine of Siena, a hundred spouses of Christ, founded several convents, hospitals, and orphanages, and her memory is held in benediction both at home and abroad.* Which of these two experienced the truth of the Apostolic saying, that all things are ours? You will say, Surely the first. Surely such wealth as his must have been able to command everything. Yet we read that during the latter years of his life, he suffered a continual apprehension that he should die a pauper; that he used to be driven every week to the scene of the labours of his early youth to receive weekly wages, as though he were still a menial, and so on. You will say, he had lost his senses and was the victim of a delusion. Of course he was; and for aught I know, he may have led an excellent and charitable life as long as he was in his right mind.

---

* *The Life of Mary Margaret Hallahan* (Longman) has been translated into the French and German languages, and had a large circulation in both those countries.

Nevertheless, this need not prevent my using these histories as an illustration of my thesis, that those only are the real masters even of this world's goods, who despise and reject them, or use them with a view to the end of the next world; the rest, so far from being masters of all, are slaves of all. The only true liberty is the service of Christ. All things have been made for us, only because we were made for Christ; let us live ever mindful of that end. We are Christ's by right, let us take care that we be His also in will, and in deed, that so we may remain His throughout all eternity.

IV.

WISDOM, NOT KNOWLEDGE, THE END OF EDUCATION.

> "Wisdom have I loved, and have sought her from my youth, and have desired to take her for my spouse, and I became a lover of her beauty."—WISDOM viii. 2.

SINCE last we sat here assembled to listen to the Word of God, we have been separated, and we have been reunited; we have gone different ways each to his own home, we have lost sight of each other, we have found the time which in anticipation we had dressed out in many pleasing colours, glide ruthlessly away, letting fall its burden of transient joy as the rain cloud passing overhead, and we have come again, obedient to a common calling, to find a common home within these walls. Christmas was the term of our aspirations. Christmas has come and gone. Now, perhaps, Midsummer limits our visionary future; that, too, by God's providence, will come and go. Would it not be better to make the term of our future, death? Nay, rather, would it not be better to extend the span of our vision till it rest upon God and eternity?

What playthings we are of time! Like a light boat upon the billowy ocean, we rise, and fall, and drift hither and thither, with the rise and fall of seasons, days, and years, laughing when time looks gay, weeping when it looks stern, content to vary with its changeful hours. But vary as we may in spirits, in health, in place, and in work, in one thing we never change; in our personality and that which depends upon it, our individual responsibility, we are ever the same. Though the day of yesterday is not to-day, we who were yesterday are the same to-day; and to yield to regrets that the time which of necessity passes is gone, is to make ourselves the slaves of an inconstant mistress who should be our handmaid. Time is ours, while it lasts, to labour at a work for which all times are suitable. Earnest labourers would measure its course by the fruits which they reap from it, fruits to be garnered in the spirit, and in the mind, and to endure for eternity, not by the number of times the sun has risen and set, or the earth has gone round the sun. These revolutions measure the length, not the value of our lives, and are to be computed rather to know how much nearer we are to death, than how long we have lived. As the future glides into the present, and the present into the past, so it will be until the term of life, whether it be in the present year or fifty years hence. We who now watch the waning of life are the same who will experience its extinction, and we shall live beyond through endless ages ever the same, ever one in our personality.

But such reflections we do not like to make; we fear the end, say what we may, and what we fear we are tempted never to confront. The future is elastic, we extend it at our will, and the terrible truths of life we stow away in its ample folds. It will hold all our resolutions to amend, keep till they are wanted all considerations upon such truths as death, and judgment, and hell; it will contain all our expectations and mighty purposes; what is better still, it will never grow less roomy, never overstocked, so that, if we may judge from what we see, even when we are old (should years be granted to us) and toppling into the grave, it will be still of indefinite extent. This is a fallacy which we can escape only by confronting the great truths of life, and making them springs to action in the present. The film of deceit will one day be removed from every man's eyes, and the naked truth will stare him in the face. Let us not wait till the truth comes laden with the sentence of condemnation, but receive it now when it comes laden with the burden of mercy. As the last three weeks have flown by, so will the next six months, and by God's good providence we may be all sitting here to hear the last discourse of the half year, when, day and night alternating through month and month, the six are complete, as we are assembled to hear the first: and my purpose in suggesting these considerations to your minds, is to make you ready to pluck the fruit of the hours as they fly. We have talents, we have a field to exercise them in, we shall have, by God's disposal, time in which to labour, and certainly a most precious treasure awaiting our acquisition. This treasure which we should do well to buy at the cost of all else, is the priceless jewel of wisdom. Listen to the words of the wisest of men. "To you therefore," says Solomon, "are these my words, that you may learn wisdom, and not fall from it. Wisdom is glorious and never fadeth away, and is easily seen by them that love her, and is found by them that seek her. He that awaketh early to seek her shall not labour, for he shall find her sitting at his door. I called upon the Lord and the spirit of wisdom came upon me: and I preferred her before kingdoms and thrones, and esteemed riches nothing in comparison of her. Neither did I compare unto her any precious stone; for all gold in comparison with her is as a little sand, and silver in respect of her shall be counted as clay."

We are here professedly to seek wisdom. The first thing for us to do is to desire it, and the better to desire it, let us "know the gift of God."

What is wisdom? There are many men of great talents, which they have assiduously cultivated and expended in constant study upon some branch of science, till they are proficient in it, masters of it, admired of men. They are not therefore wise, though we are sometimes weak-minded enough to fall down in worship before the splendour of their knowledge, as if it were wisdom. There are some who study the wonderful mechanism of our body; and devoting (and rightly) to each single limb and operation, the homage of all their mental powers, they will observe the rudimentary forms of a particular limb, as it is seen in the lowest species of God's animal creation, they will trace it in its development through the grades of higher species, until at length they think to have discovered the process of the evolution of the perfect limb of man. But never once during the study has their mind been raised to God in admiration of His wonderful works; in them no correspondent emotion to that of the Psalmist has sprung up: "O Lord, our God, how admirable is Thy name in the whole earth!" The study gratifies them or is imposed upon them, and they pursue it and acquire sound knowledge. Have they, therefore, acquired wisdom? We require a criterion, a touchstone to prove this, and it shall be this: true wisdom is eternal, and will bear the light of God's countenance. Solomon tells us how that he thought within himself, and pondered in his heart that "wisdom is allied to immortality," and that therefore "he went about seeking her that he might take her to himself." But the mind of the studious man may never have touched upon things eternal, and the simple truths of wisdom may be revelations to be made to him in the hour of judgment, when mercy has given place to justice. He may have never known God, nor served Him, and can, therefore, never be happy with Him. His mind may have been estranged from God, he may know Him only then, when it is too late, when the knowledge is fearful, and reveals in himself the cause of his own damnation.

But worse, some there are who pronounce their own condemnation upon earth, who have studied the nature of man, and are accounted men of vast learning, and withal have so far stifled the aspiration of their own soul after immortality, that they are content to esteem themselves little better than the beast of the field; "the fool has said in his heart there is no God," and denying the Father who made him, and the Son who has died for him, and the Holy Spirit who would sanctify him, no wonder he should come to deny the dignity and honour of human nature which is seen fundamentally in the relation of the soul to God. Such men may have knowledge, they have not wisdom. The laws of the visible world are plain to them, in it they are content to rest, but the figure of this world passes away, and they too shall pass with its figure. They have not known Him, before whom "the whole world is as the least grain of the balance, and as a drop of the morning dew that falleth on the earth," and they cannot enter into His eternal glory.

True wisdom, that wisdom which we seek, is, in the words of Solomon, "allied to immortality;" it transcends the visible and sensible world, and considers all things in the mind of God who created them. It is the highest attribute of the mind. It arises to the uncreated on the ladder of the created, and descends again to contemplate the world around with a pure and deep insight; above the penetration of the most learned of men who rest in carnal science; within the compass of vision of the most unlearned of men who seek God. The attribute of wisdom is above those of understanding, and of knowledge, judging of the principles of our intellect, testing, ordering, elevating the conclusions of science. Its office is to rise to the final cause of all things, which is God; and from so sublime a standpoint to judge of all science as it is in God's sight. It considers this created world in its relations with its Creator, judges before all of the relations in which we who are human stand to God, and in the light of the purpose of our being and the sphere of our duty, judges of the claims of this branch of science and of that to the studious application of our mind. It judges of God Himself by the impression of His wisdom and power and glory, which the eye of the wise man discerns upon each thing of God's creation. This is the wisdom to which we aspire, this is the spirit which we would imbibe; whose taste will give a relish to all knowledge, lending a quiet power and a determined will to thread our way through the mazes of all sciences, empowering us to find food for the mind and soul in subjects otherwise the driest. Again the experience of Solomon will confirm my words: "And if a man desire much knowledge (as we do), she knoweth things past and things to come; she knoweth the subtilties of speeches, and the solution of arguments, she knoweth signs and wonders before they be done, and the events of times and ages. When I go into my house, I shall repose myself with her, for her conversation hath no bitterness, but joy and gladness;" and again he says, "Now all good things came to me together with her, and innumerable riches through her hands. And I rejoiced in all these, for this wisdom went before me, and I knew not that she was mother of them all." To possess wisdom, then, is to have the recipe how to find pleasure in every lesson, and to draw honey from the most abstruse science.

Such is wisdom. How are we to find it? We must first believe that the fear of the Lord is the beginning of wisdom. A little reflection will convince us that it is so. No man can rise to the height from which wisdom looks down, by the effort of the powers which he has of nature. Human tendencies in their issue are proved to be downward towards sin and darkness, and the rise to the summit from which there is to be had a just view of created things, must be on the wings of purity of heart and simplicity of mind, in the light and faith, the strength and grace of our Redeemer. To whom does God give His grace, to whom can God give efficiently His help? Only to such as being humble are in a situation to be exalted; to such as being aware of their origin from God, and their relation to Him of absolute dependence, stand before Him in the attitude of a creature, in the attitude of reverence and fear. And to such the first grace of God serves to confirm and increase their fear, for it is always the grace of self knowledge, the knowledge of God's majesty and their own nothingness. It is a revelation of the boundless goodness of God, and their own scanty recognition of it in word and work, eliciting the sense of shame and humiliation; of the infinite majesty of God, and their own frail being and lowliness, producing awe; of His perfect holiness and purity and their own offences against Him, piercing them with a fear of His judgments. So situated in relation to God, not only in truth, but in belief and confession, we are able to judge of transient things, and to see that vain is the knowledge of earth and sky, so long as we do not judge aright of ourselves, our life, and our business here. As soon as we know this, all sciences furnish a harvest of salvation, being seen in their true light, and falling in our thoughts into their due relation. This light which enables us to order our knowledge, and casts around it the light of eternity, is "the true light which enlighteneth every man that cometh into this world," and which has come itself incarnate into the world to expel the darkness of sin from the soul by raising it again in power of vision to the dignity of the sons of God. Nay, in the mercy of God, not only is the truly Christian man enlightened in his intellect by God, but he is made a possessor of the substantial Wisdom of the Father, and the Splendour of His Substance, Jesus Christ.

Such in brief is the nature, the source, and the mode of acquiring wisdom. In urging you to love it and seek it, I speak with the advantage of having listeners who are under the roof of a college dedicated to Mary. She is in a singular manner identified with wisdom by the Church, and for a plain reason: She is the *Sedes Sapientiæ*, the Seat of Wisdom, not only as having borne in her womb and on her knee Eternal Wisdom, but as having been governed herself in every thought, word, and deed by its dictate. God governs Himself by His wisdom, and she so reflected the same wisdom in her life as to be found worthy to govern God Himself Incarnate without prejudice to His Holiness. Hence in using words concerning wisdom from the Sapiential books, I use words which may be, and are, continually applied to her. Indeed, in the Liturgy of the Church it is the utterances, description, blessings, of wisdom which are employed to express the qualities and offices of Mary. Thus while in the person of Wisdom I may say to you, "I love those who love me, and they who watch in the morning for me shall find me," I may with justice say again in the person of Mary: "I love those who love me, and they who watch in the morning for me shall find me." Let us be assiduous, therefore, in prayer at her feet who sits enthroned by the throne of God; let us beg of the Eternal Father that He will send down His uncreated Wisdom into our souls, and at the Mass of the Holy Ghost with which we begin our studies, let us beg of the Spirit of Jesus that He will come and teach us to be truly wise. Nor let us fail to her whose festival we keep this day, S. Agnes, that she would help us by her intercession to become wise like her. She was almost as young as the very youngest of us, and yet she knew how to triumph over the insidious arguments of age and experience, and at the age of thirteen to earn a martyr's crown. This is the burden of one of the responsories in our office this day. "At the age of thirteen she destroyed death and found life: for though she was counted an infant in years, in her mind was immensity of age." Truly if we love the wisdom which is "allied to immortality," though we are called away on the threshold of life, we shall be found "to have fulfilled in a short time a long life."

V.

THE CHRISTIAN STUDENT'S PRAYER.

"Bonitatem et disciplinam et scientiam doce me."
"Teach me goodness, and discipline, and knowledge."—
PSALM cxviii. 66.

IT has been said of the Psalms generally, that they are that portion of the Sacred Volume which more than any other both reveals and supports the hidden life of the servants of God in every age; and it is only another way of expressing the same truth, to say that all the servants of God, of whatever age or condition in life, and under whatever circumstances, spiritual or temporal, whether in sorrow or in joy, in sickness or in health, have always found in them both the food and the medicine best adapted to their needs. And if this is true of the whole Book of Psalms in general, it is specially so of this psalm in particular from which our text is taken. Bellarmin says of it that as it surpasses all others in length and artistic arrangement, so also in general usefulness; and indeed this is only what we should expect, from the history of its composition. We are told that it was composed for the pious meditation of the children of Israel as they came up from all parts of the country on their three yearly pilgrimages to the temple of Jerusalem; just as the Gradual psalms also were used whilst they ascended the steps of the temple itself. And this is why it was divided into those twenty-two octaves of verses, corresponding to the twenty-two letters of the Hebrew alphabet, each verse of every octave beginning always with the same letter, evidently as a kind of *memoria technica* to facilitate the remembrance of it. Hence it is not surprising that its prayers and aspirations, its praises and thanksgivings, should be of such universal application as they are, and that the Church should have appointed it to be used by her ministers every day, as being quite as genuine and suitable an expression of the wants of the Christian now, as it was of the pious Israelite then.

The particular verse which I have selected for our meditation this morning, my brethren, seems to me to express briefly indeed, yet fully, with very peculiar force, yet with most exquisite simplicity, the whole prayer of a Christian scholar; it asks for all he needs; it is an expression in words, and as a prayer to God, of all that he proposes to himself, and should strive to acquire as the end and fruit of his whole scholastic life. I don't know that these words were present to the mind of the royal founder of the largest of our English public schools; but King Henry's short address to his Eton scholars expresses almost identically the same ideas as our text, when he said to them, "Be good, boys, gentle and docile, servants of Christ." *Bonitatem, et disciplinam et scientiam doce me.* *Bonitas,* or *goodness;* not in the sense of piety towards God, which is a duty binding upon us equally at all times, but in the sense of kindness or gentleness towards our neighbour—a virtue which there is very great need, and at the same time there are very special opportunities, of exercising amid the trials of scholastic life. *Disciplina;* the very sound of which as long as we live carries our thoughts, spite of ourselves, back to our younger days, and is acknowledged on all hands to be of the essence of a solid education; and lastly, *scientia,* or knowledge, which in like manner is equally the end of all systems of instruction, and the especial acquisition looked for from all schools and colleges.

Let us say a few words upon each—and first of *bonitas,* or goodness. The word is used here in the same sense as in the verse preceding, as equivalent to kindness, gentleness, consideration for others; one of the first virtues most necessary to be acquired by the young, and which life in a community such as ours is calculated and intended to teach. By nature we are all more or less selfish; in our earliest years by the very necessity of our being, we are the objects of most tender affectionate care at the hands of others, so that, except in the case of very wise and thoughtful parents, this natural selfishness is often most seriously increased. Any peculiarities of bodily weakness, or unusual sensitiveness of character, or the accident (so to speak) of being an only child, or the defective judgment of an over-easy and indulgent parent or nurse, or too long confinement to the narrow circle of home, may often still further increase this natural tendency to selfishness, and that even where lessons of piety towards God, truth, and purity, and justice, are not overlooked or forgotten, until it becomes odious and unbearable, even in the eyes of our fellow-men, to say nothing of our guardian angels and of God. Well, the first lesson we learn at school is the necessity of conquering this fault, and happy they to whom some kind friend points out the necessity, and who have the courage at once manfully to yield to it. Yes, my young friends, depend upon it, *bonitas* is the foundation of all goodness, as well as of all happiness, in the scholastic life. I am assuming of course that you have been taught, as I have said, your duty towards God, and are trying to perform it. But next to this, your first duty towards your neighbour here is *bonitas*, kind, easy, gentle manners, that conciliate the affection, because they respect the feelings and desires of others, and this will render you as pleasing in the sight of God as acceptable to your neighbours: since it is written, "He will teach His way to those who are gentle and humble" (Ps. xxiv. 9), thus raising amiable manners almost to the rank of a theological virtue.

It was remarked long ago about men generally, and it is specially true about boys, that the worst kinds of unhappiness, as well as the greatest amount of it, come from their conduct to each other. The social life of a community like this depends, first of course on the discipline that is maintained in it; but next, or hardly next, its character depends upon the spirit of kindness or unkindness with which that discipline is administered on the one hand, and received on the other. One who is habitually kind and thoughtful towards others, putting others in the place of self, treating others as he would wish to be treated himself, whether he be a superior or a subject, whether dealing with his equals or his inferiors, is a source of endless joy and consolation to those with whom he lives. It is not much he may be able to do; but it is the way in which he does everything, that gives such comfort and gladness. On the other hand, there are those who seem never to be so content as when they are in an attitude of strife and contention against something or somebody, who seem to feel a positive pleasure in contradicting and giving pain. Such conduct is as much a breach of good manners as it is of Christian charity. "It is almost a definition of a gentleman to say he is one who never inflicts pain;" who "carefully avoids whatever may cause a jar or a jolt in the minds of those with whom he is cast; all clashing of opinion, or collision of feeling." You will not misunderstand me, my brethren, as though I were advocating a careless, thoughtless acquiescence in anything and everything proposed to you by another, merely because it is proposed to you by another, and without considering whether it be not also forbidden you by another, and that a far higher authority. God forbid. This quality, which the world sometimes calls good-nature, often proves a most fatal gift, a most evil nature indeed, evil to itself, evil to all who come in contact with it; but I am recommending general amiability of conduct, gentleness, and a readiness to give way to others, where nothing but your own wishes or convenience are sacrificed by it, in a word, that you should unlearn the love of self, and throw open the portals of your heart to an unfeigned love of others, as the fruit of the love of God. *Docet Deus suavitatem*, says S. Augustine, which is the same thing as *bonitatem* in this place, *Docet Deus suavitatem inspirando charitatem.*

We come next to *disciplinam.* What shall we say of this? It is a word used in different parts of Holy Scripture in many different senses; sometimes it stands for learning, sometimes for coercion or correction, sometimes for custom or mode of living, sometimes for moderation. S. Antoninus says that it must be taken here for that external virtue which is necessary for the avoidance of any kind of intemperance or want of moderation in anything, and for maintaining uprightness and propriety everywhere. Blessed Humbert defines it as the orderly correction of our manners, and says that it is taught by practice rather than by precept, and therefore is more easily felt and recognised than defined. Of course the word is used here for the fruit or effect of what we usually call discipline. When we ask God to *teach* us discipline, we mean "teach us, impress deeply upon our souls all those lessons which it is the end and object of all discipline to teach," docility, obedience, respect for others, hatred of all disorder and confusion, self-restraint, wise moderation, patience and discretion, and all those other virtues which do not come to us by nature, nor (without care and culture) even by grace, but can only be learnt by a wise and well-ordered discipline. Discipline is ordinarily begun even in our infancy and in the nursery; but it is in a more especial manner the exercise of youth, and the characteristic of scholastic as distinguished from domestic life. Where it is absent or imperfectly and capriciously used, great are the disorders which ensue. As we have had the happiness of being born of Christian parents and nurtured with something at least of Christian care, it almost startles us, or makes us laugh, to listen to the old heathen philosopher's description of youth. Plato, no mean authority on the facts and principles of mere human nature, compares young boys to the beasts of the forest, and says that "they are of all beasts the most difficult to manage, crafty and keen, and above all things insolent, so that it is necessary to bind them as it were with many chains." This is what comes of the innocence of children and the natural chivalry of boys, when they are not directed by sound Christian discipline. But as fire fails and is extinguished when it is continually kept down and not suffered to put forth its flame, so all these natural tendencies are weakened, and in the end destroyed, by the custody of Christian discipline, repressing all outward manifestation of inordinate thoughts and desires. We cannot now enter into an enumeration of all the fruits of discipline, as S. Bernard does when he says that it bows the haughty neck, restrains the wandering eye, binds the idle tongue, checks the appetite, moderates laughter, represses anger, and gives firmness and modesty to the whole look and gait of a man. I will only say that it is this which in an especial manner sets a seal upon a man's life, for good or for evil. An undisciplined youth sows the seeds of a lifelong misfortune, or of a hard and bitter repentance. But as Holy Scripture says, "It is good for a man when he hath borne the yoke from his youth" (Lam. iii. 27). Daily then and hourly should the Christian scholar pray, *Disciplinam doce me, Domine.*

But, lastly, he is to pray also for *scientia*. This (in one sense of the word) is what he is sent here to attain: and although at first sight to insist upon it might seem to belong rather to the chair of the professor than the pulpit of the preacher, yet in truth there is a closer connection between it and goodness than men commonly think. Sin darkens the understanding as well as depraves the will; and moderate abilities, accompanied by goodness and obedience to discipline, will achieve much more than splendid talents deprived of such assistance. This, however, I cannot now dwell upon; knowledge is so manifestly and confessedly the end for which you are sent here, the object at which in the present stage of life you are bound to aim, that there need no words to dilate upon it. Only remember ever to keep steadily before you the true Christian motive for attaining this *scientia.* "Some men study to know," says S. Bernard, "that they may be known; and it is disgraceful vanity. Some for the mere sake of knowing, and it is idle curiosity; others again for the sake of making money by their knowledge, and it is base covetousness. Others that they may build up or edify their neighbours, and this is prudence; lastly, others that they may be themselves built up or edified, and this is charity." In you, my dear brethren, the labour after knowledge is true charity, if charity consists in keeping the commandments, for this is the special commandment given to you, "*Stude sapientiæ, fili mi.*" We do not put it in the *first* place, because without goodness and discipline, knowledge only puffeth up, and is worse than useless. But we may not pass it over, because it is not enough for a Christian student to be kind to his companions, and obedient to his superiors, unless he be also diligent in acquiring knowledge. To know little or nothing at the end of your scholastic life of the very things in which for years you have been instructed, is a shameful and thankless waste of time and opportunity; and these are talents for the use of which you will one day have to give a strict account.

VI.

RELIGIOUS PRINCIPLES IN CONTACT WITH THE WORLD.

"What shall it profit a man, if he gain the whole world and suffer the loss of his soul."—St. Mark viii. 36.

MY DEAR BRETHREN,—We live in an age, when the supernatural world seems to be utterly fading from men's minds, and the sordid interests of earth are fast blotting out of remembrance the eternal truths of God. Material prosperity, the eager search after riches, the desire to shine in the tinsel society of life, are freely spoken of as the only objects worthy of a man's ambition, and it is scarcely an exaggeration to say, that virtue and vice are only distinguished in the language of the present day, inasmuch as they interfere with the temporal interests of society. Even in this country which affects such a Pharisaical regard for the sacred words of Holy Writ, we have been informed that the virtues of the gospel, poverty, chastity, and obedience, have ceased to exist; that the sublime counsel of Christ the God-Man, "If thou wilt be perfect, go, sell what thou hast and give it to the poor, and come, follow Me,"—that those words of His Apostle, "He that giveth his virgin in marriage doth well, and he that giveth her not, doth better,"—no longer suit the temperament of the present day; they may have been adapted to a bygone age of superstition, but in the present advance of civilisation, mankind can, and in fact have, dispensed with them. They are, in a word, dead virtues, they have ceased to exist. Worldly prosperity, the heaping up of wealth, position in society, these are the standards by which everything is weighed and measured; and every noble and generous Christian sentiment is subjected to the biting sarcasm of the worldling and the libertine. Nay, even Catholics, if Catholics they may be called, are sometimes heard to take up the same tone of conversation, and to speak in a similar strain, as though the words of God's eternal truth could alter with the ever-changing opinions of men. Such, at any rate, is the language, more or less openly expressed, to which you will sooner or later be exposed; such is the leaven of that society with which you will one day have to mingle.

We are always liable to a great danger of adopting the tone and principles of the society with which we mingle, it is a natural tendency of poor frail humanity, and therefore it is well to arm ourselves beforehand with the right principles of the law and gospel of Jesus Christ, that law and gospel whereby we shall hereafter be judged. Now our Divine Master has spoken on this subject in the plainest and most unmistakable terms; "If any man will follow Me," He says, "let him deny himself and take up his cross and follow Me; for what shall it profit a man, if he gain the whole world, and suffer the loss of his soul? Or what shall a man give in exchange for his soul? For he that shall be ashamed of Me and of My words in this adulterous and sinful generation, the Son of Man also will be ashamed of him, when He shall come in the glory of His Father with the holy angels."

My dear brethren, the principles of the world are not the principles of Jesus Christ; we must make our choice between the one and the other; God or Mammon—not both,—"we cannot serve two masters." Time and eternity, hell and heaven are realities, stern realities, though men affect to forget them, though men talk as if they existed not. Amidst all the boasts of material prosperity, amidst all the triumphs of scientific discovery, amidst all the records of this world's pageants, of which we daily read, one unpleasant truth is constantly forcing itself forward; death will parade in the front the long list of its untimely victims. Ten, twenty, thirty, perhaps for a few, forty years, and then—eternity. Will these weigh together in the balance? Shall the petty interests of this mere speck of existence be compared for one instant with the mighty interests of an endless eternity? Oh! if a thousand years were the span of life, as it was to the patriarchs of old, surely every reasonable man would conclude that it was all too small and insignificant to be contrasted for one moment with the boundless extent of eternity. What becomes then of that miserable term of years which we now call life? And yet men will contrast the two, nay, will give the preference to that which is so fleeting and deceitful!

Still life, when in prospect, does appear long, especially to the young; when we look forward to that apparently lengthened vista of years, which, we flatter ourselves, shall be ours, it does appear long, and the deception, for a deception it surely is, is carried on through life; even when we become advanced in years, life still seems long, while we look at it in prospect. But if we reverse the picture, if we contemplate the period of life which has gone by, does the illusion hold still? The ten, twenty, or thirty years, as the case may be, which have fled from us, to return no more, do these appear long? Nay, rather do they not appear like a dream, which flitted before our imagination in a single night? So even more fleeting shall life itself, aye, even the longest life appear, when viewed from that sober scene of reflection, the bed of death.

But this wretched life of ours is not only so short, it is so fearfully uncertain. We are here to-day, tomorrow we are gone. Neither health, strength, nor youth can guarantee us a single moment. What fearful examples of this appalling truth could I lay before you, even from among those whom I have myself known at this college, in years flown by, who once filled those very seats which you now occupy.

My mind pictures to me individuals whom I once knew as intimately as I now know you, and who, in a moment, from youth, vigour, health, and every prospect in life, were summoned by death. No priest, no sacraments, no consolations of religion; God only knows whether there was time and recollection sufficient even for an act of contrition, ere they were hurried away to meet their eternal Judge—and by that judgment must they stand or fall for eternity. And is this the life we cling to? Is it for such a life as this, and its petty interests, that we would sacrifice the prospects of eternity? Eternity, that fearful word, and still more fearful meaning; eternity, the thought of which has driven crowds into the desert, has exiled thousands from the courts of princes, has forced the king himself from his throne into the narrow cell of the ascetic, has strengthened the confessor and the tender virgin amidst their austerities, has nerved the martyr to his death-struggle! Have the terrors of eternity vanished in these our days? Faith in its terrors is, I fear, departing from the hearts of men, but I speak to those who believe and profess its appalling truths, and to such the word eternity speaks as strongly as it did to the saints of old. It is not, however, my wish to persuade you, my brethren, to imitate the example of those whom the thought of eternity has induced to give up all, and consecrate themselves to a life of austerity and prayer. Far from it, if you have not received a vocation from God to that state of life, heaven forbid that you should ever embrace it; that state of life requires peculiar graces, which all do not receive. No, we must take our position at that post to which God has called us, and if that post be in the world, to the world must we go, and work out our salvation even there with fear and trembling. But what I do wish to impress upon your minds is this important truth, that while we live in the world, and enjoy the goods of the world, we must never allow the interests of the world to interfere with the interests of eternity and of our immortal souls; we must resolve with a lifelong resolution, that no consideration of the love or fear of anything on this earth shall ever induce us to act against what our conscience tells us to be the Holy Will of God, to offend the Majesty of Heaven by grievous sin. Religion and the duties of religion must always hold the foremost place, the world and the interests of the world only the secondary place in our thoughts, words, and actions. All this does not entail the sacrifice of any real success in life, or of any true happiness. It does of course entail the necessity of considerable self-restraint, it will demand at times the bold avowal of our religious principles; occasionally, if God so wills it, it may require a very great sacrifice; but it does not preclude the highest success in life, the noblest aspirations to which our talents and energy can be directed. It does not include moroseness of character nor unfitness for mingling in society; on the contrary, it is perfectly consistent with all the qualities of a true English gentleman; nay, more, it is the only groundwork on which true eminence and real happiness can be based.

There is a character in our own English history, which by these very qualities has earned for itself the praise and admiration of all writers, Catholic and Protestant, and I know not any example that could be laid before young men entering upon life, which is more appropriate as a model, or which more clearly displays the practical carrying out of true Catholic principles in dealing with the world. I refer to that high-minded statesman and martyr, of whom England may well be proud, Sir Thomas More. This truly great man was no recluse whose austerities might repel us, as being beyond our strength, no worker of miracles that would place him apparently out of our reach, not even a canonised saint; but he was a simple-minded, highly principled Christian and Catholic, who, taking that position in the world to which God had called him, by his own energy, by his talents, and by his integrity, worked out for himself a career, which would satisfy the ambition of the most aspiring. In his profession of the law he rose from the position of a simple citizen of London to the highest dignity which an English subject could at that time attain, that of Lord High Chancellor of the kingdom; and by his integrity, his steady application to the duties of his office, and his eminent success in that distinguished post, he has earned for himself an undying reputation. As a member of Parliament he became the leader and speaker of the House of Commons, and by his unflinching maintenence of the rights and liberties of the subject in that age of debasement and political slavery, he formed a striking contrast with the miserable servitude of that wretched semblance of a Parliament, which crouched before the tyranny of our Tudor kings. As a courtier, he was honoured with the especial friendship of his sovereign, and continued as one of his principal ministers, until that impious monarch made his own service inconsistent with the service of God. His cheerfulness of disposition and sense of humour have become almost proverbial; he assembled around himself a society of all the most intellectual spirits of the age, and the ablest and most distinguished men of the world at that period were proud to own the friendship of Sir Thomas More. He was a man, too, that was remarkable for his devoted attachment to his family, and the affectionate regard which subsisted between himself and his favourite daughter, Margaret, has been the subject of much admiring comment. What greater success, or what more distinguished qualities, as a citizen and a man of the world, could he have displayed? Sir Thomas More was all this, but he possessed still nobler qualities, which were the real groundwork of his brilliant career. He was a thorough Catholic, deeply imbued with the highest principles of religion. " Every line of his writings, every word that fell from his lips, bespoke a habit of mind, that had completely accustomed itself to dwell on the next world as the only reality, and on the present life as merely a waiting season, the tediousness of which he sought to wile away by a pleasant humour, but which, save in its relation to what lay beyond, was utterly worthless in his eyes. Life was to him so truly a pilgrimage, that he was wont to express his wonder, how any man, who was travelling to his own home where he should have abundance of all things, could think it worth his while to turn ostler in an inn by the wayside and so die in a stable." He was thoroughly religious and devout, he heard Mass daily, he made his daily meditation, and it was his constant habit, before undertaking any matter of importance, to confess, to communicate, and to hear Mass. He made no secret of his religious sentiments, he was proud of showing that he served his God even more zealously than he served his king. He took the part of cross-bearer in the public procession of the Blessed Sacrament on Corpus Christi, and sang with the rest in the choir of his parish church, even when he was Lord High Chancellor of England ; and when, on a certain occasion, the Duke of Norfolk reproached him with it, saying, with a sneer: " What, is my Lord Chancellor turned parish-clerk ? You dishonour the king and his office ; " Sir Thomas More mildly replied, " Not so, the king, your master and mine, will surely not be offended by my serving his Master and mine." Still, his devotion was, as far as possible, removed from anything Puritanical ; he was a man who enjoyed himself, and liked to see others do the same, and who relished a joke, to use the words of a biographer, " as much as he did a quotation from Plato." He lived, moreover, in times very closely resembling our own, when religion was exposed to raillery and contempt, and the freedom of religious opinion was beginning to be everywhere agitated; and so nearly did this spirit reach his own doors, that his dear friend, the celebrated Erasmus, and his own son-in-law were deeply infected with that scoffing and irreligious tendency; but Sir Thomas More was of too earnest a religious feeling to be thus moved; the only effect upon him was that his friendship for Erasmus became considerably cooled, and that he ceased not to pray for his unfortunate son-in-law till he had completed his conversion. At length it pleased Divine Providence to put his faith and virtue to a severe trial. The question of the king's divorce was quickly followed by that of his spiritual supremacy, and Sir Thomas More was called upon to subscribe to that which his conscience forbad. Then did the true heroism of his character display itself to the world; he was stripped of his goods and deprived of his liberty; he was torn from the embraces of his family; but he remained firm to his religious principles, and he finished a glorious life by the still more glorious death of a martyr to the cause of God and Holy Church.

VII.

SANCTIFICATION OF DAILY WORK.

*"All whatsoever you do in word or in work, all things do ye in the name of the Lord Jesus Christ."—*Col. iii. 17.

THERE need no words, my brethren, to show you how the name of Christ is the life and centre of our holy religion, the key to all its ceremonies, the summary of all its dogmas, the life of all its devotions, the object to which it ever looks, the centre round which everything turns, the object at once of our faith, our hope, and our love. All our prayers are offered up in this Name, and all our blessings, whether of persons or of things, are given in no other. This Holy and Blessed Name it is into which we were all baptized in our infancy. "Was Paul crucified for you?" asks the Apostle (1 Cor. i. 13), "or were you baptized in the name of Paul?" "Do penance," says S. Peter to the penitent Jews, "and be baptized, every one of you in the name of Jesus Christ, for the remission of your sins" (Acts ii. 38). And as it is with the beginning of our spiritual life in Baptism, so is it also with the other sacraments, and with every ordinance of the Church. All is done in the name of the Lord Jesus Christ. Do we preach to you God's Holy Word? "We are ambassadors for Christ," says S. Paul (2 Cor. v. 20), "God as it were exhorting by us; for Christ we beseech you, be reconciled to God." Do we stand at the altar to celebrate the holy sacrifice of the Mass? Whose words do we repeat? In whose name do we act? You know, dear brethren, for you were taught it in your Catechisms, that we do nothing there in our own names, nor in the name of any man; we but repeat the words and the actions of Jesus Christ; He is the great High Priest in that tremendous sacrifice; we are His ministers and representatives. Or again, we join two persons together in Holy Matrimony, and it is the name of Jesus that blesses and sanctifies the union. Or we sit in the tribunal of penance: a sinner kneels before us and pours into our ears the sad history of the sins by which his conscience is burdened; and by and by, the gracious words are spoken—"*Dominus noster Jesus Christus te absolvat*, and I by His authority absolve thee." Or again, we kneel by the bedside of the sick and dying; and it is the name of Jesus which gives them peace in that hour of trial: we bid the dying soul go forth out of this world "in the name of Jesus Christ, Son of the living God, who suffered for thee;" and finally, when we commit his body to the dust, the name of Christ still follows us to the grave: it is He whose voice is heard there, bringing soft and sweet words of unspeakable comfort to the Christian mourner—"I am the Resurrection and the Life ; he that believeth in Me, though he be dead, still liveth."

Thus in every circumstance of our religious life, in every detail of our worship, we do all whatsoever we do in the name of our Lord Jesus Christ. The whole cycle of the Christian year does nothing else but bring before us the whole round of His life upon earth; it is one continual commemoration of His name. We enter upon it in the season of Advent, with pious meditation on His first and patient expectation and watchfulness for His second coming: then we celebrate His Nativity, His circumcision and manifestation to the Gentiles : in Lent we commemorate His sacred Fast; in Passion-tide His bitter sufferings and death : at Easter, and throughout the Pentecostal season, His glorious Resurrection and Ascension, and the sending of His Holy Spirit according to His promise. And not only in these great feasts, but even the lesser ones also, in every birthday of every Apostle, Martyr, Confessor, and Virgin, it is the glories of Jesus and of His grace that we really celebrate ; His works that we adore, and them only as of and in Him.

However, all this, true and important though it be, falls very far short of the full scope of the Apostle's meaning, when he bids us do all, whatever we do, in the name of Christ. He is speaking not of mere acts of religion, strictly so called ; but of all our acts: not what we do or say in church only, but of everything that we do or say everywhere and always, every day and all day long; in our work and in our play, as well as in our prayers. And my dear brethren, this is a very important lesson which the Apostle often repeats in his different Epistles, but which the Devil is continually striving to put out of our minds, or at least to prevent us from putting into practice. It is one of his most common and most successful devices for the ruin of men's souls, to teach them to separate religion from the daily affairs of life. It is his aim to bind us to this earth. The world and the affairs of the world, whether great or small, pleasure or business, industrious employment or frivolous amusement, all these things are his instruments for keeping us away from God. He is too wise, however, to set them always in open opposition to one another, to offer direct resistance, and to deny God's claims upon our time, our thoughts, our affections. No, he only professes to wish to set a limit to that claim. "Everything," he would seem to say, "everything in its right place; religion in the church, business or pleasure in the world. God in the church, pleasure at home, Mammon in the shop and the market place. God on Sundays, and perhaps for a few minutes in the mornings and evenings of other days; business on week-days, or pleasure, if you are able to afford it: but don't mix them up together; keep them always distinct, or you will involve yourselves in many scruples and difficulties." This, I say, is the language of the Devil; and alas! too frequently it is the prac-

SANCTIFICATION OF DAILY WORK.

tice of men; of men who deceive themselves, and fancy that they are doing all that is necessary to save their souls, because they fulfil some outward exercises of religion occasionally, though the thought of God is habitually absent from their ordinary occupations (1 Cor. x. 31). They vainly imagine that they can do what our Lord has declared to be impossible, viz., unite the worship of God and Mammon, giving to each its due, and so becoming entitled (in the end) to receive the reward of both.

It is in opposition to this too common practice of the world that the Apostle's injunction is directed, bidding us do all things in the name of the Lord, and "to the glory of God." He insists on the necessity of our glorifying God *in* and *by* our daily occupations. And in the Middle Ages—in the ages of faith, as they are called, it is wonderful to see how literally and exactly our Catholic forefathers fulfilled this precept. Then in public and private life alike, and in every department of both of them, in peace and in war, in the school and in the market, in the family and in the Parliament, in the chamber of birth, at the bridal and at the funeral, every act of any moment had its own special consecration. Nay, the mere business transactions of individuals, the seaman's bills of lading and the merchant's articles of agreement, the testaments of the dying and the monuments of the dead, all were blessed and hallowed at that time by solemn invocation of the name of Jesus or of the ever adorable Trinity. Even to this day, in the

Tyrol and some other Catholic places, the ordinary salutation of simple peasants, as they meet one another in the road, is distinctly Christian, and contains an act of faith, of praise and thanksgiving. Such practices, however, are extinct among us, and in our actual circumstances, it would be unwise, and indeed impossible, to revive them.

Nevertheless, some outward and visible acts of religion are most useful, not to say essential, if we would observe the Apostolic precept faithfully. For one great secret of the power which the world and the world's occupations have over us is that they are sensible; that we can see, touch and handle them, and so they gain the mastery over the mind through the channels of our senses. Moreover, they are always around us; they close us in on every side, and are never weary of inviting us; they gain our attention, and in the end our affections, by their continual presence and never-ending importunity. The Church, therefore, has provided certain remedies which shall counteract this power of the world and turn its weapons against itself. We spoke just now of her yearly festivals; but over and above these, every week of every year brings before us the same high and sanctifying memories, shedding across our daily path holy thoughts, a bright vision of joy and peace through the name of Jesus. Sunday is, as it were, a weekly Easter; Friday, with its law of abstinence, fixes our eyes and hearts once in every week on Mount Calvary: Thursday, to all good

Catholics, is full of thoughts of the Blessed Sacrament; Saturday, of Christ's Virgin Mother, and so of the rest. Yea; even more than this, the hours of every day of every week, whilst to others they pass unheeded, and are alike allotted to schemes of worldly business or empty mirth, are made by the devout Catholic so many breathing-places and helps to his spiritual advancement, inviting him to withdraw for a moment from the outward scene around him, and to renew and strengthen his inward and hidden life in Christ. First, every Catholic child is taught as soon as he awakes to sign himself with the sign of the Cross and to call upon the name of the most Holy Trinity; next, he is invited and encouraged to begin the day, if possible, by assisting at the holy sacrifice of the Mass, by making a short meditation on some mystery of faith; three times a day in a Catholic country, and now in many places of our own, the Angelus bell invites him to thank God for the great blessing of the Incarnation, and to pray that he may be made a partaker in its fruits; then again grace before and after meals, the prayer before each period of your study, the visit to the Blessed Sacrament after dinner; all these things give you an opportunity, nay, oblige you from time to time to lift up your hearts and minds to God in the midst of your daily work, and so to sanctify it. And besides these public practices which the general order and discipline of the house impose upon you, doubtless many of you have also other pious practices of a similar kind, taught you by a devout mother perhaps, or picked up from the life of some saint, or suggested by the preacher at some retreat, and you have learnt from your own experience how useful these helps are for keeping alive in your souls a continual sense of the abiding presence of God. The end to be aimed at, the sanctification of our daily lives, is an inward and a spiritual work, and therefore no mere observance of outward forms or ceremonies can secure its being done well; and yet it will hardly be done at all without such outward forms.

An old mediæval writer has quaintly said that God cares more for adverbs than for substantives; by which he means that God looks not so much to the outward act as to the inward motive; that it is not the thing itself done, so much as the way in which it is done, the reason and the manner of doing it, which pleases Him and which He rewards. Thus, it is quite possible to perform even our religious duties in a cold and heartless way, as a mere matter of routine, without any real act of faith or love or reverence. Contrariwise, it is possible by a momentary lifting up of the heart to God, by a short ejaculatory prayer, or by a silent aspiration of the soul, to ennoble and sanctify our most secular, and even trivial, occupations: and it is this duty which I would urge upon you to-day. At the beginning of every work, remind yourself that you are doing it for the love of God and because He has commanded you to do it. In the course of the work, frequently renew this pious intention, and when the work is done, thank God who has enabled you to do it. Learn to see God in everything, to recognise and adore His Presence; so will you begin and maintain that union with Him here, the continuance and perfection of which is to be the reward of the blessed for ever.

VIII.

THE RACE OF LIFE.

"Know you not that they that run in the race, all run indeed, but one receiveth the prize? So run that you may obtain."—1 COR. ix. 24.

WHEN S. Paul wrote these words to the Corinthians he was addressing a highly civilised and intellectual community, proud of its philosophical speculations, and refined, after the evil pattern of paganism, that is, in sensualism and sin.

The danger to the Christian converts in such a community would be, that their old habits would tend to make them *theoretical*, rather than *real*, Christians; full of words, empty of deeds. Already, in fact, their contentions, together with grave scandals which had occurred, had brought upon them the severe though loving rebuke of the Apostle. In this passage then of his epistle he makes use of an illustration which would bring home in a most telling way the lesson he had to teach them.

Among the pleasures of their time those of which they seem to have been most passionately fond were the sports of the Circus, the Isthmian games, in which were included the chariot races and all kinds of manly exercises. The Apostle turns to these for his argument, and we will try to follow it.

We must remark, to begin with, that it consists of two parts; one in which he reminds them how and with what spirit their fellow-citizens contend in the arena, the other, in which he shows them, from the example of his own life, how he would have *them* strive, with a like ardour, for a nobler prize.

The argument may be summed up in this way:— Your life is a race and a contest, and heaven is the prize. If they who run in your games, where only one receives the crown, so strive as you know, what should be your strife for the everlasting crown? If " every one who strives for the mastery " in these contests " refrains himself," that is, bridles his inclinations, withholds himself from self-indulgence and enervating pleasures, and this for a victor's wreath, a poor fading crown of bay leaves and the applause of his fellow-citizens, what struggle with ourselves and our passions shall be too great, what self-denial too severe, for us who strive, not for a fleeting honour or an empty name, but for a crown and a kingdom such as God holds out to us.

But, because he knows that example is better than words, the great Apostle, in that perfect humility which is not afraid to manifest its own excellence where all the glory is given to God, goes on to show that in his own life he practises these lessons which he is teaching them. "I therefore," he says, "so run. I so fight. I chastise my body." But he tells us more. He tells us *how* it is that he runs, *how* he fights. And in this lies the pith of his lesson. "I do run," not as at an uncertainty, not vaguely and blindly, like the reckless charioteer in your races, who, mad with excitement, and thinking only of the rival at his side, misses the goal and wanders from the course. No! with the victor's keen gaze my eyes are fixed unceasingly on the goal of my life, its end and crown. To this my soul is turned and all its energies are bent on reaching it; the distractions that beset me on either hand cannot draw me aside from my course.

"I fight," but how do I fight? "Not as one beating the air," not with aimless blows that, falling wide of my adversary, waste their strength in air; but I strike home, straight and true. My foe is my rebellious nature. That I chastise and subdue. And not in times of temptation only, when the actual contest is begun. No! but as your own competitors, who, weeks and months, years perhaps, before the day of trial, have trained and exercised themselves with hard fare and stern self-control and untiring practice, banishing excess and luxury from their lives, *so* "I chastise my body."

Is it necessary to say how all this comes home to ourselves? This life we are living, is it not for each of us the same race and strife as S. Paul's was, and for the same goal and prize? How then are we striving? How do we run? How do we fight? Let us look at our lives and see! Three words will almost sum them up:—Prayers, studies, recreations. From

THE RACE OF LIFE.

the way in which we are doing these we may tell what part we are taking in the contest of life, and what is our chance of heaven.

What meaning then have prayers with you? Are they in truth speaking out of your hearts to God, or opening a book and thinking of everything else but God? It is true that perfect prayer, unbroken by distractions, is beyond the power of most among you, but it is equally true that you can, if you will, call to mind that you are kneeling in God's presence, and make some attempt to thank Him for His gifts, and ask Him for what you need. To those who try to do so honestly He is a merciful and most gentle Father, who pardons a thousand imperfections if only our good will is there. But if to any one of you the time of prayers is a time of decorous idleness, in which he ignores God while he pretends to worship Him, and insults Him by deliberately turning his thoughts away from Him, let such a one ask himself how far *this* part of his life will help him to attain his end, and if he is not rather running wide of the course and missing the goal.

To some their studies may seem to have less to do with the matter, and their playtime not at all. It is a grave mistake. What did S. Paul mean when he said to those same Corinthians (1 Cor. x. 31), " Therefore, whether you eat or drink, or whatsoever else you do, do all things for the glory of God"? Just this, that if you would keep before yourselves the goal of your life, its purpose (and your faith tells you it is to please God and save your soul), every one of these little ordinary actions of your day would help you on towards heaven.

But life is not only the race in which we must run with eyes fixed upon the goal; it is the contest in which we must fight, fight with the determination to conquer. So to run and so to win, we must be resolved to turn aside for no pleasure that would draw us from the way of what is true and right, to strike down with determined will the temptations that would wrestle with us to rob us of our prize. Which amongst us is without his tempter and his adversary, and who is there that does not know his enemy? Time after time he has named him in confession. Time after time he has striven with him; and alas! too often he has been vanquished in the strife. It is this habitual fault, confessed so often and still unmended, that we must fight and master if we would win our crown.

Is it an impatient temper, a bitter tongue, a habit of sloth or of untruthfulness? Is it worse than these? Look your foe in the face and pray God for strength to overcome; this at least you can do. As often as you kneel at Mass and bow your heads, as the bell warns you that God is come once more to His mercy-seat upon our altar, you can say to Him: "Give me, O my God, the grace and strength to fight this day's fight, to overcome this day's temptations, to keep my heart fixed upon the goal and prize which I must win at last if I would not lose all!" Try to practise this much at least of St Paul's lesson. You cannot *drift* into heaven. You must *strive* for it. For remember "the kingdom of heaven suffereth violence, and the *violent* bear it away" (Matt. xi. 12). Therefore, once more I say to you, "so run," so strive, that you may win your everlasting crown.

IX.

THE VICE OF SLOTH.

"Why stand you here all the day idle."—S. MATTHEW xx. 6.

THE householder went out, at different hours of the day, in quest of labourers for his vineyard. Each time he found men loitering about the common market-place, apparently too idle to get employment, and wasting the precious time of day in waiting to be hired. He reprimanded them for their idleness; and they excused themselves on the plea that no one had, as yet, offered them work. In this is presented for our instruction and profit a very concise but faithful picture of the vice of sloth, and its consequences. A few moments' consideration will be sufficient to show that the same rebuke is perhaps deserved by many among us.

The hours of our day are the particular times and seasons when God visits us with some very special favour for the good of soul or body. Education is one of these many gifts of God, and by no means the least important; and from time to time the same searching question is put to us, as to the idle labourers in the gospel. Can each of you, my brethren, listen to those words of rebuke, and tremble not at the answer you must give? You cannot say "No man hath hired us;" for you have been called, each one distinctly; and you have each had your work allotted. You are already in the vineyard; and the question you have to answer is, whether you are faithfully doing that portion of labour assigned as yours. Let not your conscience shrink from the examination, however unpleasant it may be; let your answer be candid and honest. The knowledge that you will gain of yourself will be most beneficial, and tend to make you work henceforth with greater earnestness. Occasionally to look back on what has been done, very often suggests a better mode of working for the future.

We have met together once again, my dear brethren, to resume the labour of the past year. We have had our resting-time; and refreshed, must now in earnest continue the work of our education, which we were sent here to receive. That education is of a threefold nature: the training of the soul in the ways of virtue and religion; the training of the mind by the infusion of knowledge; and the training of the body by the necessary restraint of sound discipline and healthful recreation. Each part is the necessary complement of the other; and you are indeed happy in having such a training, for outside the Catholic college, you will find that education is but an empty sound, a meaningless term, for it professes now-a-days to do without God and His revelation. Yet, says the

Holy Spirit, "the fear of the Lord is the beginning of wisdom."

But, my brethren, there are some of you who very closely resemble the idle labourers in the Parable, and to such would I more especially address my words. I would ask such the householder's question, "Why do you stand here all the day idle?" Idleness and inactivity, one would think, were the very purpose of your life. This evil habit, this noxious vapour, like a slow poison, is doing its work of mischief amongst you, and is robbing you of that spirit of emulation and energy which should be characteristic of every student. This is no delusion; your work proves it; your outward demeanour betrays it; it is amongst you in every degree, both of carelessness, of indifference, of indolence, of sluggishness, of self-indulgence, and of downright slothfulness.

You will marvel, perhaps, how it has come amongst you; whence it had its beginning. In most cases, the first appearance of idleness is in spiritual matters; the training of the soul is the first to suffer. "An enemy hath done this." The devil, ever busy, watches his opportunity, and lays his snare successfully. He makes your conscience easy and pliant. He falsely persuades you that a little fatigue, which might easily be overcome, is quite a sufficient excuse to omit now and again, or at least for once, this or that good practice; and so, you are deluded into thinking that you have been too particular, too severe with yourself, and that a greater latitude is allowable than you had before imagined. Once triumphant, he returns to the attack with greater force ; and by degrees, you become careless in your daily examination of conscience ; one devotion or religious duty after another is given up ; and the mischief is soon complete.

It is very seldom that a boy becomes remiss in his studies first of all ; for a conscientious student would soon remedy any defect of this kind : goodness and idleness never walk hand in hand. Lay then the axe to the root, and begin your work again. It requires a strong will and much sacrifice to give up what you have so long indulged in, what has now become a second nature to you ; but it can be done, and prayer and the grace of the Sacraments will assist you. Kneel in God's presence, but not in a lounging, careless, disrespectful manner ; take up your prayerbook and use it ; it cannot be wearisome to join with others in answering the prayers ; pray then, for you and all men need prayer ; show that you are a disciple of the cross, make then the sign of the cross at the proper time, you will thereby disarm the devil's power ; make your daily examination of conscience carefully, you will then be very different from what you are.

"Why do you stand here all the day idle ?" may again be asked you on another point, the training of your mind. You were sent here by your parents for the purpose of acquiring that knowledge which is to fit you for the great world outside. They are anxiously waiting for the return you intend to make. Your education is undoubtedly in many ways a great sacrifice to them, and they alone know what a parent's pain and grief are, when their child defeats their object, and returns to them no better, but rather worse, than when he left them. My brethren, you commit, and it is no exaggeration, a serious injustice to your parents if you neglect your work and waste your time; and injustice that is grave implies a restitution equally grave. The thought is terrible. You are not required to do too much. Your recreation and your study time are judiciously arranged; but the fact is, you set yourself against study, simply because it is work. You spend too much of your time in day-dreaming; and this, of all things, is most harmful. It so stultifies the mind, and its great powers and faculties, as to render it absolutely incapable of thinking upon any subject, even for a few moments, except on its own vain or idle fancies. This experience tells us is a very common fault; and the habit becomes so deeply rooted, that you cannot tell when you are under its influence. It is most deceptive to others also; because, however intent and studious you may appear, it is most likely you are wandering far away, abstracted from all sense of duty, existing only in your own delusions. It cannot bring any good whatsoever to you; rather, it makes you childish, inconstant, foolish, ignorant. Little do you know the difficulty there is in eradicating deeply rooted habits. It is, moreover, a direct road to your spiritual ruin; for you harbour at times evil thoughts; and neither the presence of God, your lessons, your games, or the society of others, will prevent you indulging in your folly, until at last you have destroyed every spark of energy and the very life of your soul. And it would be well, if it staid even here. Your example, unfortunately, influences those among whom you associate: and, unconsciously though it may be, still you poison an atmosphere that others have to breathe. It destroys the energy of those who have been working and enduring the burdens of the day and its heats, and chills the ardour of those who have just entered upon their work. The tree that is healthy and promising is destroyed by the withering blast of bad example; and the fruit that was good to look upon, and fair to touch, is snatched away with a stealth that no hand can stay. My brethren, how serious a thought is this; and yet, perhaps, it has never entered your mind before how fearful an injustice is done to your parents, your superiors, your companions, yourselves, by that which a strong resolution would soon overcome.

The education of your body is none the less important, whether it be attained by the discreet restraint of others, or your own individual activity. Here is another large field of work, and of pleasant, easy labour; and yet this too is sadly neglected; though, judging from the complaints raised against the irksomeness of prayer and the wearisomeness of study, one would conclude that this third part of our education would be a great relief to an idle boy. But, says the Holy Scriptures, "the slothful man wishes, and wishes, and knows not his wants." No work of any kind is pleasant to such a one. His pleasure is in his dreams, and "dreams," says the Holy Spirit, "lift up fools." Recreation is not lounging about cloisters and doorways; it is not creeping about from place to place; giving up your games and amusements on the plea of indisposition or physical weakness. If you wish to be strong and healthy, you must do that which God has intended you to do; you must live and work under that regular discipline which has been planned out for you, the object of which is, by strengthening the body, to invigorate the mind and perfect the powers of your soul. If you give way under every fatigue; if you do not join in the games, and take your regular outdoor exercise; if you insist on always being ill, and take a seeming pleasure in being thought so, you will become effeminate men, weak in mind, weak in body.

Therefore, my brethren, exert yourselves; rouse yourselves to labour energetically this half year. Throw off that morbid state of indolence that characterises your every action. Be determined that the traditions of your Alma Mater shall not suffer in your hands, and hand them down uninjured to those that come after you. Show to the world the manly spirit that has ever been a prominent feature of this college.

You have now a long half year before you, which will, however, pass away very rapidly if you work well and earnestly; very slowly and tediously, if you dream away the day in idleness. The pleasure and happiness of life consist in employment; and I am sure the happiest day of your life was, as it ever will be, that which was spent in having something to do. Work whilst you have the day; the night cometh when no man can work. Determine your course of action; and begin it, not to-morrow, not a month hence, but to-day: yet trust not in your own strength of will and purpose, but ask for God's aid.

There is a passage in the Psalms, which embodies all I have said, and it may be aptly called the student's prayer—

"Bonitatem, et disciplinam, et scientiam, doce me, Domine."

It is said every day in the Church's office. Do you also say it every day. Pray for goodness; pray that you may understand the use of work, for he that worketh not, can never be good; pray for a right understanding of what discipline is, so that you may be an earnest, hardworking disciple in the school of Christ; pray for knowledge; go to Her, who is the Sedes Sapientiæ, the Seat of Wisdom; sacrifice five minutes of your playtime in kneeling before the statue of Her who is the Patroness of this place and you, and she will teach you the same lessons that Her Holy Child deigned to learn from Her lips.

X.

SCANDAL.

"And Cain said to Abel his brother: Let us go forth abroad. And when they were in the field, Cain rose up against his brother Abel and slew him. And the Lord said to Cain, Where is thy brother Abel? And he answered: I know not. Am I my brother's keeper? And He said to him: What hast thou done? The voice of thy brother's blood crieth to Me from the earth."

GEN. iv. 8-10.

THESE verses carry the mind away to scenes far off, to times long past. They just suggest a thought of Adam and Eve in their melancholy retirement, and then take us after their only children in what seemed to begin a pleasant walk. That walk led them round the very threshold of lost paradise, and they were alone. Save the two whom they often found weeping at home, they had none to think of or to love except each other,—and save the angels good and bad who were busy about them, and Almighty God who still hovered with anxious love around His fallen favourites, there was no one to look upon them. In such a scene, with such a company, what should we look to find but brotherly affection, and brotherly emulation to bind up the broken hearts at home, and brotherly encouragement and help to grasp after and secure the good which might still be theirs, which God held out to them, which their own hearts yearned for and told them was best. But when they were in the field, Cain rose up against his brother Abel and slew him, and then with unfeeling sullenness asked, Am I my brother's keeper? whilst God who had already cursed the parents now cursed their only child.

It is a humiliating passage in the history of our race, the record of this walk of Cain and Abel; excepting perhaps the unsuspicious love of Abel, there is nothing on which the mind can rest itself with pleasure. Still I have chosen to read it to you, because it will introduce not inappropriately one danger which I wish to tell you of, and one duty which I wish to impress upon you. It might sound to you like the burden of an old song—at least you would probably think you had heard something like it before—if I said that here, at your age, with your companions, with your duties and pleasures, and the influences about you, you are nearer to the gates of paradise than the after stages of life will ever carry you. At all events I may say you are in a very pleasant place, in very brotherly company; and with respect to one particular sin, I would put you on your guard; and for your dearest interests here and hereafter, I would beg you ever to be upon your guard against the entrance of a Cain amongst you.

There is a vice which permeates and pervades the

whole world like its atmosphere; it seethes around us and against us wherever our steps lead into the ways of men; it hangs above us an ever-thickening cloud of abomination between our good God and His ungrateful earth; angels move through it in their ministry of mercy; and sometimes in some places it even rolls close round the tabernacles of our Jesus; a vice which shouts aloud in cities, and men and women take up its cry, and give it to the echoes whilst they prostrate themselves its votaries; a vice which robs its lightness and its laughter from boyhood, and leaves its hideous characters among the furrows and snows of age; which banishes graces from the hearth of home, and confidence from friendship, and every sweet charity from human life. Here I dare hardly call it by its name, because your sweetest and noblest virtue would hang its head and blush at the sound. But under the mantle of our Mother Mary, and with thoughts on dear S. Aloysius, we will speak, as if with bated breath, not of the great world and its sinfulness, but of our little world and its most cruel danger.

It may be that there is amongst you one who, at some time in the past, in an unguarded moment, at the suggestion of the devil, who at the time did not seem a devil, or from a curiosity which he had not learned to fear, or at the solicitation of one whom till then he had loved to look upon as a friend—put forth his hand and plucked the forbidden fruit. And God came to him in the evening time, and he was afraid and knelt; then thoughts of happy childhood came upon him, thoughts of home and of those with true hearts who loved him there and prayed for him and hoped in him; and with a burning shame he hid his face and wept; he looked up, and in the face of his God he read forgiveness; and he looked around him, and realised to himself the battles of his school-boy life, and stood up in the power of God and the help of Mary to walk right on and conquer, and he sits amongst us still penitent, still victorious.

My brethren, let us thank God for such a one; his presence amongst us is like a benediction; his battle for himself like a continual prayer for us; and you, O Christian brother, if indeed you are amongst us here, look up through your silent sorrow for the past, through the anxieties and uncertainties of the present, through the gloom and dangers of the future, look through all to the highest seats around your God. They are thronged with such as you; men and boys who sinned in thoughtlessness and sorrowed in love. Put the past and what it has carried with it at the feet of your Jesus; be happy in the present, you are very near His Sacred Heart; go forth to meet the darkening future in His strength and with a manly heart.

But again it may be there is one amongst you who in like manner has taken a gratification offered to him by his own corruption, or by the devil, or by a worse companion: and now in the blindness of his poor foolish heart believes himself a God knowing good and evil. Sin seems to him a brave thing, and the knowledge of sin he thinks a glorious insight into doings around him; and because he has lost the innocence and the bloom, and the cheery, candid, bold heart of boyhood, he struts before his fellows, in the sight of God and His angels, and thinks himself a man. And he talks of that great world without, and of life, and of the pleasures of life in the world, and, where he may, of the opportunities and sins of the world; until, in an evil hour, the devil finds him the occasion, and he takes an innocent child of God, and in one moment a brother's murdered soul shrieks before the judgment seat of heaven, and another Cain walks the earth, and walks amongst you under a heavier sin and a heavier curse than he who slew his brother in the beginning.

O my brethren, it is a dismal sight, and you have seen it; it is a dismal sight, it seems to choke life in the heart, to see the lifeless body of a boy lifted high on the shoulders of his companions and carried away, away from the sunshine and laughter and love of early life, and hidden deep in the silent grave where the rain falls and the snows gather, but where the feet of those he loved best shall never tread. But what must it be to the angels, to Mary, to Jesus, to look down upon a home like this, and see a young and spotless soul snatched by an evil companion and hurried away, in all its life and beauty, where there is sin and loathsomeness and death, where the smile of Jesus cannot follow it, where the love of Mary can hardly reach it, where good angels and good men can never be with it?

Perhaps you will think I ought not to speak so, that I have hard thoughts about you; that I ought not to dream of such a possibility in such a house.

It is indeed a hard saying. Still we may not forget that in a happier place and a happier time, when two walked together in all the strength of unfallen nature, one sinned and then seduced the other. The devil passed the gates of paradise, and we must expect him here, though God and Mary and the saints be with us.

But, my brethren, I will say no more. I do not wish to speak more plainly or more fully, I do not wish to fill your minds with thoughts that will pain you before Almighty God, or make you less confiding in each other. I only hint at a danger which may beset you even in an abode like this; and I speak of the *danger*, that you may understand and accept the *duty*. Now, if ever it be the misery of your day in college to know one who invites others to go abroad, and then rises up against them and slays them, you must give the alarm; in plain words, if ever you know that one companion is undermining the virtue of another, you must *tell—you must tell*. Look the duty well in the face; it is unwelcome, it is repugnant; yet you must tell the master—the bitterest cross to the schoolboy, but in this the most sacred obligation of the Christian. I know the objections, the protests which are on each one's tongue, and they do credit to your kind and noble hearts, but nothing more.

1. He would have to go, and why should I bring that on one who never injured me? "Am I my brother's keeper." He would be expelled, and it's an awful thing that last drive from a place to which one's

heart has grown; it's a dismal thing to go without one good-bye, or one kind look, or one word of cheer for the long uncertain future. It is, brethren; and more dismal still is the meeting with friends at home. Depend upon it, that blank look of a disappointed father will come before him at many a cruel turn on the road of life. And those hot, silent, reproachful mother's tears will be upon his soul to scald it when his own griefs are more than he can bear. Still the duty is the same, and you must tell.

2. But, a hundred voices urge upon me, "to tell the faults of a companion is mean and meddling, against the laxest principles of schoolboy honour." O brethren! if there is on earth a human code venerable for its antiquity, and sacred in its origin, worthy of jealous guardianship and loving obedience, it is those laws of truthfulness and sincerity, and self-sacrifice, and endurance, and mutual help, and unselfishness, and generosity, and loyalty to each other, to which right-minded boys subscribe and call their honour. It is the only chivalry now alive; cherish it, each of you, as you wish to have happy days in youth and pleasant memories in age. But be sure you have the right interpretation of the code. He who with the arm of friendship on his brother's shoulder reads that brother's heart, and uses his confidence against him, or, as it has been put, "fawns on men and after scandals them;" he who prys into a brother's house and finds the skeleton there, and brings the world to see it—whether it be poverty or domestic trial, or

moral weakness, or bodily defect—he who catalogues a brother's shortcomings, and harmless tricks, and petty lawlessness, or wild adventure, to gain the favour of a master as unprincipled as himself, that boy is unworthy, dishonourable, and mean. He is a sneak, and God in His goodness never sends us more than one in a lifetime. Look out for that, find it if you can, then put it away from you; keep it in a corner, torture it, starve it, until it goes or dies: you have warrant for it. "Six things there are which the Lord hateth; the seventh His soul detests, and that is a tongue which sows discord among brethren" (Prov. vi. 19).

But he who shall see the young and timid and almost helpless children amongst us in danger of pollution because they are timid and helpless; he who shall see the generous and noble, yet unthinking, being gradually tainted because they are unsuspicious, and with a true heart and upright conscience shall remove the danger; if *he* is mean or unmanly, why, O God, was Joseph so pleasing in Thy sight? His brothers put him in the well, and sold him to the Ismaelites, because he had accused them to his father of a very wicked thing, and Thou didst lead him forth to the second seat in Egypt.

Brethren, I have kept you long on a distressing subject, but do not go away and think I have said hard things, or that I have said them because they are hard, or because they are opportune. I almost feel that I am speaking out of time and out of place.

Go then, and forget all, except the principle; let it be with you the most binding article in your code of honour, not to stand by idle or afraid while a friend of your friend Jesus is ill-treated and wounded to the death.

XI.

THE CONFESSIONAL.

"Whose sins you shall forgive, they are forgiven them."
S. JOHN xx. 23.

THERE is probably no institution of the Church which has been so maligned as the Confessional, or which is capable of evoking against us so large a measure of unchristian bitterness. People affect to despise the Church for her extreme sensitiveness, for instance, in all that concerns the faith and purity of her children; or they would pity her for her old world ways, so much out of keeping with the tone and temper of the age; or, again, they profess to laugh at her pretensions to infallibility, and are indignant with her for what they deem her uncharitable bigotry in maintaining that she alone is Christianity, and the one divinely-appointed guide to heaven. And thus her teaching on these and such like questions serves to draw down upon her the scorn, or contempt, or pity, or anger of the unbeliever; but in regard to the doctrine and practice of Confession, the attitude more generally assumed towards her is one of simple hatred. Some of our opponents indeed seem incapable of approaching the subject without sinking to the level of mere vulgar slanderers. Their hatred seems so to warp the natural intelligence within them, that they see in Confession only an enemy to personal morality, and domestic peace, and social security. The charity which "thinketh no evil" is turned to gall and wormwood; and in their eyes the aiders and abettors of Confession, and much more the confessors themselves, must either have lost, or are fast losing, all sense of decency and true religion. Indeed, certain sections of the community seem absolutely beside themselves at the bare thought of this hated institution becoming once more a power in the land. And they are nowise ashamed to ignore their professions of liberality, and remind us, and threaten us with a recurrence, of the summary process by which, as they say, their fathers stamped out and utterly abolished the Confessional in England.

Nor is this hatred confined to the unreasoning Protestant; it is shared by the immoral and the irreligious everywhere; and to the red republican of the Continent, equally with, perhaps more than to the English Evangelical, the very thought of Confession is a source of most foul and most unjust suspicion, and stirs up within him all the malice of his unregenerate nature.

Why this should be so is hard to understand, unless on the supposition of a diabolical origin. For what, after all, is Confession, and of what does it stand convicted, that its very name should let loose such torrents of bitter invective? Were it a desecration of all that men most reverence on earth, it could hardly excite more unmeasured hostility. Certainly, it would seem that at this moment, a man may more safely, and with much better chance of a patient hearing, deny the Divinity of our Lord Himself, than seek to prove that He instituted the Sacrament of Penance. It would excite less horror to deny the inspiration of the Bible altogether. Nay, it may well be doubted if the great organs of public opinion in the country—if the pulpit, the press, and the platform—would contend more zealously for the existence of God Himself, than they do for the mischievous nature of Confession. Certain it is that there are men amongst us who have questioned these vital truths, and have not been visited with one tithe of the obloquy which has been so unsparingly heaped on the heads of those, who, as ministers of God, maintain they have received from Him the power to forgive sins. Let a Protestant clergyman, for instance, but inculcate the practice of Confession, and he is treated as he never would have been had his preaching been of a tendency directly atheistic. And this, surely, is enough to make people, who are Christians at all, pause in their headlong opposition, and ask themselves if in this matter they are zealous only for God and His truth. And this, all the more, because, as I have said, much of this opposition comes from those who disclaim religious convictions of any kind whatever. Something good surely there must be—something divine even—in Confession; else why should it be signalled out for the special hostility of those who insult Him whom we claim to be its founder? Protestants, indeed, may say that we do Him no honour in crediting Him with an institution of this kind. But then if it were so—if Confession were really unworthy of our Lord, and injurious to the interests of His kingdom on earth, would not its continuance be a subject of thankfulness and joy to the infidel, and not, as it is, a matter for scorn and hate? It is, however, labour in vain to seek, even in the interests of Christianity, for a fair hearing from the class of Protestants who are engaged in this anti-confessional crusade. In their blind fury any weapon that comes to hand is a welcome one if only it serve to strike a severer blow against the Church. Sheerest unbelief, in fact, is far less offensive in their eyes, than even a mildly-expressed preference for Confession.

And yet amid all this utter recklessness as to consequences, our opponents are loud and vehement in their protestations of jealous regard for God's rights and power. "Who," they are continually asking, "who can forgive sins but God alone?" Long ago the same question was asked, and not by those who were well disposed towards our Lord. For ourselves, brethren, we prefer to imitate the simple-hearted, sincere-minded multitude that "feared and glorified God that gave such power to man." With these we gladly take our stand; and while we know, and confess, and proclaim that God alone by His divine power can forgive sins, yet joyfully and gratefully we recall those ever-blessed words of His, in which He has been pleased to make over that power to His Apostles and their successors—"Whose sins ye shall forgive they are forgiven them."

And a wonderful power it is, brethren, which our Lord has thus confided to His Church. For, think for a moment what is involved in the simple words of absolution pronounced by the priest over a repentant sinner.

Nothing on earth can compare in beauty and loveliness with a soul in the state of grace. It is no longer, indeed, a mere thing of earth: God Himself is within it, adorning it with His own marvellous gifts: nay, making it in some deeply mysterious, but most true and real way, a very partaker in His own Divine nature. There it is before Him, basking in the sunshine of the light and the love of His presence: shining with more than a borrowed light, for He, the uncreated Light, is shining within it. And so to the angels and saints in heaven, who see it as it is, the sanctified human soul must be an object of joy, and delight, and awe-inspiring reverence.

Yet, let that soul but commit one mortal sin—let it but deliberately offend God in a matter of grave importance—and in a moment all its beauty, and glory, and loveliness, and sanctity are gone. From a friend of God, united to Him by the closest and dearest of ties, it has made itself His declared enemy; and He who was its life, and its joy unspeakable, is driven forth to give place to the evil one. No doubt our Lord still loves it, seeing that He died, and if needs be, would die again for its sake. Still it must be to Him an object of unutterable repugnance, for knowingly and willingly it has that within it which He cannot but hate with all the awful intensity of His Divine nature.

And the poor wretched sinner himself, heedless of all that he has lost, and bent only on gratifying the wild beast within him whose nature has been roused by the taste of blood, rushes on in his mad career, heaping sin upon sin, dragging himself still deeper down in the mire of his passions, until he presents hardly a trace of what he was, perhaps but a few short years ago. Conscience, however, will insist upon making itself heard; and, it may be as a final effort, will put before him with a terrible distinctness the certain consequence of his crime. Oh! in such a moment he may be sorely tempted to give up the thought and the hope of better things. Or he may seek to deceive himself, and fortify himself in his criminal indulgence, by asserting to himself that his passions are stronger than he can resist; while all the while in his inmost soul he knows that he lies. And so his attempted self-deception but serves to cast him back in completer wretchedness upon the consciousness of his guilt.

Oh who will bring peace and calm to that troubled heart? Who shall restore to it its lost beauty, and make it taste again the happiness of innocent boyhood? Surely only He who is infinite in love as He is in power. And daily and hourly are such miracles being worked in our very midst, though we heed it not. Daily and hourly is God's grace triumphing over the devil's malice, and strong passions, and long formed habits of sin—enticing in a thousand unnoticed ways, and urging and strengthening the sinner to come there where he will find rest to his soul, and recover the joy he has lost. Humbled and subdued, he casts himself before God's minister, and pours into his ear a story of sin and of shame which he would not breathe to the truest and dearest friend he has on earth. And God, in that moment of sorrow and abasement, bends lovingly over the child He had lost, and draws nearer to him than ever, and fills the crushed and broken heart with a happiness keener even than his unsullied innocence had ever known. Hardly are the words of absolution pronounced over him, when he rises from his knees, even outwardly changed,—with a sense of relief that gives elasticity to his step, and lightens up his countenance with joy and peace. But the great change has taken place within,—a change so great, that the angels would fail to recognise him, did they not know what God has been doing for him.

Who then shall say that what this repentant sinner has just done was a useless act, or one unbecoming his manhood, or one that tends to beget weakness of character?

Putting aside the supernatural effect of Confession altogether, is it a thing of no account for the guilty, sorrow-laden heart to unburden itself, if only for the sake of sympathy and advice? Is it not an unspeakable gain to the sinner to enable him to break through the terrible secrecy in which certain crimes shroud themselves—crimes which can only live and thrive in darkness. Is not the revelation of them an essential condition of their cure? And in lesser perplexities and entanglements, surely it is no light blessing to have access to some one in whom we can confide, and before whom we can speak of the secrets of our conscience without reserve? We all feel the need of some such friend and adviser: and in the Confessional the need is supplied us in a higher, and truer, and safer way than were otherwise possible. Nor is there anything unworthy in a man thus disclosing the secrets of his soul, and seeking sympathy and direction there, where he knows they may be had with most perfect safety. No doubt it involves much humiliation; but what right-minded man is there who will not say, that the sinner avowing his crimes before God, and for God's sake, before a sinner like himself, is not an infinitely nobler spectacle than he whose pride will hardly permit him candidly to acknowledge his guilt even to himself? Never is a man more manly than when he is his own accuser. Far from such a habit being a sign or a source of weakness, it is evidence of true bravery, and in its turn tends to foster real strength of character. Let those who doubt even the merely human help that comes of Confession, test for themselves its value, or if not, let them believe those who have. They will then come to acknowledge that far from being an enfeebling degrading tyranny, it is full of strength, and peace, and consolation, and supplies an urgent want of our nature, and is in strictest harmony with our better thoughts. For after all, confession is but nature's own remedy for the sin-laden heart, and its answer to its cry for help, only raised, and refined, and supernaturalised by our Lord's power and love.

For ourselves, brethren, let us value our privilege, and recognise the greatness of the mercy that is placed within our reach. Use this sacred remedy frequently, but use it circumspectly, remembering that God has made it one of His Sacraments, and, that if profaned, it will bring a curse, when it was meant to convey a blessing. So use it, therefore, that you may merit the reward promised to those who wash their robes in the blood of the Lamb, that you "may have a right to the tree of life, and may enter in by the gates into the city."

XII.

REVERENCE, THE TEST AND MEASURE OF RELIGION.

"I honour My Father."—S. JOHN viii. 49.

THIS is the honour for which God and man had been waiting for so many ages. This is the fruit, of which it was said in prophecy: "The Lord will give goodness, and our earth shall yield her fruit." Almighty God had been seeking this fruit of the human race from the beginning, and our Saviour, in uttering these words, *Honorifico Patrem Meum*, makes known the fulfilment of God's expectation and of man's.

He declares with His own lips that character of His life, which S. Paul in the Epistle to the Hebrews ascribes to Him: "He was heard for His reverence." The two declarations, one of the Master, and the other of the disciple, express the same truth under different aspects, and they both sum up the life of Christ. S. Paul, as our Lord Himself, is gathering the whole life of Christ under its leading feature, for he says of Him: "Who in the days of His flesh with a strong cry and tears, offering up prayers and supplications to Him that was able to save Him from death, was heard for His reverence." And though of course there is a distinction between honour and reverence, yet they are inseparable; they mutually imply each other, and cannot be disjoined if either is to exist: and this is especially true in the things of God, for in what other disposition of heart can we render honour to His Supreme Majesty but in that of reverence?

That feature reigned necessarily in our Lord's life, as He who came to render and alone could render a worthy service and honour to the true God. Service of false gods was the predominant feature of the heathen world, it was the reigning vice of His chosen people; idolatry, I mean, which is a reverence shown to idols and irreverence to God. It is only natural, therefore, that David, when filled with the spirit of God, should sing in the "*In exitu Israel*" a song of derision against those false gods who have eyes and see not, ears and hear not, hands and feel not. He was already full of the spirit of his Redeemer, in pouring his heart out in reverence before the true God, the God of Israel. But it is strange, at least it is wonderful, to find God Himself taking up the parable of reproach against the idols set up in His room. "Thus saith the Lord (by Jeremias): the hand of the workman hath cut a tree out of the forest with an axe. He hath decked it with silver and gold; he hath put it together with nails and hammers that it may not fall asunder. They are framed after the likeness of a palm-tree and shall not speak, they must be carried to be removed because they cannot go. Thus then shall you say to them :˙. . . "The gods that have not made heaven and earth, let them perish from the earth, and from among those things that are under heaven. He that maketh the earth by His power, that prepareth the world by His wisdom and stretcheth out the heavens by His knowledge," He is the Lord.

God is jealous, jealous by reason of His love of man, jealous of the honour and reverence of His own creatures, which are His by every title of creation and love. Hence it is that He speaks of this going after idols as a going after strange lovers, and calls their crime by the opprobrious name of fornication.

Such being the predominant sin of the heathen world, such being the special vice of His own people, and the object of His peculiar abhorrence, it is no wonder that when the Son of God came in manhood to render as the head of our race due service to God, He should come with the feature of reverence written upon His person and life, no wonder that it should reign in a like express manner in the life of His Mother. The majesty of the silence of her life is eloquent of reverence, and if you ask how in those numberless offices of motherhood which she did for Jesus, she preserved her place as His creature, the answer is that, exercising a mother's right, as she did, in questioning our Lord, for instance, when she found Him after three days' search in the Temple, she yet listened with reverence to His words. Is it not plain, therefore, that one who would be with our Lord a son of His Eternal Father, or a child of His Blessed Mother, must be reverent.

Reverence is almost too simple a word to need defining. The sense of reverence is so clear and strong in all, and especially in the young, that in talking of it one has the advantage of speaking of what is well understood. Still, feeling, though it be as in this case so simple, so lasting, and depending upon conditions always present, needs instructing and confirming by the understanding. Reverence then springs from the consciousness of a higher presence. The presence of one much our superior in dignity, to some almost the presence of any one, serves to abash us; that is the witness of our nature to this sense, which is one we can hardly lose and remain good.

The higher presence upon which divine reverence depends, is the presence of God, and primarily that presence as it is made known to us in our conscience. Reverence for conscience and reverence for God go hand in hand; they are one, and depend, to be just, upon the consciousness of the nearness of that God "in whom we live, and move, and be;" and extend to all persons and things—to the Pope, to the Bishop, to priests, to nuns, to every Christian, to every man, to chalices and vestments, to all persons and things in proportion as they are related to God.

Hence it follows that reverence covers the same ground as religion; it is the bloom upon the fruit; nay more, it is the relish of it; it is the measure of its strength and its soundness.

Reverence is the measure of religion, and one easily applied, to gauge each one his own. All religion consists in communion with God, it is walking in the presence of God in word and deed; at least it is the often bringing of ourselves into that presence; and the sign and measure of our sense of God's presence, and our sensitiveness to His voice, is our reverence.

But, my dear brethren, this is a world of faith, and therefore it is a world of signs; it is a world of signs which are the testimony of faith, such as the unity of the Church, of signs which are the efficient instruments of faith, as Baptism, of signs which are the visible expression of its life, as the sign of the cross, a statue, bowing at the Holy Name. Religion, as it is a visible worship, is made up of signs, and in proportion as the sphere of religious truth and worship widens, signs and ceremonial must increase. Therefore a supernatural religion will be fuller in rite and ceremony and sign, than natural religion; at least all that sphere of truth which is above the natural will require new signs of testimony, of efficient instrument and of expression; and one who believes in it is, as compared with a rationalist, in quite a new mode of life. Two men, for instance, in presence of the Blessed Sacrament, one with faith and one without, are so much severed in thought and conduct, that no earthly distinction of man and man can compare with it. This, however, is the danger of one who lives in England, where the coldness of Protestantism keeps down the warmth of Catholic worship. He lives in an atmosphere which must repress in some way the outward signs of his faith, and which will infect his spirit, if he is not on the watch, so as to make him less disposed to confess it by outward sign. A man should love the farthest hem and fringe of the robes of the Church—even the least, I mean, of her practices, and ceremonies, and signs; but to do this in England, he had need have the most sensitive love of the Church and of things ecclesiastical, or to have become imbued with the spirit of his forefathers, or to have gone and drunk in her spirit among the fervent people of some Catholic land.

However, it is not only from the coldness of Protestantism that a man in England is liable to an undervaluing of certain signs of the Catholic religion, it is more perhaps from the insidious working of its root principle, by which it attacks supernatural religion on the ground of the natural.

The sphere of a Protestant's faith is very small, consequently its need of signs very little, and it has been a leading line of action of that religion, or irreligion, from the beginning, to flaunt its own nakedness before men's eyes as an excellence and a beauty, and to attack Catholic ceremonial and signs on the ground of their opposition to what it is pleased to call pure Christianity; that is, they have denuded their form of religion first of faith, then necessarily of sign, and, to justify themselves, have made an onslaught upon the outward signs of the Catholic faith as being idolatry. They hate them because they express a faith beyond their own, and consequently condemnatory of their own. This is really setting natural religion against supernatural, though God is the author of both, and the higher supposes the lower; it is setting what is sometimes termed common sense, which cannot rise above the natural, against the supernatural sense, which is a grace of God, and by which therefore we do rise above the natural.

Now, my dear brethren, such a spirit is not among us, where there is of course only Catholic faith and love and reverence. And yet it is possible for us, standing as we do, a remnant, though a growing one, amidst the unbelieving mass of our estranged countrymen, to fail of the supernatural; the cold atmosphere of their negative religion may affect us in some little, and there is no room for surprise if it does.

Now believing, as one ought and does, in your present desire to rise to the standard of Catholic youth, believing in that rich undergrowth of holy desires which spring up in every Catholic boy's heart (any one of which only needs conscious cultivation to grow into a strong tree of virtue), believing in a responsiveness to noble deeds and great plans for God's glory, to which an appeal may always safely be made, I believe too that when faults creep in unwittingly, the best way is to speak of them with candour, and to appeal for their correction to this religious sense.

When then a boy is seen preceding a priest to the holy mysteries of the Altar, not with hands joined and eyes cast down, but with hands dangling at his side, and eyes wandering, that is a fault of irreverence, due either to the nearness of Protestantism or to simple neglect. When again, on days on which it is necessary to come up to the steps of the Altar, as on Good Friday and Palm Sunday, a boy is seen returning with an air for which jaunty would be too hard a word, but one by which he disguises the sense of reverence of which he is plainly conscious, that is a fault of irreverence. It is natural; but that is both its excuse, if it has one, and its fault. It should be supernatural. He should express by his manner that supernatural sense which he has. It is not any mere attention to mere external conduct, which is needed, but the due expression of that sense of the Divine Presence, which a youthful soul ever has, ever finds within itself, and may ever appeal to, as I appeal to it. The sense is certainly not wanting. Born as we have been in the Church, we have been fed with her life, which is the presence of God. It is the privilege of Catholic youth, especially so long as they are uncorrupted by any malice, nor can bear the consciousness of such sin as frailty leads to, that the presence of God is part of the consciousness of life, and that arguments to prove the existence of God, however necessary, seem to them but as holding a candle to the sun. A Catholic youth, indeed, hardly knows how to draw a distinct line between his consciousness of himself and that of God. This is the dear, the precious boon which the Church, the fair and immaculate Spouse of Christ, has to give to hers. She nourishes them at her breasts, and there flow therefrom the streams of her own life which is the abiding presence of the Spirit of God. No, it is not the sense that fails, it is the little acts corresponding to it. It is by inattention to these that we are beguiled into hasty genuflections, random departures from the chapel, careless taking of holy water, crossing of the legs in presence of God in church, which we should not do before our earthly superiors; and by omission, into keeping our head unbowed at the name of Jesus, entering church to make public prayers and not making them, but remaining silent. I am not saying that each single act or omission is sinful in itself; through inadvertence there is, perhaps, but little guilt in it, and yet each fault springs from an evil root, and is a step in the formation of a habit of irreverence, which is so far a habit of irreligion. A religious act done with reverence is a strength to the soul, and a glory to God; the same act done without reverence is neither, and often repeated is sure to be of great harm.

Now, by reason of the regular recurrence of our daily religious duties, there is incessant call for reverence; it is a radical virtue, a necessary accompaniment of all religion, and the measure of it; it remains for us, by acting upon the sense, to acquire the virtue of it.

That word *acquire* is the most important that can be named to young people. Unless we acquire when young, we shall find the grace, the spontaneous religious sense, and unbidden virtues of childhood and boyhood disappearing, and their room not supplied by the robust virtues of manhood. To be saved, to grow, each must acquire singly for himself. Each stands alone in the world, with a thousand helps, natural and supernatural, around him, from the star in the sky to the pebble on the road, from the Incarnation to the holy water in the stoup, but he alone can use them. They are helps, he is the agent. God, it is true, must begin with him every good act, and go along with him in it, and help him to finish it, and yet the man alone can do the act, and he alone is responsible. Rulers and superiors may bring him to the chapel ; a Catholic college, an Alma Mater, as the term is, a true fostering mother, is constrained, out of love to God and him, to offer him the means of becoming soundly and nobly religious, but he alone can use them, he alone can pray, he alone can be reverent in his heart. The freedom of his soul is a sacred trust, unconstrained by any law of God or man. And so, my dear brethren, if you choose to love God, having yet the terrible power not to love Him ; if, having the power to transgress you choose not to transgress ; if, having the power to do wrong you choose not to do wrong, set about acquiring virtue which alone supplies the constant power of loving God, and not doing wrong against Him ; and first set about acquiring reverence, not merely as a sense which I know you have, but as a conscious virtue. God's name is a power upon the lips of a reverent man, and is the power most needed in these times. Of one thing no one is allowed to doubt, that frivolity and irreverence are the curse of the time, and that God's name is ceasing to be a power, except in the Church of God. Under cover of newspapers, or under the supposed necessity of being familiar with what are called the open questions of the day, the most elementary truths, not merely of faith, but of the natural conscience, even the existence of God, are discussed as topics of ordinary conversation, as if mankind had still to make up its mind about them, and God's name were a term of science only. His reign in the individual conscience is fearfully enfeebled; He is absent there, and therefore He is absent from the pages of natural science; for no one can ever believe in the God of the heaven, the God of the land and sea, unless he believe in the same God in his own individual conscience, "in whom he lives, and moves, and is." But that from which God is absent is vain; and the loud voice of the gossip and the scientific literature of the day, we have thus to account idle as the wind. How shall we do so but in the power of that God whose name and sovereignty it assails? We may not be familiar with the writings of men of science, we may not have separated the truth in them from the falsehood, it matters not. "*Quoniam non cognovi literaturam, introibo in potentias Domini.*" "Because I have not known literature I will enter into the power of the Lord." Yes, my dear brethren, we must enter into the power of the Lord, our armour must not be as theirs, it must be of God.

Let us fashion it ourselves now; that is the work of every Catholic youth. Let us weld it together strongly, for the strife is unto death. A Christian is a warrior. S. Paul saw him in the eye of his soul as a soldier clad in armour, with his breast-plate on his breast, and his shield upon his arm, and his sword in his hand, and his helmet on his head. But the armour was not of penetrable brass; it was of invulnerable virtue: he calls it the armour of God; the breast-plate is justice, the belt round the loins is truth, the feet are shod with the teaching of the gospel, the shield is faith, the helmet is salvation—the crown of all, and the sword, is the sword of the Spirit which is the Word of God. Labour at this armour, that you may be able to resist in the evil day, and stand in all things perfect; and then, though the spirit of this age, as it will, erects itself a Goliath in your path, clad in brazen impudence against God, and defies aloud the armies of the God of Israel, you like David will know how to hurl at its shameless front the irresistible truths of God, and cleave it through head and trunk with its own sword of perverted truth.

Only let us be reverent, and we gird ourselves round with a wall of defence, proof against our enemies: *Firmamemtum meum, et refugium meum es Tu,* "Thou art my strength and my refuge," at the same time that we widen the freedom of our soul, and the spaciousness of our steps: *Dilatasti gressus meos subtus me,* "Thou hast broadened my steps under me." By reverence we are made sensitive of all truth, by it we learn to judge of all that is beneath our senses, while we are saved from judging of that which God has reserved to Himself, the guilt of any man; by it we learn how to govern ourselves and dispense with rule;

by it we should know how, though there were no precincts to the Church appointed by rule beyond which no word should be said, to make such for ourselves; by it we learn, and safely learn, our singleness before God and our independence; by it we learn at the same time modesty in carriage and manner and voice; by it we enter into that deep sense of God's being which alone will stand the stress of youthful passion; by it we enter into the knowledge and power of God, and "taste and see that the Lord is sweet."

God is ever old, yet ever new, and the soul that lives in His presence finds every day like every other indeed, yet ever new and fresh, opening out new fields of work and thought, yielding new vigour of heart and understanding, and leaving him at the close one day nearer, it is true, in company with all nature to his end, but one day too nearer to his rest.

XIII.

THE NATURE AND GROUNDS OF CHRISTIAN FAITH.

"This is the victory which overcometh the world, our faith."
1 S. JOHN v. 4.

"Jesus saith to him, Because thou hast seen Me, Thomas, thou hast believed; blessed are they that have not seen and have believed."
—S. JOHN xx. 29.

THESE two passages of Holy Scripture which the Church has selected for our instruction this day, both speak of Christian faith; of that fundamental virtue or habit of the soul infused into it by grace, by which it believes without doubt or hesitation those unseen truths and mysteries which have been revealed to us by God; and by which it not only assents to them as undoubtedly true, but, as we say, realises them; that is, regards them as present, actual realities, much in the same kind of way as sight or touch makes evident to us the reality of what we see or handle in the world around us. It is of this latter property of faith that an Apostle speaks, when he says, "Faith is the substance of things hoped for, the evidence of things not seen."

It is of Christian faith, then, that both these

passages of Scripture speaks; S. John in the Epistle, teaching us that it is this faith which is the victorious principle within us, by which we overcome the world; and our Lord in the Gospel, reproving S. Thomas for having wished to rest his faith on the evidence of his senses, the testimony of which it ought to have superseded, and pronouncing those blessed who, not having seen, have believed.

Following, then, the train of thought thus suggested to us, it may be profitable to dwell a little this morning on the nature or essential properties of Christian faith. For in an age of general scepticism, such as this we live in, nothing can be of greater moment than to understand thoroughly what Christian faith is, and on what it rests. And though the subject may not have for some of you the attractiveness of the higher parts of religion, yet since it is the foundation on which all the rest is built, it is the most important of all. It is in the superstructure of a building that we look for beauty; it suffices for the foundations that they be strong and solid.

1. The first essential property, then, of Christian faith is that it believes supernatural truths, simply on the authority of God who has revealed them. For it is a virtue of which God is the immediate object, and rests on His divine infallibility and truthfulness, and on the right which He has to command the submission of the created intellect. Many of these revealed truths are, as you know, obscure and incomprehensible in themselves, and do not carry with them to the human reason their own

intrinsic evidence; but this makes no difference as to the certainty with which they are held by Christian faith, which believes, not from the weight of intrinsic evidence, but simply and entirely on the Word or authority of God.

And it is in this, that *divine* faith differs essentially from *human* faith, which, whether the object be a natural truth or a truth of religion, believes with just that degree of certainty, neither more nor less, that the evidence seems to warrant. This is the faith of heretics who pick and choose among the truths of religion, and believe some because they think they see sufficient intrinsic evidence for them, and reject others because they cannot see such evidence, and are doubtful about a third class because the evidence itself seems inconclusive. Christian faith, on the contrary, is absolute, positive, and unhesitating. There cannot be any degrees of certainty; anything of more or less of certainty in it. It is as certain about one revealed truth, however incomprehensible, as it is about another, however obvious to the reason; and this certainty as to the whole body of revealed truths remains to it at all times constant and unchanging. All it asks, in the first place, is, "Has God taught men this truth? Is it one of the mysteries He has revealed?" And if the answer be "It is," then at once the will demands of the intellect unhesitating faith; a faith which is thus borne on the truth of God Himself, and which is therefore as absolutely certain to the mind, as it is absolutely certain that God can neither be deceived Himself, 'nor deceive His creatures. Observe, the will commands the intellect to believe; for faith is both an intellectual act and a moral act. It would not be the former if we did not believe with the intellect; it would not be the latter if the will, the moral part of our nature, did not enforce that belief. And it is precisely for this reason (that an act of will is necessary for faith) that we are responsible for our belief, and that acts of faith are meritorious, and acts of unbelief mortal sins. Moreover, since the act of faith is not only an intellectual and a moral act, but also a supernatural act, that is, one which directly conduces to salvation, and one therefore which is above the power of mere nature, God Himself by His grace inclines and empowers the will thus to exert its authority. When the will has freely yielded to this divine inspiration, and commanded of the intellect a firm assent to a truth, as to one revealed by God, then at once an act of divine faith is made.

2. But we have not yet a full and complete notion of all that is necessary for Christian faith.

I said just now that all faith asks in the first instance is, whether this or that mystery which is proposed to it has been revealed or not by God. Now this, it is obvious, is an altogether essential step in the process. For if we cannot be certain that God has revealed a particular truth, neither can our faith in that truth be certain, for this, as I have said, rests simply on the fact of the revelation having been made by God.

But how are we to find out with absolute certainty what God has revealed? We do not hear a voice from heaven telling us what we are to believe. And though we have the Sacred Scriptures, which are the written Word of God, we cannot make out for ourselves from them a scheme of belief, a list of *credenda;* first, because they were not written for this purpose. They were originally addressed to men who were already in possession of the truths of faith by means of oral teaching; and though they allude to many of those truths in various ways, they nowhere give, or profess to give, a complete account and summary of them. Some leading dogmas of revealed religion are indeed so clearly contained, and so often repeated in the New Testament, that as to those we might be certain, if we had otherwise sufficient grounds for certainty that these writings are indeed the Word of God; but as to other truths, all those truths, for instance, which are necessary to the full explicit belief of their leading dogmas; which distinguish them from error on this side and on that; as to all these, and many others, we should be left to the speculations of our own fallible intellect.

Secondly, therefore, we cannot gather with unfailing certainty what God has revealed from Holy Scripture, because our intellect is fallible, that is, liable to error. Absolute certainty as to the fact of particular truths having been revealed by God, supposes not only that the writings in which they are thought to be contained have been inspired by God, and thus preserved from all doctrinal error, but also that the person who interprets the meaning of these writings cannot possibly err in that interpretation. But this infallibility we know does not belong to any human mind, even when it speculates on those natural truths which properly fall under the cognisance of human reason; still less, therefore, is it an attribute of any human mind, as such, when it speculates on the mysterious supernatural truths of religion, or endeavours to deduce them from the hints and allusions which are scattered through Scripture.

And this is not only a conclusion which we are entitled to draw from the very nature of the case,—from the form, I mean, in which the sacred writings are cast, and from the acknowledged fallibility of the human intellect,—but one also which actual experience attests to us; for we have around us in this very country a multitude of sects, all of which profess to have derived their doctrines from the Bible, and yet no two of these agree in holding the same doctrines, most of them differing very widely as to truths of great importance. Nay, since each individual, or at least each public teacher, in these sects, claims for himself the same right of working out his faith from Scripture, each sect is itself, in its turn, broken up into several divisions or parties, the members of which hold together for convenience' sake, but scarcely any two individuals of which hold precisely the same views as to revealed truth.

If then an unerring certainty that God has revealed certain truths be necessary, in order to have Christian faith in those truths, it is perfectly clear, from these examples before our eyes, that the Holy Scriptures, as interpreted by the fallible human intellect, cannot give, and were never intended by God to give that certainty, at all events, as to the whole body or complete circle of revealed truths.

How then, I ask again, are we to know with absolute certainty all that God has revealed? The youngest of you, my brethren, knows the answer. Because God who has revealed these truths through His Son Jesus Christ, has committed them to an ever-living Guardian and Expositor of them, His Holy Catholic Church, and charged her with the office of teaching them to all men as truths which have been revealed by Himself; and, in order that she may fulfil this office without failure or error, to the very end of time, has pledged Himself to be with her by His Holy Spirit as she thus teaches, " all days even unto the end of the world." Thus, though no man of himself, and no body of men, as such, but only God is infallible; yet in thus giving Himself, the Holy Spirit of Truth, to His teaching Church, He has made her by this participation of Himself, infallible to the end of time, in thus discharging the office of teacher He has laid upon her. And thus it is that we too, by humbly submitting ourselves to the teaching of the Church, may know with infallible certainty what God has revealed, and therefore be capable of believing with an absolute and unwavering faith, not one or two truths only, but the whole body of revealed truths. And hence it is that among the children of the true Church, and among them alone, there are no degrees of certainty as to particular revealed truths, but all alike are held with the same absolute certainty, because all alike rest on the same foundation, the truthfulness of God revealing; and because all alike are transmitted to us by that infallible witness and exponent whom He has appointed as the medium by which these truths are made known to us as revealed by Himself.

3. Now this, as to the fundamental matter of faith, might seem enough for all our wants. We have an infallible God revealing, and we have through His appointment, an infallible means of knowing what He has revealed. God, moreover, on His part, is ever ready with His grace to give us the necessary supernatural assistance towards the actual exercise of faith, so that nothing farther might seem wanting. And doubtless, for those who already, on some sufficient ground, believe that God has made a revelation to man, and has appointed the Church to be the unerring witness and exponent of that revelation, nothing farther is necessary.

But, then, is it always the case that we do believe in these two essential pre-requisites of faith on sufficient grounds? Is it not possible that some of us may have accepted them as mere matters of course, or at least on insufficient grounds, as for instance, because we have been born and bred among Catholics, and because every one around us accepts them? Now I do not say that such a person is not capable of some kind of Christian faith, for there is a probability that he is capable. But this I say, on the authority of the doctors and theologians of the Church, that his present faith is defective and imperfect, and that for the future he stands in no small risk of losing it altogether. For suppose the circumstances of such a person to be changed, as they will be changed in the case of most of you; suppose that after leaving college or home, he goes out into the world, and finds himself surrounded, in his everyday life, no longer by Catholics, but by those who do not believe in the Church as the Guardian and infallible Teacher of God's revelation, nay, perhaps by those (for there are thousands of such now-a-days) who do not even believe that God has made any revelation at all to man. Then it is obvious, that the very same principle by which he believes in revelation and the Church now, namely, an easy adoption of the opinions of those around him, will incline him to scepticism and unbelief then. He may begin to say within himself, "These dogmas of Catholicism are most obscure and incomprehensible in themselves, and though I believed them without difficulty when I took for granted God had revealed them, and that the Church which teaches them is His infallible Messenger to man, yet was I really justified in those two great assumptions? and if not, what is my faith worth? May not these incomprehensible dogmas after all be only the inventions and speculations of men as fallible as myself?" It is thus, I fear, from this thoughtless and unreasoning acceptance of these two essential pre-requisites of faith, from this ignorance of what theologians call the "*motiva credibilitatis*" of our religion, that doubt, and at length perhaps a settled unbelief, find entrance into many a soul.

To what has been said already, this then must be added, that if not for all faith, at least for complete and perfect faith, there is necessary a clear conviction of the natural reason, produced by a sufficient consideration of the proper motives or evidences, that the truths of our religion have been revealed by God, and that the Church is the unerring and infallible exponent of them to us; and it may be further added, that this intellectual or rational conviction is necessary, in proportion as the mind is capable of understanding and weighing these evidences. The reason is, that faith is an assent of the intellect to the truths of religion as revealed by God, firm, decided, positive and unchanging; and from the very nature of the human intellect as created by God, such an assent cannot be enforced by the will, or at any rate permanently enforced, unless there be sufficient *rational* grounds for believing that God has revealed these truths and that we are in possession of them.

It is true that for poor simple persons, or for young children, who are not capable of appreciating the force and weight of these evidences, it is not necessary that this rational conviction should be full and complete, or that it be derived immediately from the consideration of these evidences themselves; it suffices that it exist in some degree, and that it be derived immediately through the conviction and teaching of others. But then such persons, as they cannot understand the arguments *for* religion, neither can they understand those which are urged *against* it; and therefore their faith is not exposed to danger, and thus, though not perfect, it may yet be undoubting and constant. Besides, the habit of faith which God infuses into the soul at Baptism very much assists such persons towards acts of faith. In proportion, however, as the mind through age and culture becomes capable of reflecting on the grounds and motives of its belief, the very nature of faith itself demands that these grounds and motives be made clear and evident to the reason, so that a conviction which is self-gained, and not a mere reflection of the conviction of others, be formed in the mind, not only that there are abundant evidences for believing that God has revealed supernatural truths, and made the Church the infallible Teacher of them, but that these evidences have an indefinitely greater cumulative weight and force than any arguments whatever which can be adduced to the contrary.*

Now certainly it is our own fault, or the defect of our education, if we grow up without this rational conviction ; for the means of gaining it have been abundantly furnished us by God Himself, Who never demands faith of man in any supernatural mystery without first giving him the necessary rational grounds for believing with certainty that the mystery proposed has been revealed by Himself. Thus our Lord said to the unbelieving Jews, that if He had not done among them works that no other man had done, they

* See Suarez de Fide, Disput. iv. Sect. 2; and De Lugo, Disput. v. Sect. 1 and 2.

would have been without sin, but that after these miracles they had no excuse for their unbelief. And St Paul asks certain of the Hebrew Christians who were in danger of apostasy, how they could escape condemnation if they turned away from a faith which was first declared by the Lord, and confirmed unto them (these Hebrew Christians) by those who heard Him, " God also bearing them witness by signs and wonders and divers miracles" (Heb. ii. 4).

And the case is exactly the same with us; for although we did not see with our eyes these miracles of Christ and His Apostles, yet we have the accounts of them in the writings of men who did see them, and who were convinced by them, and who laid down their lives in attestation of their reality. And if in this respect of not having actually seen these miracles we may have a somewhat less convincing degree of rational evidence than the first Christians had, yet it should be remembered that in other respects we have far stronger and more convincing evidence than they had.

For example, all those wonderful prophecies of the Old Testament, which predicted not only the Advent of Christ, with the circumstances of His Birth, Passion, and Death, but also the future glories and triumphs of His Church, and the dispersion over the whole earth of the Jewish nation for rejecting Him, were for the first Christians fulfilled only in part—only as to the actual Advent of Christ; whereas for us they have been fulfilled, and are still fulfilling, in all their compass and extent. Every Jew we meet is a living evidence of the truth of Christianity, as striking to every thoughtful mind as any miracle can be. For it is a fact which stands alone in the history of mankind, that one nation should be scattered among all other nations, and yet for eighteen centuries remain indelibly distinct, "a proverb and a byword to all people" (Deut. xxviii. 37). And yet this singular and unparalleled fact was predicted by Moses 1500 years before the destruction of Jerusalem, and that in books which the Jews themselves have preserved for us. This then is an instance in which our evidence far exceeds that of the first Christians. Another is the very history and continuity of the Church herself, which for the first Christians was in her infancy. They saw but the tiny rill issuing from the earth; we can trace the majestic, ever-widening river through eighteen centuries of its course. And when we reflect what the history of the Church has been; by what feeble human agency she was propagated from nation to nation; the obstacles she has encountered from the persecutions of the Roman Empire, from heresy ever springing up in new shapes and attacking one sacred dogma after another, from the devastating inroads of ruthless barbarians, from the jealousy of national spirit towards the Holy See, from the worldliness and tepidity of her own children,—when, I say, we reflect on this history, and compare this steadfast onward progress through all these obstacles with the words of Christ, "Thou art Peter, and upon this Rock I will build My Church, and the gates of hell shall not prevail against it," then we have before our very eyes a palpable evidence of the truth of our religion, which from the very nature of the case the first Christians could not have had. St Augustine, at the beginning of the fifth century, avowed that one of the chief motives of his faith was the continual succession of Bishops in the chair of Peter, to whom Christ had entrusted His flock. And if that continual succession for 400 years was so strong an evidence to him, what ought not to be that same unbroken succession of 1800 years to us?

When these and a variety of other evidences (which I have not time to speak of now), that God has revealed supernatural truth to man, and constituted His Church the Teacher of them, are viewed together as one argument, their cumulative force is such as to bring the clearest conviction of these two things to every rational and honest mind; and such conviction, as I have said, or at least some sufficient degree of it, is necessary to perfect faith from the very nature and definition of it.

When there is a lurking suspicion in the mind that faith is irrational, that the grounds on which it rests will not bear scrutiny, in such a mind there is not faith. Reason herself, which is God's gift, sends us to faith, which is His supernatural gift; and thus an act of faith is the highest possible exercise of human reason.

Be not then afraid, my brethren, of strengthening and confirming your rational conviction in these two pre-requisites of faith by every means within your reach. God would not have afforded these evidences in such abundance if they had not been necessary for us; nor would He have so wonderfully provided that where, in any age, from the necessity of the case, these evidences should be in some respects less convincing, there, in other respects, they should be more convincing.

Only remember that this rational conviction, though necessary for faith, is not in itself faith, but that faith itself is the unfaltering submission of the intellect to truths which are above and beyond reason, or those which have been revealed to us by Him Who is the Eternal Truth, and made known to us by an infallible Teacher accredited by Himself. And thus, whilst on the one hand you will hold your Catholic faith intelligently, and without fear or misgiving, — "ready (as St Peter enjoins) to satisfy everyone who asketh you a reason of the hope that is within you;"—on the other hand, every act of that faith will be that implicit submission of your intellect to the voice of God, which is the truest recognition and worship of His divine authority, and thus merit for you the blessedness of those who have not seen and have believed.

XIV.

CHRIST TEACHING BY HIS SPIRIT IN THE CHURCH.

> "I have yet many things to say to you; but you cannot bear them now. But when He, the Spirit of Truth, is come, He will guide you into all truth."—S. JOHN xvi. 12.

THERE is no part of the Gospel narrative which so touchingly portrays to us the tenderness and compassion of the Sacred Heart of our Redeemer as this last discourse of His to His Apostles (the last, that is, of His mortal life), from which three of the Sunday Gospels have been taken at this season.

That discourse was spoken on the eve of His Passion, a few hours only before the Agony in the Garden. His prescient mind was then keenly alive to every pang which so immediately awaited Him. His man's nature shrank from torture and death, just as we should shrink from them if close at hand; nay, far more, because what we should only vaguely apprehend was distinctly present to His mind in all its cruel details. And yet, throughout all this long discourse, He hardly alludes to His own Passion and Death, or alludes to them in the lightest terms, as

His "leaving this world" or His "going from them for a little time."

Even in that hour when His human heart craved for sympathy, He asked not for sympathy, but He gave it to others. The delicacy of His love made Him draw a veil over His own most bitter sufferings, and devote His last hours to alleviate the lighter distress of His Apostles in the trial of separation which awaited them. He knew, moreover, that, during that trial, they would be wanting in fidelity to Him, that fear would get the better of love and duty, that one would thrice deny that he was His disciple, that all would forsake Him and flee; but the foreknowledge of this did not diminish aught of His love for them, aught of His tender interest in their coming bereavement. He waited only till the traitor had gone out from them on his infamous errand, and then to the rest, whom, though weak in courage, He knew to be true in loyalty and affection, He poured forth all the sympathy of His generous heart, suggesting to them motive after motive for hope and encouragement, consoling them cheerfully and tenderly, rather as if they were just going to suffer for Him, than Himself to agonize and die for them. His former tone is quite changed. He no longer addresses them as the Lord His servants, or even as the mere Teacher His disciples. He calls them by endearing names, His "children," His "friends," His "chosen ones." He tells them that, though going from them for a time, it is only that He may prepare a mansion for them in His Father's

Home; and that He will come again and take them to Himself, that where He is they also might be for ever; that meanwhile, whilst still wayfarers amidst the trials and persecutions of the world, they were not to be left orphaned and alone, for that He will send them another Paraclete and Consoler, Whose office it would be to receive of His and shew it unto them, Whose presence with them and in them would make Him, their Lord, Himself present with them and in them—present in a higher, more intimate, more uninterrupted mode than He had ever been present before—present with them and within them as their guide, their peace, their strength and solace, till their wayfaring should be ended, till they should be reunited to Him visibly in the still resting-places above, and their sorrow be turned into endless and unbroken joy.

And during the forty days which intervened between His Resurrection and Ascension (this very Paschal time we are keeping now), it was this same great truth of His spiritual presence in the Church that He was gradually bringing home to them and enabling them to realise.

From time to time during these forty days (twelve times in all) He appeared to them, and conversed with them, and instructed them as to His Church, and removed their doubts, and calmed their fears. But His visits then were not as His presence with them before His Passion. They were strange and unearthly, having almost the character of spiritual manifestations. He came when they were least expecting Him; and when they saw Him, there was hesitation and uncertainty in recognising Him. Twice He stood suddenly in the midst of them when they assembled in the upper chamber with closed doors, and they were troubled and affrighted as if they had seen a spirit. The two who were walking to Emmaus found Him by their side, and though their hearts burned as He conversed with them, they knew Him not till He broke the bread and vanished. When He appeared to them on the shores of the lake, and invited them to a mysteriously prepared meal, "none of them durst ask Him, Who art Thou, knowing it was the Lord." Even Mary at the Sepulchre mistook Him at first, till that familiar voice had pronounced her name. In the long intervals between these mysterious visits, they knew not where He was, or how occupied. When they saw Him, they could not say whence He had come, or, when He disappeared, whither He had gone. It was as if the air had yielded Him to their sight, and as if the air had received Him back. His presence with them *then* was ruled by other laws and conditions than His presence before His Passion. It was something intermediate between material presence and spiritual presence, between local presence and Divine Omnipresence.

Surely then all this was intended to prepare them for a new and higher mode of His presence with them in the Church than that visible presence which they had so much feared to lose. It was designed to teach them that there was possible for them a more certain knowledge of Him, and a closer and more intimate communion with Him, than that which sight and sense afforded—a communion of spirit with spirit, of the Eternal Spirit of the Father and the Son with their new-created spirit; and that when that Divine Paraclete had been sent, then He, their Lord and Life, would be nearer to them than ever, and dwell with them and in them, and thus fulfil towards them, perfectly and fully, those very offices of grace which He had commenced whilst visibly among them during His mortal life on earth.

Those gracious offices were manifold; but I wish now to speak of one in particular which the Gospel of this day suggests, and the consideration of which is peculiarly suitable to our present circumstances.

He had been their *Teacher*, one who had taught them not like other teachers, but with divine and infallible authority, infallible because divine. He had revealed to them, so far as they could receive them, "the mysteries of the kingdom of heaven." What to others He had veiled in parables, to them He had conveyed clearly and explicitly. But it was not much that they could *then* receive. Their understandings were dull and earthly, their memories treacherous and confused. The very announcements which He made to them of His future Passion and Resurrection, which to us, as we read them in the Gospels, seem so plain and simple, were misunderstood by them, or at least forgotten when those events occurred. His very enemies remembered His predictions better than His chosen disciples, and took their precautions accordingly. Even up to the last evening He spent with them before His death, He had still many things to say to them, which He could not say, because they could not bear them then.

But see these very men but ten days after the Ascension of Christ, when the Holy Ghost had been sent to this earth, and had become the Life of the new-born Church. They are no longer the dull, forgetful disciples, but themselves the inspired teachers of mankind. Penetrated with divine truth to their inmost being, every word their Lord had uttered clinging to their memory, all that He would before have taught them, if they could then have borne it, supernaturally infused into them, they go forth from their retirement, changed themselves, to change others, fearless and persuasive to convert the world!

For the promised Paraclete had come, and had come (as He had been promised) as the Spirit of Truth, to guide them into all truth, to bring to their remembrance all that their Lord had taught them, to empower them to teach others with the same infallible authority as that with which He had taught them Himself, and with a success immeasurably greater.

For before they had been taught from without, but now they were taught from within. Before, their Divine Teacher had been separate from them, and human words were the only vehicle of communication: now, by His Spirit He dwelt within them, and spoke directly to their spirits; and the light within them was His Light; and when they addressed themselves to others, it was not they merely who spoke, but the Spirit of Christ Who spoke by them, and through them, and drew the hearts of their hearers to faith and conversion.

And thus it was that their Lord's promise was fulfilled when He had solemnly commissioned them to be the teachers of the world. "All power," He said, "is given to Me in heaven and on earth. Go ye, therefore, and teach all nations, baptizing them in the name of the Father, and of the Son, and of the Holy Ghost; and behold I am with you all days, even to the consummation of the world."

But was it to the first teachers of the Church, to the Apostles alone, that that commission and that accompanying promise was made? No; as its very terms imply, it extended itself to all to whom they should hand down their sacred office—to the "Teaching Church;" "all days," that is, continuously, without break or interruption—to the Teaching Church for ever, "to the consummation of the world," to the end of time. And so again, when the Holy Ghost was promised as the Church's Guide and Teacher, the very words of the promise declare the perpetuity of the gift: "*Manebit vobiscum in æternum.*" He, the Spirit of Truth, "shall abide with you for ever."

This you know, my brethren, is the very foundation of our faith as Catholics. We believe whatever the Church teaches with the same absolute certainty as if we had personally received these truths from the lips of Christ Himself. Not to do so, would be to disbelieve in Him Who has pledged His word to teach by His Church always, and to the end of time, and Who has said to those whom He has sent: "He that heareth you heareth Me, and he that despiseth you despiseth Me." To doubt any single article which the Church declares to be of faith, would be to doubt in the faithfulness of Him Who has promised to His Church the Spirit of Truth to guide her into all truth, and to abide with her for ever.

The world outside the Church is irritated and incensed that the Catholic Church claims for herself infallibility, and that she claims to be heard and obeyed by all. Its hostility to her would cease at once, if, like the sects around her, she confined her ministrations to certain portions merely of the earth, or, like them, professed views and opinions only probably true; but it cannot bear that she should assert for herself, as they say, "a monopoly of truth," that she should assert her right to teach all men, and that too with a pretence to absolute certainty and divine authority.

But such persons should surely consider this: that unless the Church were intensely conscious that she has a mission, not to this or that nation only, but to every creature under the sun, and acted on this consciousness; unless too she claimed to teach with superhuman authority, knowing herself, in virtue of the guidance of the Holy Ghost, to be secure from all error in matters of faith, she could not possibly be the continuation and representative of that Church which the Bible sets before us; of that Church which was commissioned by Christ to teach and baptize every creature, with the promise that He would be with her in her teaching all days to the end of the world; of that Church concerning which He said to the chief of the Apostles: "Thou art Peter, and on this Rock I will build My Church, and the gates of hell shall not prevail against it;" of that Church which was to possess "the Spirit of Truth for ever to guide her into all truth."

The very fact, then, that alone, of all existing religious bodies, the Roman Catholic Church,— Roman, because Rome, the See of Peter, is her centre of unity; Catholic, because the circumference of her mission is only limited by the earth itself,— the very fact, I say, that this Church alone, of all existing religious bodies, lifts up a voice to all peoples and nations, and not a faltering and timid voice, but a voice of certainty and authority, asserting her right to be heard as the one Messenger from God, and to be obeyed as His unerring Teacher of mankind,— this very fact ought to go far (I might even say, ought to be enough) to convince all who believe the word of Christ, that she, and she alone, *is* God's Messenger, and *does* teach with His authority. For there, and there alone, is His guiding presence, and His Spirit of Truth, and His teaching, and His infallibility, where it is felt to be, and known to be, and fearlessly claimed and asserted.

And, indeed, this is what our Blessed Lord Himself said at the very time when He promised to the Church the Holy Spirit of Truth. The world, He said, would refuse to believe that the Church possessed this gift, because, being the world, it would judge of the Church, as it judges of everything else, by sight and sense, by mere external phenomena, and not by faith in Him. It would not receive this great truth, simply because it could not see with its eyes this invisible Guide and Teacher. The Church herself, on the other hand, would always know that she possessed this Divine Spirit of Truth, for the very reason that that Divine Spirit would be with her and in her. "I will ask the Father" (these are our Lord's words), "and He shall give you another Paraclete, that He may abide with you for ever, even the Spirit of Truth, Whom the world cannot receive, because it seeth Him not, neither knoweth Him. But you shall know Him, because He shall abide with you, and shall be in you."

For us, my dear brethren, who already by God's grace are Catholics and believe in His true Church it may still be of use to be reminded of these elementary truths on which our religion rests; especially now, at this eventful time, when the successors of those Apostles to whom this promise was made are assembled in general Council, themselves collectively the heirs to the same promise and to the same gift.

At times, it may be, the thought has crossed our minds, that our faith now is exposed to a severer trial than was the faith of the actual disciples of Christ, that it is harder for us to believe in the teaching of His Church than it was for them to believe in His own personal teaching. But it is not really so. The object of faith is now and always, as it then was, what is impervious to sight and sense; nay, what, in a manner, seems opposed and contradictory to these.

Our Lord, before His Passion, said to His Apostles, "You believe in God; believe also in Me." He Who spoke was to sight and sense a man like themselves, and nothing more. But He had given them sufficient proof that He was more than man—proof enough to make an act of faith in His Divinity, and they made it; made it, notwithstanding the testimony of their outward senses, which revealed only a human nature in Him, and apparently only a human person. And now the same Lord says to us and to every Christian, "You believe in Me; believe also in those whom I have sent, and whom I have promised to teach and guide by My Holy Spirit to the end of time."

We cannot see with our eyes the Divine Teacher and Guide Who dwells in the Church, any more than the Apostles with their eyes could see the Divinity of Christ. We see only in the "*Ecclesia docens*" a body of men compassed about like ourselves with human frailty and infirmity. But the evidence afforded us of Christ's continual presence in the Church is at least as great as that afforded to the Apostles of our Lord's Divine nature and person. To omit all other proof drawn from the history of the Church itself, we have the evidence of Christ's own words—words express and oft repeated. If, therefore, we really do believe in Him, this His word will be enough for us. As it would have been unreasonable for the Apostles and first disciples, believing as they did in God, not to believe in Christ, He having given them sufficient evidence that He was sent by God and came from God, so it would be equally unreasonable for any one who always believes in Christ to doubt the word of those whom He has sent to teach in His name, for He has pledged Himself to be their continual Guide and Instructor, to be with them in their teaching all days, even to the end of the world.

But if the nature of our faith itself is the same now as it was in the case of those who saw Christ and conversed with Him, ultimately resolving itself now, as it did then, into faith in God; on the other hand, the truths of faith, the mysteries on which faith can rest, are now for us far fuller and clearer, far more copious and explicit, than they could have been if we had lived when our Lord was visibly on this earth, and if we had ourselves been admitted to His instructions. For then there would have been many things He could not have taught us, because we could not then have received them; and those truths which we could perhaps have received would have been vague and dim and confused, compared with our present knowledge of them, because not then drawn out in explicit detail, and co-ordinated in their relation to other truths, as they have since been by the co-operation of the Spirit of Christ with His Church during eighteen successive ages.

Thus, excepting of course the Apostles themselves, who after the Advent of the Holy Ghost had a peculiar gift of inspiration and infused knowledge, it was not those who lived nearest to the source who had the clearest and fullest knowledge of revealed truth, but those, like us, to whom the stream has descended in ever-widening and deepening volume. For the Church at large, it is by degrees only, and as it were step by step, that the Holy Ghost guides her into all truth. The very words, "He will guide you," imply this, and the whole history of the growth of dogma in the Church bears witness to it.

Lastly, let us not forget, that as it is the Holy Spirit of Truth Who has been, and is, the invisible Agent under Whose guidance and co-operation the mysteries of faith, once for all revealed by Christ in germ, have been thus gradually unfolded, so it is He too Whose gracious office it is to prepare and dispose the minds of the faithful for the reception of those developed truths.

Let us then be docile to His inspirations; and as day by day we repeat the "*Veni Creator Spiritus*," let us pray that He will guide and assist not only the Supreme Pastor and the Fathers of the Council by His divine light and wisdom, but us too by His grace, that we may now and at all times receive the Church's teaching, "not as the word of man, but as it is in truth, the word of God Himself."

Note.—This sermon having been preached during the Session of the Vatican Council, it is obvious why the particular *organ* of the Church's infallibility is not here discussed.

XV.

THE TRANSFORMING POWER OF THE LIFE OF GRACE.

"Be not conformed to this world; but be transformed in the newness of your mind; that you may prove what is the good and acceptable and perfect will of God."—ROMANS xii. 2.

IN these words the Apostle teaches us three things; first, something we are to avoid; secondly, something we ought to aim at; and thirdly, the means by which we are to avoid the one and to attain to the other.

What we ought to avoid is conformity to this world; what we ought to aim at is a clearer knowledge of what God wills of us, and a more perfect fulfilment of that will of God,—"to prove" (as he says) "what is the good and acceptable and perfect will of God," —the will of God, that is, in its three ascending degrees of comparison; and the means by which we are to avoid conformity with the world, and to attain to the more perfect knowledge and fulfilment of God's will, is the transformation of our new or regenerate nature, or (as St Paul expresses it) by being "transformed in the newness of our mind."

The subject, then, that is suggested by these words is this: how, by the transforming power of the regenerate life within us, we can, and ought, to detach ourselves more and more from the love of the world, and attach ourselves more and more to knowing and doing the will of God.

And, first of all, let us endeavour to understand what the Apostle means by "not being conformed to this world," and by "proving what is the good and acceptable and perfect will of God."

When St Paul teaches us "not to be conformed to this world," he certainly does *not* mean that we are to make ourselves singular and outwardly distinct from the rest of men by adopting any peculiar outward badge of our own. Some persons, apparently supposing that worldliness consists chiefly in showy dress and in insincere speaking, have adopted, you know, a peculiar dress and phraseology of their own, —hoping, I suppose, thereby to shut out the world. But the hope is not well founded. For "the world" which the Apostle tells us to avoid is a temper or habit of mind, that is, a spirit; and this spirit, like every other spirit, is very subtle; it can find its way everywhere, and penetrate into every form, and may lurk beneath the gravest dress as well as beneath the gayest, and find expression for itself in the boldest forms of speech, as well as in the most superfluous compliments.

Nor, again, does the Apostle mean that we are to cease to take an interest in the pursuits and avocations of this world, that we are to be indifferent as to the events passing around us, and spend the whole day in prayer and meditation. This, indeed, is the duty and privilege of a few whom God has called out of the world to serve Him in the contemplative life; but St Paul is writing, as I am speaking, to those whose vocation is to serve God *in* the world; and therefore, since their duties lie in the world, they must necessarily be occupied in its concerns. Nay, he himself tells us in this same chapter, not only that we *may* occupy ourselves in the business of life, but, moreover, that it is our duty to be "*diligent* in business."

On the other hand, by "not conforming ourselves to the world," the Apostle means *more* than that we are bound to abstain from the vices and immoralities of ungodly men, from those gross forms of sin which exclude him who commits them from the kingdom of grace altogether. Many a worldly man is what we call a "moral man;" and in a Christian, worldliness, though it, of course, tends to the loss of grace, may yet be very strong within a soul which keeps out of mortal sin, and therefore is still in a state of grace.

What, then, is this "worldliness" which as Christians we are bound to avoid? It is a temper of mind which makes us interest ourselves wholly or chiefly in the things of this life, without referring them at all to the will of God. It does not consist, as I have said, in the amount of time or thought which we give to the business of the world, but in doing this business from a wrong motive — not because it is the will of God, but only because it is *our* will, not that therein we may serve God, but only that we may serve ourselves.

An example will explain this. Two men, both of the same calling, may work at their calling the same number of hours every day. Their lives outwardly may be very similar. They may both be moral men, chaste, sober, just, peaceable, and industrious. They may both punctually fulfil the external obligations of religion, both keep Sunday holy, and come with equal regularity to the Sacraments, and both be in a state of grace. And yet there may be a very wide difference between these two men. One may be very worldly, the other a man after God's own heart. And the cause of the difference is this, that one works only for himself, the other works for God; one in his daily toil has no end in view but money—wages, or at least a temporal reward of some kind or other; whilst the other directs his chief attention to the will of his Father in heaven. You see, my brethren, the worldliness of the one man does not consist in his doing this world's work, but in doing it for a merely worldly or natural end; and so the unworldliness of the other man does not consist in abstaining from this world's business, but in doing it for an end which is unworldly and supernatural.

And not only in the toils and cares of life, but in its pleasures and relaxations there is the same difference between the worldly and unworldly man. The worldly man makes his own enjoyment the *sole* end of these, and therefore, since he has only enjoyment in view, with no purpose before him of anything higher, he is often led, by that lower nature which he follows, into acts of sin, dissipation, intemperance, quarrelling, unseemly language, or still worse sins. The unworldly man, on the other hand, does not, because he is unworldly, refuse to recreate his nature with proper enjoyments (for he knows that God has so created his nature that these are in some measure necessary for it), but in his enjoyment he does not lose sight altogether of something higher, of the will of God, and that acts as a check to extravagance and dissipation. Whether he eats or drinks, or recreates himself with his friends, or takes repose and sleep, or whatever he does, he does all to the glory of God.

You see then, my dear brethren, what St Paul means when he tells us not to conform ourselves to this world.

He means that we are not to live as if this world were our all; as if success in life, or "getting on in the world" (as people say), were the one thing needful; but whilst we are diligent and painstaking in our daily tasks of work, or while we rest from our work for refreshment of body and relaxation of mind, to have a higher end in view than the mere temporal reward of our work, or the mere enjoyment of our animal nature,—the end, namely, of following God, and doing in all things His holy will.

He means that we ought not to be so absorbed in the things of life, however necessary and innocent they may be in themselves, as to lose sight of our relation to our Creator and our Father, but ever bearing in mind that we are His creatures and His redeemed children, to live as under His eye, soberly, honestly, and contentedly; offering our daily work to Him because it is His will that we should work; offering to Him also our pleasures and refreshments, because it is His will that we should recreate ourselves; living, in short, for God, and not for self or for the world.

Now the man who has learnt thus much, has learnt to take the first great step towards Christian perfection.

He has begun, as the Apostle says, to prove the *good* will of God, that is, to consider in his common daily life what God wills of him, and to have a practical insight into the relation in which he stands to God as a creature to his Creator, and as a child to his heavenly Father.

And if he be faithful to this conviction of the claims of God upon him, he will in process of time, and under the teaching of grace, go on to still greater perfection, and gain a still deeper insight into the will of God. He will prove what the Apostle calls "the acceptable will" of God; that is to say, he will learn to make a continual offering to God, not only of his work in life, and of his pleasures and refreshments, but of his troubles and sorrows and hardships also. Whatever happens to him, poverty, sickness, pain, bereavements, humiliations, the prospect of an early death,—he will be resigned and content; not because he does not feel these things,—not because he is hard and callous,—but because he has learnt to know that these too come to him from the hand of God,—that they are expressions of his Father's will,—bitter medicines but wholesome, designed for his real good.

And when patience has thus had her perfect work, then patience will give birth to joy; and strange to say,—that which will occasion the supernatural joy will be those very trials and sufferings which once it was all the man could do to bear without murmuring. He will begin to rejoice that he is counted worthy to suffer, knowing that the steep and rugged path of suffering is the shortest way to the possession of God. His lower nature, his flesh and blood, will feel the suffering still, but his spirit, taught by God's Spirit, will feel thankfulness and joy that God is thus honouring him with the richest tokens of His love; for "whom the Lord loveth He chasteneth, and scourgeth every son whom He receiveth."

And when he has thus learnt to bear pain and sickness and poverty and humiliations and contempt, not only with resignation, but with a full heart of thankful joy, then he has learnt the highest lesson of all. He is conformed not only to the good, not only to the acceptable, but to the perfect will of God; and he has come to the very opposite—to the direct contradiction of conformity to the world; for that which the world hates and shuns as the greatest evil, that by God's grace he has learnt to love, and even to seek as a means to the highest good.

And now, my dear brethren, the practical question for us is how, in any measure, in the lowest even of these three degrees of Christian perfection, we may be enabled thus to live for God and not for self or the world ; how we may loosen our hold by degrees of the perishing and unsatisfying things of this life, and tighten our grasp upon that which is unending and full of blessedness, the will of Him Who is Eternal and All-Blessed. "For the world passeth away and the concupiscence thereof, but he that doth the will of God abideth for ever." The mere knowledge that the things of earth, its occupations and possessions and enjoyments, are all hastening to an end ; or the experience that these things, even when they go well with us, cannot fill to the full the wants and aspirations of our souls—this knowledge, I say, and this experience are not of themselves enough. They may affect us for an hour, while we are listening to a sermon, or when we are seriously ill, or when we come into contact with death, but the impression soon passes away, and leaves us just as absorbed in the world, just as thoughtless of the will of God as we ever were.

If we would really grow more conformed to the will of God, and less to the spirit of the world, this must be by God's grace and in God's own way, in the way that the Apostle hints at in the text, when he bids us be "transformed in the newness of our mind."

And now let us see what he means by this. He means that we must yield ourselves to that transforming power, that power of metamorphose (for this is the very word he uses) which we have within us in virtue of our regeneration, in virtue of our union with Christ as members of His mystical body. At our baptism we were really and truly united to Him as branches are united to a vine, as limbs are united to a body. His life then passed into us. He came, by His Holy Spirit, to live within us as God and as man; and if we be in a state of grace, He thus lives within us still. And He came to live within us, and He now lives within us, that we might become new creatures, that we might have a new mind about all things, that we might begin to think differently about the things of this life, and about the will of God, than we should have thought if we had remained heathen. "For if any be in Christ, he is a new creature, the old things are passed away, behold all things are become new." He came, in short, to live within us, as God and man in one Person, that we might be enabled to live on earth as He lived in the days of His flesh; that we might be enabled to think of this world and its aims and its maxims, and of our Father in heaven and His will regarding us, even as His blessed human soul then thought; that we might be enabled to *do* the will of that Father even as He did it, throughout a life of trial and sorrow, and even outward temptation, which only ended with the sharp cross itself. When He came, He chose a lot on earth humbler and more painful than that of the lowest and most suffering amongst us; for He would be an example to all, and especially to those who are so dear to Him, His poor and suffering members. And what I would now impress on you, my dear brethren, is this, that He is not merely an example to us of perfect conformity to the will of God by His life on earth, but that by His life in us now He can and He will (if we only do our part) enable us, in our measure, to live as He then lived; enable us in our daily work of life to go about our Father's business even as He did; enable us to overcome those temptations of the world which the devil dared to offer even to Him; enable us to make it our meat and drink, the very refreshment of our spirit, to do the will of Him Who has sent us into the world; enable us, even when nature is shrinking from the thought of suffering or humiliation, to say, as He said in the Garden, "My Father, not My will, but Thine be done," and then to go forward with willingness and joy to bear our lighter crosses after Him.

Yes, this, by the power of His life within us, He will enable *us* to do, even as He has already enabled thousands and tens of thousands in every age to do, if *we* only do our part now, as they then did theirs.

And what is our part but this—first of all, to know and feel at all times that in ourselves and of ourselves we are weakness itself; but that in Christ and by His strength we can indeed overcome nature, and, in the face of temptation, do the will of God? This is the first thing we want, and what we ought daily to pray for—greater diffidence in ourselves, and greater faith and confidence in the power of Christ strengthening us, and acting, as it were, in us and by us. This was the great lesson which St Paul had himself so perfectly learnt. "I can do nothing by myself (he says), but I can do all things through Christ strengthening me." And what was true of him is equally true of us. A saint naturally is not different from any other man, from the most ordinary Christian. He differs only in this, that he has learnt thoroughly to distrust himself, and so to depend upon Christ's life within him, that when he acts Christ acts in him and by him. "I live," exclaimed this same great Apostle, and then he corrected himself—" No, not I, but Christ liveth within me." And again, "To me to live is Christ." And again, "Gladly will I glory in my infirmities that the power of Christ may dwell in me."

This, then, is the first thing requisite, to feel very intensely convinced of our own insufficiency and helplessness, as regarded in ourselves, and equally convinced that through the power of Christ within us we can, if we depend on that alone, do all things. The next thing, of course, is to *act* upon this conviction, and to act upon it as constantly as we can, not waiting for great occasions, for extraordinary difficulties or temptations, but acting upon it in the common events of our daily life, especially in those which require a little self-denial, such as rising in the morning, temperance at meals, patience over our work, command of our temper when we are put out of our way, obedience when we are commanded by parents or superiors.

On these occasions, and the like, try, my dear brethren, to recollect yourselves, to breathe a moment's prayer to Him Who lives within you by His Holy Spirit, and then go forward to the duty in His strength and under His directing power, and you will find not only that the duty will be done, but that the repugnance which you would otherwise have felt in doing it will be overcome, and give place to peace and content of soul. You will not feel pride or self-elation, for you will know that you did it, not of your own native power, but that He enabled you to do it Who Himself, when He was in this life, rose early in the cold mornings, Who Himself fared hardly, Who worked for many years with His own hands at a mechanic's toil, Who was ever patient under injuries and affronts, Who submitted as a child and youth to the authority of Mary and St Joseph.

And if you thus learn, by an active practical dependence on His life within you, to do the will of God in these smaller daily trials of life, He will prepare you for doing or suffering it in those greater trials which await us all in this school for heaven, in the moment of strong temptation, in the hour of bereavement, in days of loneliness, languor, disease, and pain, and in that last great trial which will come to each of us, the prospect of approaching death. If you be but faithful to Him, and continually dependent on His grace, His strength within you will ever be equal to the occasion. It will increase with the greatness of the trial, and it will manifest itself in that calm unshaken peace, that more than willingness to suffer, that actual joy in suffering, which only He

Who has suffered for us can give to the soul in which He dwells. And thus, by the transforming power of His life within you, you will indeed be enabled to overcome the world, and to be conformed in all things to the blessed will of your Father in Heaven.

XVI.

ENGLAND AND ROME.

"When the Lord brought back the captivity of Zion, we became like men comforted."—PSALM cxxvi. 1.

MY DEAR BRETHREN,—The Bishop of the diocese has expressed a wish, and his wishes are commands, that we should occupy ourselves to-day with the subject of the hierarchy, so that, coming to a fuller understanding of it, we may appreciate it the more, and make a more sincere thanksgiving for it. But his Lordship, in his late pastoral, has himself dealt with the nature of the hierarchy so explicitly, and exhibited the results of its restoration in England, especially in his own diocese, so fully, as considerably to abridge the subject. In brief, the hierarchy is the sacred order of Church government, and, in respect to our immediate subject, is that part of the universal hierarchy confined within the limits of this kingdom, consisting of thirteen dioceses, thirteen bishops with their cathedral churches and chapters, empowered to meet in synod under the presidency of the Metropolitan of Westminster, to legislate for our local wants.

That the reinstitution of this regular order of government has proved a benefit, is a matter of plain observation, and has, moreover, been exhibited to us in figures by the pastoral of our Bishop. That it must be a benefit in itself, in comparison with the pre-existing order of ecclesiastical administration, may be seen by reflection upon such principles as these: The constitutional government of the Church is in itself to be preferred to the personal administration of His Holiness, living as he does in Rome, even though he be a Pius IX. and most devoted to our interests: an organic body of bishops invested with ordinary power, and legislating in the country for its local wants, is preferable to a body of Vicars Apostolic holding only delegated power, and therefore unable to meet needs and dangers as they arise, without long processes of consultation and explanation: a permanent order of things is to be preferred of its very nature to a temporary expedient. In saying that constitutional government is in its nature to be preferred to the administration of the Pope, you will not misunderstand me, and suppose that any disrespect is intended to the Holy See. We are bound to understand the principle, in order to appreciate the benefit of the hierarchy, and to have a due sense of our debt of gratitude for it as in some sort a gift from the Holy See.

The Pope is, first of all, Bishop of Rome, and as such he administers his own diocese, as the Bishop of Birmingham administers his, except that he has no superior. He is not the Bishop of Birmingham, nor of Paris, nor of Cologne; but as Bishop of Rome he is the successor of St Peter, Vicar of Christ and Pope; and in his capacity as Pope has immediate jurisdiction over the universal Church, over sheep and lambs, over bishops, priests, and laity. Hence, in countries where no hierarchy has as yet been established, he has the immediate administration of ecclesiastical affairs; and in countries where the hierarchy has ceased to exist, he has the same direct administration, for they have (to use a feudal term) escheated to him. Such was the case in England at the extinction of the Catholic hierarchy, by an abuse of royal power under Elizabeth, and the same condition of things continued until the year 1850, when, by an exercise of supreme jurisdiction, the Pope again erected the hierarchy of England, and earned the personal gratitude of us all. By such act, apart from abuse on our side, he was of course advancing the interests of the Church, which is the salvation of souls; and, therefore, it is required of us not only to understand that the constitutional or normal condition of Church government is a higher state than that of dependence on the personal administration of the Pope, but to acknowledge that every reason of attachment to the Holy See is stronger under the former than under the latter, or at least not diminished. If it be a question of personal love of His Holiness, his generosity and paternal care of us can only increase it: he has added not a few to the many reasons this country has for special devotion to the Pope and Rome. If it be a question, and this is the main one, of attachment to the Pope as such, that is, as Head of the Church, and to the Holy See as the centre of jurisdiction, this surely ought and naturally would be strengthened by the reinstitution of the hierarchy. Union should be closer and firmer when its natural bonds are in force than when any less perfect mode of connection is resorted to. Devotion should flow more strongly and regularly through the ordinary channels than along any temporary course of communication. However, this is a point for consideration. It occupied the attention of the English bishops and Rome before the concession was made; it may occupy ours with profit; for if by abuse a blessing should be perverted, and made to serve in any way to weaken our relation to the Holy See, this would be to prove that they were right who argued against the ecclesiastical policy of granting it.

Cardinal Acton, who lived in Rome, and was one of the counsellors of the Pope many years ago, though in part, at least, an Englishman, opposed the concession on the ground that it would diminish the attachment of England to the Holy See. Cardinal Castracane supplies the reason for such conclusion in an answer he made to the present Bishop of Birmingham. Drawing his knowledge of our history mainly from Lingard, he affirmed of us: "You have always been a nation inclined to withstand authority!" Let us take a survey of our history, and see how far such conclusion is just.

In such a survey, the first fact to come before the

mind is the Reformation, which in this country means a national apostasy. Now, my dear brethren, this apostasy turned upon the point of the Papal authority, not merely as any and every act of abandonment of the faith is at the same time an act of separation from the Holy See, but as its explicit ground and motive. A long series of acts by which the Papal power had been crippled in this land, summed up under the name of an iniquitous statute called *præmunire*, was completed at length by a distinct Act of Parliament declaring the king to be supreme head of the Church in England, by a royal proclamation abolishing the power of the Pope, and by the imposing of an oath requiring the acknowledgment of the king's supremacy, and renunciation of the Pope's, under pain of death. The king, who delighted, as his successors have done, to wear a title conferred by an exercise of Papal prerogative, fretted under the exercise of the same prerogative when he could not bend it to gratify his ungovernable passion. The Papal power, whose office is to uphold the sacred authority of conscience, was in the lists on a question of conscience against the royal power pressed into the service of a lawless passion, and in the conflict the Papacy, which conquers by persuasion, found itself opposed and unseated in this country by cupidity allied to brute force.

Of a piece with this is the fact that hostility to the Church in this country has been summed up in the cry of *No Popery*; a cry which has entered as deeply into the political as the religious life of England, and which unprincipled statesmen, such as Shaftesbury in the reign of Charles II., trading upon the prejudices of the people, have used as the means of advancing their ambition for political office.

From the same ill-will to Rome have come what are at once the names of our reproach and our glory; I mean *Papist*, adherent of the Papa, Pope, or Father of the faithful, as it is our grace and our pride to be, and *Romans*, or liege subjects of the spiritual sovereignty of Rome, as every true Christian is.

In fine, Protestantism has concentrated all its power and its virulence into one cry, *No Popery*—has condensed its deepest emotions into a mortal hatred of Rome, and has ceased to have any common dogma but the negative one that the Pope is not the Vicar of Christ, and therefore an usurper.

Such is one side of the picture, and surely they spoke with reason who declared that we have always been a nation inclined to withstand authority. There is, however, another side to the picture, and it was on this side that the promoters of the cause of the English hierarchy looked to kindle their hopes. Before that they could only hang their heads in grief and confusion; before this they looked up with hope, for it is a spectacle not only of allegiance, but of allegiance strong unto death.

In the Saxon times,—I mean the times preceding the Norman Conquest; for in spirit, language, blood, we are Saxon still in the main,—what is conspicuous is not rebellion against the Holy See, but allegiance to it. Ceadwalla, one of the dynasty of the kings of

Wessex, which became the royal line of England, went to Rome, a pilgrim of faith and love, and died there. "This year king Ceadwalla went to Rome," says the Saxon Chronicle, "and received baptism of Pope Sergius; he gave him the name of Peter; and in about seven days afterwards, on the 12th of the kalends of May, while he was yet in Christ's garments, he died, and he was buried in St Peter's Church." Ina, of whom only praise is heard, and his queen, sovereigns of the same dynasty, resigned their kingdom that they might retire to the Eternal City, and lay their dust in the consecrated dust of Rome. Alfred the Great went with his father to Rome when very young; but, says perhaps the most popular manual of English history, "he was not too young to receive lasting impressions from his visit." What impressions they were is sufficiently shewn in the character the same manual gives of him: "he possessed and cultivated every virtue, public and private, belonging to a man, a Christian, and a king." Cnut, the Dane, went to Rome, and among the influences which changed him from a fierce warrior into a just king, must first be counted his Christian devotion, which led him also on pilgrimage to Rome. His letter thence to his people breathes the spirit of the place: after letting them know that he had spoken with the freedom of a son and a king to the Pope concerning a grievance to his subjects experienced through the practice of the Papal court, and obtained not only redress of it, but "all he had asked for the advantage of his kingdom from the sovereign Pope," he says that he has vowed to God and determined to reform his life, to govern piously and justly, maintaining equal justice in all things; and he therefore commands his ministers to see that, neither through fear of himself or any person in power, any injustice should be done or suffered towards any man, rich or poor. Edward the Confessor, the year of whose death is the closing year of these Saxon times, vowed to go on pilgrimage to Rome, but out of regard to the objections of his council that the country required his presence, he got his vow commuted by the Pope. He was directed by Leo IX. to build a monastery in honour of St Peter; and Westminster Abbey, where his successors are still crowned in his chair, is the testimony of his obedience. "And King Edward," says the Saxon Chronicle, "came to Westminster at midwinter, and there caused to be consecrated the minster which himself had built to the glory of God and of St Peter, and of all God's Saints; and the Church-hallowing was on Childermass day. And he died on Twelfth-day eve, and they buried him on Twelfth-day in the same minster."

Surely no one can say of our ancestors in these times that they were inclined to withstand Papal authority.

Along with the succeeding dynasty came in that spirit of jealousy of the authority of the Pope which culminated in the apostasy under Henry VIII. So much we must confess with shame and sorrow; but our country had still its glories. It was this spirit of opposition, set in motion from the throne, that gave occasion to the English people to produce from its ranks him who is the very martyr of the immunities of the Church and the rights of Rome. St Thomas à Becket contended to death for the freedom of Papal and episcopal administration, fighting, dying, and conquering in a struggle to defend the Church against a usurpation such as that made successfully by Henry VIII. He is therefore the elected patron of the immunities of the Church and of the Roman congregation of Cardinals instituted to maintain and guard them. There is also—and let his name never be forgotten—that champion of the Holy See's rights and upholder of episcopal responsibility, Bishop Grossteste, who, maintaining in word and deed the highest faith and reverence for the prerogatives of the Pope, yet had nobility of character enough to represent how injurious to souls in England some Papal appointments were, and even to withstand them, once earning thereby, it is said, the public praise of the Pope for so doing. The great Clerk of Lincoln, as he was called, was held in more than ordinary veneration so long as England had the faith; but under cover of ignorance Protestantism has tried to rob us of his name, and in our own days he has been heard of as its champion, that is, as an opponent of the Papacy.

But how should Protestantism, the creation of royal tyranny and its slave, understand the free spirit of a Christian bishop?—who, therefore, expostulated with the Pope because he knew his own responsibility, and knew and in the act recognised the far higher responsibility of the Pope, on whose shoulders is the government not of one diocese only, but of the Church. But fortunately there has been an official publication of his letters, and what is more, the editor, a clergyman of the Anglican Church, has had the sincerity to declare: "No one can exceed Grossteste in his reverence for the Papal power, and for Innocent IV. in particular," the very Pope whom he is said to have withstood. Once for all, he is on the right side, and a foremost figure on it. As well might they lay claim to the champion of orthodoxy, our own Founder, Dr Milner, as to Grossteste of Lincoln.

In the disastrous reign of Henry VIII., it is true, the bishops fell through not maintaining the dogma of Papal supremacy; but it is also true that with one exception they stood true under Elizabeth. It is true, and this indeed is something to set off against England's apostasy, and that God has weighed in the balance against it, that this is the one nation which has offered up to God martyrs, called traitors by their country, martyr upon martyr to the faith of the Papal supremacy. And who were the first? Two dignitaries, one of the clergy, one of the laity: a cardinal, a bishop venerable in years, John Cardinal Fisher of Rochester; and an English gentleman in the fulness of his powers, an ornament of literature, a Speaker of the House of Commons, a Lord Chancellor of England, Sir Thomas More. They lead the van of the great company of martyrs for the Papal supremacy.

Such was the glorious response the representatives

of English Catholics were able to make in answer to the charge that an extension of our liberties would diminish our attachment to the Holy See. These are the glories of England: they are not meant to, they cannot, disguise our shame. God forbid that any one should try to palliate the ignominious, sinful apostasy of the pastors of the Church and of the country under the Tudors. But on this day, when we are considering the resurrection of the Church in England, the multitude of our Almighty Father's mercies, and not His judgments which we had deserved, it is natural to point to the signs of hope.

And in this spirit let it be confessed as an undeniable truth, that if our shame proceeds from our infidelity to the Holy See, our glory proceeds from our fidelity thereto—the fidelity of many martyrs, the fidelity of a long-tried and suffering, yet hopeful remnant. It is sinful with the deepest malice that the Vicar of Christ has been so hated, mocked, belied, slandered in this country, but from the depth of her sin there springs this ray of hope, that vices spring by perversion from the same ground as virtues, that they who can hate well can love well, and that if she has shewn her hatred when, in the lurid light of her passions, she saw the Church of Rome as the harlot of Babylon, and the Vicar of Christ as Antichrist, she has in the day of her sound vision seen in the same Church the joy of her heart, and died for her faith in the Pope.

Such is the picture on one side and the other, of our shame and our glory. It is well to look at it on both sides. It has its lesson of encouragement, and its lesson of warning. It teaches us this truth, that the evils of our country have sprung from infidelity to the Holy See; that her glories in the past and her strength in the present depend upon her fidelity to it, and that her hopes of the future lie in the extension, the deepening, and the continuance of that fidelity. Only in this way can the *Second Spring* verify its promise.

I have mentioned a word that must recall memories, and memories full of inspiration. From this pulpit the word was first used, by one who knew how to make a survey, as keen as enthusiastic, of the hopes and signs of the time, and to set it fast in imperishable words. Into the *Second Spring* Oscott entered as symbolising in the very building the second rise of the Catholic Church in England, the emancipation of her children, her new glories and prospects, and as being the scene of the first act of her new life—I mean the first synod. Here the new Church met, and we are therefore inseparably connected with her resuscitation. Let us cherish the memory, and it will help us to keep the true spirit of the faith which we have inherited, of devotion and allegiance to the Pope, our Spiritual Father, of childlike love and veneration for her who has been the nurse of us all, the Catholic Church.

We have heroic examples to point the way. We cannot forget to-day, nor indeed ever, those who celebrate this change of the right hand of the Most High, not merely as a glory in the history of the

Church, but as a victory won by their labour, and patience, and blood. That we think not more of them may be ascribed in part to our being too much occupied with the result to consider the means, but much more to the cunning of their persecutors. Their misguided countrymen schemed how to rob them of their due honour as well as of their lives; made them out to be traitors, quartered their bodies, and threw them piecemeal into seething cauldrons that they might not be venerated as relics; kept off the Catholics who would draw near to dip napkins in their blood, or carry away a straw stained with it; and even hindered the knowledge of the truth by publishing slanderous reports of their having yielded to torture. Such was the malignity of their persecutors. They knew the heroism of the men they were dealing with; they knew how the Catholic world at least was looking on in admiration, and with cruel malignity they plotted to rob them of even a fair reputation. There was a clear sense here how their brethren, and countrymen, and heirs ought to honour them; and should not their schemes to obscure be a spur to us to publish their glories? Remember it was they who "sat and wept by the rivers of Babylon," or rather who pressed back from the land of their exile into their own land, laboured and poured out the streams of their own blood, "when they remembered Sion." It was they who had courageous hearts to say: "If I forget thee, O Jerusalem, let my right hand be forgotten. Let my tongue cleave to my jaws, if I do not remember thee; if I make not Jerusalem the beginning of my joy." It is we who, now that "the Lord has brought back the captivity of Sion, have become like men comforted." It is we whose "mouth is filled with gladness, and whose tongue with joy." They laboured, and we have entered into their labours. They have entered into their rest among the white-robed army of martyrs; we shall enter into ours, if we follow them in keeping ourselves unspotted from this world, and prove ourselves in doctrine and in practice heirs of their fidelity to the faith, to the Church, and to the Holy See.

XVII.

NATURE, THE SERVANT OF GOD.

"By Thy ordinance the day goeth on; for all things serve Thee."
PSALM cxviii. 91.

THE public thought of the country, whether religious or irreligious, is engaged at present with the subject of the reasonableness and efficacy of prayer for fine weather. Not only in the Catholic Church have we been praying daily in the Mass that the present hurtful rains may cease, and the pursuits of husbandry be no longer interrupted, but the authorities of the Protestant Church have called upon their communion to make solemn prayer for the same object. From these acts, which are a public profession that God has dominion over nature, and governs its course at His will, occasion has been taken to make an equally public denial of the reasonableness of such appeals to God, on the ground that the course of nature is governed by stable laws, which is true, and that this stability renders them independent of any merciful change of purpose on His part such as we implore, which is false. As we are going to make public supplication for fine weather on the three following days in the litanies which we shall sing in solemn procession, the consideration of God's power and providence over nature will, for this reason also, be timely this morning.

Why is it, then, dear brethren, that the sun is shining, that the day has succeeded to the night, that the vital force of tree and shrub is coursing through the stem, that the buds are breaking, and the flowers are blowing? Why is it that the blood is circulating through the veins, that the heart is beating, and the pulse is throbbing, that power is in the voice to speak, and in the ear to hear? It is that God, Who made all things in the beginning, sustains them even as He created them; that He Who sent forth His Spirit to communicate its vital force to every living creature, *is* communicating life to it as He did in the moment of its creation; that He Who laid the law of His purpose on them all when He made them, is governing them by the same law. The necessities of creation make the being, life, and motion of a creature as dependent on God the Creator at one moment as at another, now as ever.

Moreover, every single thing is not merely sustained in being by God, but is under His providence, and the object of His knowledge and present care. A Divine Intelligence could not create without a purpose, nor could Omnipotence allow His decreed purpose to be frustrated; so that in the mind of God is the reason why everything is, the purpose for which everything is made, and in His operations is the carrying out of His purpose: in other words, everything is under the eternal providence and present government of God. We have only to believe in an all-wise Creator, and conceive in some degree what is the act of drawing a being out of nothing, and every creature becomes a witness of God's power and care. Let the thought of Creator and creature lie within the mind and reveal itself in its consequences, and the world of sight must be seen as the instrument or organ of the Divinity, every part and constituent of which, however small or secret, must have its purpose and place in the working out of God's plan. The hairs of our head would seem to be of small account. Accustomed as we are to measure things by their magnitude, and to hold as precious only what is scarce, we may find a difficulty in taking in the truth that each grain of sand has its purpose, and that each hair of our head is distinctly known to God; but Jesus Christ has said—"Yea, the very hairs of your head are all numbered" (St Luke xii. 7). Upon each, the least of His creatures, God has written His will and purpose; each is a manifestation of Himself; and nature, which is the sum of them all in their variety, unity, and law, is His witness and handmaid.

This truth is in stronger relief in the dealings of God with the Jews than in His operations under the Christian dispensation, and for the plain reason that God was revealing Himself to them first as the God of nature and only as the pledge of a future grace, while to us He is first the Author of grace, and only secondarily of nature. Not that the Incarnation of His Son was not the primary purpose of the whole Jewish dispensation, but that He was preparing their minds to receive His Son by keeping them alive to the truth that He made them and the world, and that His will was the sovereign law of His creatures. To keep them from idolatry was the first necessity in this preparation, and in the patient working out of this purpose till the fulness of time should come, His chief means were the visible wonders He wrought among them through the forces of nature. He manifested Himself in nature. Abraham and Lot saw Him in the smouldering heap which remained of Sodom and Gomorrah after He had rained His vengeance upon them in fire and brimstone; the Israelites saw Him in the hail and the locusts and the creatures, animate and inanimate, through the ravages of which He wrought their deliverance from Egypt; they saw Him in the divided waters of the Red Sea and the Jordan, in the superhuman strength of Samson, in the weak arm of David, in the thousands of Sennacherib that strewed the ground around their city; they heard His voice in the words that broke from the lips of their children when the Spirit of God suddenly came upon them and spoke by their mouths. Thus did He become in a manner visible and vocal through the organs of His creation, till the earth and the sky was known to be, as it is, full of His majesty and power. When the Psalmist contemplated the universe, it was to him the robe of God: "Thou hast put on praise and beauty, Thou art clothed with light as with a garment;" the clouds were His chariot, the winds strewed His way, the thunder was His voice, the lightning was the minister of His will, the mountains ascended and plains descended where God had founded them; it was He Who sent forth the springs in the vale, and watered the hills in the storm; it was He Who brought forth the grass for cattle, and the herb for the service of men; He brought forth bread out of the earth, and wine to cheer the heart of man; He made the moon to know its seasons, and the sun its going down; He made the darkness of the night, and set the morning sun in the heaven, that man might go forth to his work and to his labour until the evening. The Israelites saw Him behind every feature of nature, and it is the imagery which grew out of this sense that makes one chief beauty of the Psalms. It is not an imagery of the fancy, but of faith springing from a profound and enthusiastic conviction that their God was the Creator and Lord of the universe, and that in His handiwork He had reflected His own glories. "How great are Thy works, O Lord; Thou hast made all things in wisdom: the earth is filled with Thy riches. . . . When Thou openest Thy hand, all Thy creatures shall be filled with good; but if Thou turn away Thy face, they shall be troubled. Thou shalt take away their breath and they shall fail, and shall return to their dust. Thou shalt send forth Thy Spirit and they shall be created; and Thou shalt renew the face of the earth" (Ps. ciii.)

Such was the spirit of the Jewish people formed under the tuition of God, and hence it comes that the glories of God as the Author of nature are more celebrated in the Sacred Books of the Old Testament than in the writings of the New. God has now been revealed in us by His Spirit, and the visible world is not so much the way by which we ascend to God, as the evidence of the beauty and love of a God already residing in the heart, and possessed as its own by every truly Christian soul. Nevertheless our Holy Mother, the Church, though she occupies herself primarily with the spiritual and supernatural works of God, being herself spiritual and the sphere and instrument of God's spiritual dealings with mankind, does not regard the forces of nature as being in any less degree the operations of God. Nay, she regards them as through Him subordinate to her power, as her numerous blessings of natural things, such as the crops, fruit, food, water, &c., her prayers, and especially the prayer of which there is now question, declare. And while she fails not to show her faith that God does convert the laws of the universe to man's good, she can point to daily recurring instances of the miraculous exercise of His power, as a proof that God is still ready at the prayer of faith even to interrupt the course of nature. Witness the wonders occurring at Lourdes, and attested by evidence that cannot be gainsaid.

From the manner, then, in which God revealed Himself to the Jews, and kept their mind full of Him, from the belief and practice of the Church, and from the necessary consequences of the truth of creation, we see how religion, natural and supernatural, attests the presence of God in nature, and that He governs and uses it as the instrument of His will. This clears the way for us to see how it is that the laws of the universe may be made subservient to man's will, expressed in prayer; for if on the one hand he unites his will to that of the Almighty, then so far the world is his servant as it is God's; and if on the other hand God so loves man as that He will condescend to listen to his cry, and govern His own divine acts by his desires, then it is plain how in the fullest sense the laws of the universe are converted to his good by prayer.

What is man's place in God's providence? He is the lord of creation, he has under his dominion all the created world of sense, for he is the perfection of that world, and is moreover made in his soul like to God and destined to participate in His glory. What God loves among His creatures on earth, loves in that true sense in which a return of love is possible and is sought, is only man, because he alone has intelligence to know his sovereign Benefactor. How far He delights to be with the children of men is seen in the mystery by which He was made man Himself, and in that other by which He abides here among us upon the Altar. What God seeks in this world; what He lays Himself out to catch, if you will make the expression reverent, in His beauty and majesty and boundless generosity; what He has sought, not with the profuse loveliness of nature, but with His own infinite beauty as revealed in His sacred humanity; what He stretches out the web of the world's beauties and the meshes of His divine love to ensnare, is man, frail, erring, and sinful and blasphemous before his sovereign Lord, yet still in His image, and as long as this life lasts, loved and sought for in spite of a thousand crimes. No man can seek his own good as God seeks it; no man can seek in prayer as much for his own good as God desires to give; and since God wills antecedently to help us, and is ready to incline His ear to our petition, and since nature in all its laws and operations is the obedient handmaid of His will, we have but humbly to pray, and God's promises and love are the assurance that He will bow the vast compass of the universe to work our good. To some men, I know, the glorious network of influences in which the forces of nature are knit together serves as an argument to banish God from it; every discovery of a further secondary cause seems to them a removal of God one degree further from its government. But though there be not ten, but ten thousand links of cause and effect between the emission of the ray from the sun in the heavens and the ripe grain in the ear of corn, still because He, the First Cause, is in every cause, and He the prime mover in every motion and operation, He has only to will and His divine power moves along the whole chain, and what He wills is done, even as He spoke and all things were made. And if such were His will, in the twinkling of an eye, swifter than the current that flashes along the cable beneath the Atlantic, swifter than the lightning that cleaves the clouds, from end to end of the world through endless secondary causes could He despatch the message of His purpose, and silently and inscrutably accomplish it.

Therefore he who can make the will of God his by prayer, can thereby draw the clouds over the sky and bring down the fertilising rain, or disperse them before the quickening heat of the sun.

To recognise this truth even the light of reason would be sufficient, if passion or indifference did not obscure it. To know God as Creator, overruling the world, and ourselves as creatures having access to Him by prayer, is all that is required. And yet those most given to physical studies and most penetrating in detecting the laws by which God governs the world, are often those most bold in denying His providence. How comes this?

It depends upon a principle, my dear brethren, that will bear much fruit if pondered. God becomes known in His external world to each soul only just as far as He is known to it in its own inner self. To be saved, man must know God first, not as the Creator of the world, but as his own Creator; He must know Him as He reveals Himself in the conscience, as the measure of right and wrong, as the rewarder of such as do right, and the punisher of such as do wrong. The knowledge of God begins in the subjection of our will to the voice of reason, as it is the guide of our acts, or to conscience; and if we refuse this submission, and withdraw ourselves in our inmost souls from God, it is in vain to seek Him elsewhere. God can only be present without, because He is within, and herein lies the reason why so many students of the laws of God's physical world become infidel. God is not in them, therefore He is not seen in the world without. They reject God when He speaks with the imperious voice of conscience, they withdraw themselves from His law and order as made known within them, and therefore they find Him not in the law and order of nature. On the contrary, the discovery of each new law of nature removes them more from Him, not only because it is the evidence of a power above them which they have ceased to regard as God and which they worship for its own sake, but also because the discovery strengthens the sense of their own self-sufficiency, and without indeed lessening their dependence on God for everything, lessens the sense of that dependency. Such men usually vaunt highest the claims of reason, and they have least right, as every one knows from the experience of his own soul. If reason demands the obedience of the understanding when it proclaims a speculative truth, why does it demand less authoritatively our submission when it tells us what is right and wrong, and is the evidence of our responsibility to a power above us? Has he the right to talk of reason's claims who follows it only when it flatters his passions and closes his ear when it would control his conduct? Rather is he, child or man, the only true disciple of reason who bows himself to its control, who is obedient to it as well when it asserts a truth of science as when it whispers of right and wrong, of reward and punishment. Only he who thus reverences its voice at all times, when it costs him nothing and when it costs him much to follow it, has any claim to praise, or indeed any power to estimate reason. And if our judgments were not warped by the love of novelty, or of brilliancy, or of public opinion, which is so often on the side of error, should we not, when there is question of God or religion, value more the words of a child who loves God and obeys Him, than that of any learned man, who, ceasing to follow the moral guidance of the reason, or selecting from its code of laws only such as society or his own degree of self-respect enforces, declares as the result of his study of nature that God is unknowable, and His will no longer therefore the guide of our actions? Such men reject the teachings of faith, because they have first refused obedience to the teachings of their reason. Their words therefore, brethren, upon God and religion, are to be held of no account. They should serve, indeed, to make us render an account of our faith and to give it solidity and fervour, and therefore have I referred to them. So long as our faith is sound and well grounded, its encounter with falsehood only spurs our love of the truth to new acts of faith. The spirit of opposition which at times moves men to defend opinions in which they have no belief, is then rightly used, when that truth which we know and believe on divine testimony, the saving Word of God, is attacked. It should help us then, at this time of special supplication for God's blessing on the fruits of the earth, to pray with more confidence in His providence.

Let us, therefore, during the ensuing days, join in the procession with that humility and reverence which draws God to us, and with that faith in His power and providence which Jesus Christ invites. St James for our encouragement puts before us the example of Elias : " Elias was a man passible like unto us : and with prayer he prayed that it might not rain upon the earth, and it rained not for three years and six months. And he prayed again : and the heaven gave rain, and the earth brought forth her fruit." We ask not for a miracle, we only pray that God would convert the natural laws of His providence to our good ; though He Himself puts no limit to the efficacy of the prayer of faith, not even if we should say to a mountain, " Be thou removed into the sea." And, as one result of our consideration of God's presence in His creatures and His power over them, let us in this month of May raise our thoughts to her who is the first of them all, Mary, the Queen of heaven and earth. Men have refused to honour and love her as His Mother, for the same reason that they have refused to regard the world as His dwelling-place, because she brings God too near them. When love and reverence for Him grows feeble in our souls, our sense of His presence in the world around grows proportionately enfeebled; but so long as we keep our souls full of Him or of the desire of Him, the heavens and the earth are full of His glory, or rather, I should say, of the reflection of His glory, which is to be revealed only in such as die in His service.

XVIII.

THE VENTURES OF FAITH.

"Master, we have toiled all night, and taken nothing; but at Thy word, I will let down the net."—S. LUKE v. 5.

THIS account of the miraculous draught of fishes, like all the other miracles of our Blessed Lord, in addition to its more direct and obvious purport, is capable of suggesting lessons which are applicable at all times and to all conditions of persons.

The immediate design was doubtless to teach the Apostles, and especially him who was destined for their chief, and in their persons the pastors of the Church in every age, the great truth that success in their apostolic labours would depend not on mere human industry and perseverance, but on the presence with them of Him in Whose name and cause they were called to labour, and on their faith in His assistance, and on their prompt obedience to His commands, even when circumstances should seem most unfavourable and the chance of success most improbable. What mere words or exhortations could so forcibly teach them this, could so impress it on their memories, as the miraculous occurrence of which they were then the witnesses?

All night long they had been at their toil on the lake, rowing out with their long heavy net, and then drawing it in again slowly and cautiously, anxiously watching the contracting circle on the water to catch sight of the entoiled and struggling prey, but all in vain. Each time, all through that night, the net came empty to their disappointed hands. So when morning broke, they abandoned the unprofitable task, and with the patience of Easterns, sat down on the shore to prepare their tackle for future service.

As they were thus employed, their Divine Master, whose omniscient mind had watched them all through the hours of that weary night, appeared on the strand, surrounded by a crowd who pressed on Him to hear the Word of God. He called St Peter, entered his boat, bade him thrust a little from the shore, and when He had finished His discourse from that symbolical Chair of truth, desired him to pull out into the lake and to let down the net for fishing. St Peter told our Lord of their fruitless labour. "Master (he said), we have toiled all night, and taken nothing;" but, with that instinctive faith and ready obedience which ever characterised him, he hesitated not to comply with the command. "We have toiled all night and taken nothing; but at Thy word, I will let down the net." The net was lowered and drawn, and so great a number of fish were at once taken, that the net was broken, and the two boats were filled with fish, almost to sinking.

St Peter, awestruck at the preternatural event of which he had been made the instrument, and recognising in one flashing thought the divinity of our Lord, threw himself at the knees of Christ, exclaiming, "Depart from me, for I am a sinful man, O Lord." But Jesus said to him, "Fear not; from henceforth thou shalt catch men." So the miracle decided his vocation. From a fisherman he became an Apostle, and the Head and Chief of the Apostles. The broken net mattered not now. "Having brought their ships to land, leaving all things, they followed Jesus." And during his Apostolate, after that wonder-working Lord had ascended to heaven, leaving in His servant's hands the keys of the kingdom of heaven, when on the Pentecostal birthday of the Church he to whose guidance that Church had been committed went forth with his brother Apostles into the streets of Jerusalem, and stood fearless amidst the mocking multitude, and by a single discourse converted three thousand of them to the faith, when afterwards he passed to the populous provinces of Asia eastward, and at length set up his See in the great Metropolis of the West,—during all this long Apostolate, that miraculous occurrence on Gennesareth's Lake would again and again recur to his memory, inspiring him with confidence in that arduous mission of his, of which it had been made the occasion, reminding him that there was ever at hand an Invisible One guiding and ruling the Church by human agency; One Who having created the fish of the sea and lake, was able then to control their movements; One Who having created the spirit of man, is able to draw to Himself the very freedom of the human will.

And from that time for 1800 years, the same Bark, the Bark of St Peter, has ever floated on this sea of life; at times all but overwhelmed by its billows, and beaten back by sudden tempests from its onward course, but ever at the very crisis of its peril rescued by Him Whom the winds and seas obey, and Who by a word can speak the storm of human passion into a great calm; at other times spreading its nets in vain through many a dark and weary night in days of laxity or worldly policy, losing children rather than adding to their number, but still ever and anon hearing a divine command to make the ventures of faith, and by obedience to that command, and contrary to all human probabilities, winning to God innumerable souls, and training for heaven generations of faithful.

So it was, as I have said, in the days of St Peter himself, when by his mouth Jews and Gentiles, Palestine, Asia, and Italy, received the germs of faith. So it was when his successor in the Roman See undertook the conversion and civilisation of those countless barbarian races which for more than a century poured themselves as a torrent on Southern Europe. So was it when St Celestine gave his benediction to St Patrick and sent him to convert Ireland. So was it when St Gregory commissioned Augustine and his brother monks to reconvert this island of ours. So was it when the discovery of America and the conversion of its vast southern continent, in some measure compensated for the schism of the East, and the heresy of Northern Europe. So was it when England's missionary priests and the sons of Benedict and Ignatius came forth in little bands from Rome and Douay in the days of persecution, and in spite of dungeon, rack, and gibbet, kept alive in this land that little root of faith which now is again springing up into a vigorous tree. And so is it now in this day, when the Catholic missioner is everywhere penetrating into lands pagan and inhospitable, when China and Japan, and India and Africa, and the islands of the South already count their converts, ay, faithful converts too, who dare to suffer for their faith, by hundreds and thousands; and when the Annals of the Propagation of the Faith are no unworthy continuation of the Acts of the Apostles.

But not only for the pastors and labourers in God's Church is this miracle thus instructive; it has a lesson too for each of us in the conduct of our own individual Christian life. For what is it in which our trial and probation as Christians consists but just in this, in daring to make the ventures of faith, in staking all things on the word and promise of Christ, in acting on that word when sight and sense cannot assist us, when past experience can do nothing to assure us of the certainty of the result?

It was this which St Peter did. At the word of Christ, he threw the net again where he had been throwing it all night unprofitably. Sight and sense could not assure him of success. The experience of the night seemed to tell him that success was improbable; but with him one word of Christ outweighed all sight and sense and past experience. He obeyed in faith, and then sight and sense were satisfied, and a new experience took the place of the old. And so will it be with us if we do likewise. Let us understand this, my dear brethren. We say that a man "makes a venture" when he sacrifices some present profit or advantage with the view of some larger profit which he hopes and expects, but cannot be certain, will result from that present sacrifice. The husbandman, for instance, commits the seed to the earth, and thus loses all present use of it, with the hope of a large return, which, according to the state of the weather, may or may not be reaped. The merchant again embarks his property in some commercial speculation, and thus sacrifices the present enjoyment of it, with the hope of a considerable profit hereafter. Human life indeed, in one way or another, is almost made up of such ventures. And men make their ventures on human faith. The husbandman reposes faith in the general uniformity of the seasons; the merchant in the integrity of those to whom he entrusts his money.

Now the very essence of a really Christian life consists in exactly the same principle of action, only in the spiritual or supernatural order; in staking what is present and visible for that which is future and invisible, and that on our faith in the word or promise of Christ; in sacrificing something of temporal good and advantage, simply because He has assured us that such sacrifice will be for our spiritual and eternal good.

This is what our Lord Himself teaches us. He bids us deliberately to "count the cost" before we commit ourselves to Him; to see, that is, whether we have the heart and spirit to make the sacrifice which His service will entail. In other places, He tells us that unless we "deny ourselves," we cannot be His disciples. He does not merely say that unless we renounce sin we cannot be His disciples, though this of course is true; but He goes beyond this, and says that unless we "deny ourselves," we cannot be His; and self-denial does not mean the renouncing of what is in itself evil, but the renouncing of what is naturally lawful and good, for the sake of some higher and supernatural good. So again He says, that unless we "forsake all that we have," that is, unless we are ready, at His call, to abandon any temporal interest whatever, "we cannot be His disciples." And the motive He puts before us for these present sacrifices is our own spiritual interest and advantage here and hereafter. Thus He says, "Every one that hath left house, or brethren, or sisters, or father, or mother, or wife, or children, or lands, for My name's sake, shall receive a hundredfold, and shall possess life everlasting."

It is true indeed that few of us may be called to make any great sacrifice such as these; but still the principle remains certain, that we cannot be Christians ("disciples of Christ") in any real sense, unless we are venturing something simply on the faith of

Christ's word and promise; unless there be something or other of present inclination or advantage we are sacrificing, because we believe, on the strength of His word, that this sacrifice will profit us eternally.

The habit, for instance, of private prayer for ourselves and others, is such a venture; it costs us time and considerable effort of mind, and we do not always see its present fruits. We may be inclined to think that we have long toiled and "taken nothing;" but if we have faith in the word of Christ, Who promises a special reward to such prayer, we shall persevere. So again, when a young man chooses some profession in life which he knows to be safer and better for his spiritual interests, rather than another to which he is more inclined naturally, he makes a venture of faith. Almsgiving, again, is such a venture in a very special way; in giving alms we deprive ourselves of that which represents almost every temporal good, on the word of Christ that we shall thereby be laying up treasure in heaven. Imposing on ourselves some permanent penance, or denying ourselves innocent pleasures, as a punishment for past sins, is another such venture.

In short, whatever we do, or whatever we deny ourselves, which we should not do or deny ourselves unless we believed in the promise of Christ, is a venture of faith. It is taking Him at His word, and acting on that word against present inclination and immediate profit. It is thus the surest of all tokens, if indeed it be not the only real token—that our faith in Him is not nominal but real, not in word only, but in deed and truth.

Let us then examine our life by this test, and see what we have thus committed to Christ; what stake we have in the truth of His word. We doubtless all have faith enough to believe, as a general truth, that He can and will fulfil to the uttermost all that He has promised. Let us then act on that belief, and venture something on His promises. So only shall we one day draw the full net to the eternal shore. So only shall we now look forward to that life beyond the veil with a sure hope and trustfulness, with something of the holy confidence of Christ's Apostle, who as he drew near to that life could say—"I know Whom I have believed, and I am certain that He is able to keep that which I have committed to Him against that day."

XIX.

CHRIST WITH US IN THE DESERT.

"I have compassion on the multitude, for behold they have now been with Me three days and have nothing to eat."—S. MARK viii. 2.

MOST of you are familiar with the explanation of the miracle worked on this occasion by our Lord; that, wonderful as it was in itself, it was the foreshadowing of the still greater, though less obvious miracle of the Blessed Eucharist, that "table in the wilderness" (Ps. lxxvii. 19), spread by the Divine bounty to feed the hungry souls of men in the desert of this world. But besides its reference to this greater work of love that was to follow, this miracle, in its circumstances, suggests incidentally various other lessons. For instance, the mere *picture* it sets before us is *itself* a teaching about our Lord's divinity. If we were told of some one nowadays whose discourses were of such intense interest as to draw four or five thousand men away from their daily work, and so fascinate them that they would follow him miles away from their homes into the rude open country, forgetting even their bodily needs of food and rest, leaving their trade and the implements of their daily toil to take care of themselves, and hanging for hours and days in silent attention on his words, though all the while he was to outward appearance only a poor artisan like themselves,—what should we say of it? We should probably begin by disbelieving the report, we should say it was incredible. But what if, by and by, the facts were proved to be as they were stated, and new and stranger facts were added,—that this man, for example, having little or nothing of his own, had on a sudden, in a desert place, provided this starving multitude with food? We should be simply at a loss to explain it by any human calculation. Perhaps we should try to think of it as a sort of madness come upon the people, some strange infatuation or wild enthusiasm, inspired by the genius of this man; unless indeed we looked at it with other eyes, and confessed that such an explanation was only trifling with the facts, and wholly inadequate to account for them.

Nevertheless, it was probably some such explanation a Jew of the Pharisee type would make to himself of the strange news which, in the time the Gospel speaks of, came to him out of Galilee. For all this, and much more, would be told him of the doings of Jesus, the carpenter's reputed son. He would hear how the sick were being healed of all manner of infirmities, and how devils were being cast out, confessing, as they went, that He Who cast them out was the Son of God (St Matt. viii. 29). Even dead men, he would be told, had been brought back to life under circumstances that left no room for deception or mistake. Perhaps he himself had listened to this wonderful preacher, when but a short time before he was travelling on foot through Judæa, and had shrunk before His withering exposure of the falsehood and hypocrisy of his own sect. And now by that Lake of Gennesareth the words of this strange orator were calling the fishermen from their nets, and the labourers from the fields, some of them, the Gospel adds, "from afar off." Looking at their numbers, whole villages, in fact, must have been emptied of their inhabitants. Onward, ever into the desert, they followed Him; and as the words of a teaching holier than the world had ever listened to before fell from Him, they seemed to find their way into the very souls of His hearers; they took possession of them, so that house, and home, and food, and rest were all forgotten in the spell of that voice and the living words it uttered. It is a strange and stirring picture. It seems to speak aloud to us of that Master's presence, which alone could work such wonders, and so fill and absorb the hearts of His creatures that they forgot the very needs of life. Even in its mere remembrance, as it comes to us from that far-off age, now, when the world reckons itself too wise to believe, does not that scene compel us, as we gaze upon it, to strike our breasts and own with the centurion beneath the cross, "Of a truth this was the Son of God!"

Then again, take notice of the very circumstance of the *place*, for it too has its lesson. It is called the *desert* (St Matt. xv. 33); not necessarily the sandy waste we are accustomed to speak of by that name, but more probably it was a wild uncultivated spot like that desert of Bethsaida, of which St John (vi. 10, cf. St Luke ix. 10) tells us " there was much grass in the place." It was at all events a solitude, such as our Lord seems to have sought frequently in the midst of His labours, where, free from interruptions, He might speak alone with His Father, or discourse with the faithful souls He had drawn apart from the world. And as such it reminds us of the need *we* have, each of us, of our own time and place for solitary thought, when God and our soul must be together, apart from all else. This is the solitude which finds its place in every good Catholic's life, at least in the time of his daily prayers and the examination of his conscience.

But again, the desert is, as you know, used often by spiritual writers as a figure of this *world*, in which we wander as pilgrims, and in contrast with the home and place of our true rest, which is heaven.

Yet when Scripture (Ps. lxxxiii. 7, xliii. 20) speaks of this world as "a valley of tears" overspread with the shadow of death, we are sometimes inclined to say to ourselves these are strange expressions, and do not describe our *own* experience of it. For it looks, perhaps, to *us* a very pleasant world, full of bright and beautiful things,—and its chief drawback is that it cannot last. And so, especially when we are young, such expressions sound to us *unreal*.

We must put ourselves in the place of the saints to know what they mean. From their point of view, the world is indeed a bright and glorious thing as it came from God's hand; but because they were gifted with a clearer light than we are, and saw not only the beauty of God's work as He had made it, but saw too the deeds of men and their wickedness, they knew how that beauty was blurred and spoilt by the sin that everywhere was festering underneath, and looking upward with that eye of faith which could almost pierce the veil, and gaze upon the loveliness of heaven and the glory of the saints, this earth became to them, by contrast, in truth a valley of shadows and of tears.

Even to us, as time goes on, its brightness is dimmed, as loss and sorrow overshadow our lives, and we look with other eyes at what seemed once so fair. If, then, there is no cloud as yet in *your* sky, thank God and be grateful for the sunshine. But do not forget it is still the desert you are in, and that unless Christ be with you, your souls will faint by the way.

I will tell you what I mean. You are looking forward to the happiness of home. Of all God's natural gifts this is the best. It is the image of that first bright home in Paradise when as yet the world was fair as God had made it. But Paradise was fair and bright on one condition; it had its law. When that was broken and sin entered, its joy was gone. The flowers might bloom, and the birds sing, but for man there was only shame and misery and death! It is the same with *your* paradise. It has its law; see that you guard it well! Home is in truth not only your earthly paradise, but it is the test of your religious principle, and tells how much of it is real and honest. If, when a boy is free from college rule, he shows himself obedient, unselfish, straightforward, and kind, if he speaks no wrong word, and gives no bad example, if he says his prayers regularly and well,—most of all, if he has his times for confession and communion, and keeps to them; then he has stood the test. No matter where such a one may be, nor what his needs and difficulties in the desert of this life, for Christ is with him; and as He fed the multitude in the wilderness, so will He feed him with His grace, and strengthen him in times of trial, and gladden his heart with that joy without which all happiness is empty and unreal—the joy of a good conscience.

XX.

THE BLESSED EUCHARIST.

I have compassion on the multitude; for behold, they have been with Me three days, and having nothing to eat. And if I send them away fasting to their home, they will faint in the way."—S. MARK viii. 2.

OUR Blessed Saviour, my dear brethren, in working His miracles, besides the general purpose of manifesting His divine power, seems always to have had two special ends in view—an immediate end and a remote end.

The immediate end was, in almost every case, the relief of some form or other of temporal want or suffering. The more remote end was to teach us, through this temporal interposition, some eternal truth of the kingdom of grace. Thus, when He opened the eyes of the blind, or the ears of the deaf, when He restored the palsied limb to strength, or raised the dead to life, His first design was to relieve these various forms of human misery and calamity, His second was to illustrate the power of His grace in subduing the corresponding maladies of the soul, *its* spiritual blindness, and deafness, and palsy, and death. So, again, when in Peter's storm-tossed bark He woke from His slumber and rebuked the winds and the waves, so that there was a great calm, this was not merely to allay the fears and save the lives of His Apostles, but also to teach them and us that at the very crisis of the Church's peril—when her very existence seems threatened by the storm of human passion,—He rouses Himself from what may have seemed to us indifference to her danger, and by a word speaks the storm into peace.

And the same twofold purpose may be seen in His miracle of the multiplication of bread. The first and immediate design of that stupendous exercise of divine power was to recruit the exhausted strength of that great multitude, who could not without great suffering, or peril to life itself, obtain a supply of food in the ordinary way. "I have compassion," He said, "on the multitude; for behold, they have been with Me three days, and have nothing to eat: and if I send them away fasting to their home, they will faint in the way." But a further end of that miracle was to shadow forth to us the great mystery of that miracle of love which the same Lord works daily in the Church—the multiplication on her ten thousand altars of "the Bread of Life," "of His own most sacred Body."

The Blessed Eucharist has well been called a "compendium of miracles." But amongst these there are two which are most remarkable; the first being the instantaneous change of one substance into another—the instantaneous change of the substance of the bread and wine into the substance of the Body and Blood of Christ ; the second being the illimitable multiplication of that divine substance of Christ's sacred Body and Blood, that is, its presence in an indefinite number of places at one and the same time. Which is the greater miracle of the two we cannot say. That one substance should in an instant cease to be, and another wholly different take its place, and that this new substance should be wholly and entirely here, and yet wholly and entirely there, and wholly and entirely in all parts of the earth at once—these, I say, are both miracles equally wonderful to our human conceptions, which judge according to the ordinary laws of nature, and both equally easy to that God Who, having ordained those laws, can, of course, suspend or modify them when and how He pleases.

But what I wish you to observe is this, that our Blessed Lord, as if in compassion to our sense-tied intellects, did not abruptly announce to men this eucharistic mystery, or bid them to believe in it before He had prepared them for its belief. It is a miracle in which our senses can be of no use to us, for it takes place in a region into which the senses cannot penetrate—in the region, not of appearances, but of substances, which are as impervious to the senses as our own souls are. But, nevertheless, our Blessed Lord, in preparing us for belief in this invisible miracle, did vouchsafe to appeal to the sight and other senses. He wrought two miracles, of the truth and reality of which the senses *could* judge, in order that we might be prepared and disposed to believe His word with respect to corresponding miracles in the Blessed Sacrament, of which, from the very necessity of the case, the senses were precluded from judging.

The very first miracle which He worked was that of the marriage feast of Cana, when by a word He changed one substance into another,—the substance of water into the substance of wine. What was at one moment simple water, became, at the next, by His Almighty word, wine—wine which was served to all at table, and attested as such by every human sense. Having thus, as the Evangelist says, "manifested forth His power and glory, His disciples believed in Him," and had no difficulty therefore in believing His word when, three years later, He announced to them that He had changed the substance of wine into that of His own Blood, and the substance of bread into that of His own Body.

And so, also, in the other miracle of feeding thousands of persons with a few loaves, our Blessed Lord gave His disciples *ocular* proof of His power to multiply the substance of bread, that is, to make present in a thousand places at once the very substance which had before been present but in one. He blessed it, and brake, and behold the fragment He broke off contained all the bulk and substance of the entire loaf; and that again, as it was broken by His multiplying hands, was separated into new loaves, and so on till the whole multitude were fed and satisfied; and when all had eaten, the very crumbs and fragments which remained were a greater mass than the original loaves from which they had been separated. Having witnessed this amazing miracle, His disciples were prepared to believe with unhesitating faith in His power to multiply also the presence of His own sacred Body, and to give Himself wholly and entirely, as the living Bread from heaven, not to thousands merely at once, but to all the members of His world-wide mystical Body. Their senses, you see, had convinced them of the reality of the miracle of the loaves. Sight, and taste, and touch had all confirmed it, and their faith in Him superseded the testimony of sense, and assured them of the equal reality of the invisible eucharistic miracle. "*Præstat fides supplementum sensuum defectui.*"

Moreover, our Blessed Lord, as if in condescension to the weakness of man's faith, and in order that a greater number of His disciples might witness His power, vouchsafed to work this miracle of the multiplication of bread more than once, and that on an ascending scale. On the first occasion He fed 4000 persons with seven loaves, when seven baskets full of fragments remained; on the second occasion He fed 5000 with five loaves, and twelve baskets full of fragments remained. You see the fewer number of loaves were made to feed the greater number of people, and after a greater number had eaten, more fragments remained from the five loaves than those which had remained from the seven. This was doubtless to show that His power was illimitable; that what seemed a greater difficulty, with respect to the ordinary laws of nature, was equally easy to Him Who is the Creator and Lord of nature.

And that our Saviour worked this latter miracle for the very purpose of confirming our faith in the corresponding eucharistic miracle, is clear from this, that He made it the occasion of announcing to His disciples the future gift of His own Body and Blood as the food of life, the bread of heaven. The same chapter in St John's Gospel which records the miracle of the multiplication of bread, records also the promise of the institution of the Blessed Eucharist. For, when on the following day His disciples and the Jews came round Him in the synagogue of Capharnaum to ask an explanation of this miracle, He said "*I* am the bread of life. Your fathers did eat manna in the desert and are dead; this is the bread which cometh down from heaven, that if a man eat of it he may not die. I am the living bread which came from heaven; if any man eat of this bread, he shall live for ever; and the bread which I will give is My flesh for the life of the world." The Jews therefore (as the evangelist tells us) strove among themselves, saying, " How can this man give us His flesh to eat?" Then Jesus said to them, "Amen, amen. I say unto you, Except ye eat the flesh of the Son of Man and drink His blood, you shall not have life in you. He that eateth My flesh and drinketh My blood hath everlasting life, and I will raise him up in the last day. For My flesh is meat indeed and My blood is drink indeed. He that eateth My flesh and drinketh My blood abideth in Me and I in him. As the living Father hath sent Me, and I live by the Father, so he that eateth Me, the same also shall live by Me."

These words were spoken a year before His Passion. Till then, the *mode* in which they were to be fulfilled remained a mystery even to the Apostles. But when, on the eve of His Passion, after partaking with Him of the last Paschal Feast of the old law, they saw Him again take bread in His sacred hands, and again repeat the very same action which had accompanied these miracles on the mount—when they saw Him now, as then, look up to heaven, and bless, and break, —and when His words, His creative and transforming words, at last fell on their ear—"Take, eat, this is My Body." "Drink ye all of this. This is My Blood "— then, in one moment they comprehended that scheme of tender and loving preparation, the deep import of those miracles at Cana and on the mountain, the meaning of that mysterious discourse at Capharnaum, —why He had then called Himself "the bread of life," "the bread from heaven "—how, under the appearance of their daily food, He could give Himself wholly and entirely to each, and dwell within each as the common life of all.

Oh, blessed reward of child-like faith! Oh, happy they, that they had believed in the words when as yet they could neither comprehend them, nor see the possibility of their fulfilment. Happy they, that when others of His disciples had stumbled at those words and from that day had gone back, and walked no more with Him, and when He had appealed to them, the twelve, and said, "Will you also go away?" they had answered by the mouth of the loving Peter, "Lord, to whom shall we go? Thou hast the words of eternal life, and we have believed and have known that Thou art the Christ, the Son of God." Yes, blessed they, for it was their reward to receive Him into their souls as their divine food and life, and to live by Him, even as He by His eternal generation lived by the Father, till at length they lived with Him, and like Him, for ever in the kingdom of glory above.

And we, my brethren, are the inheritors of their faith, and, if we will it, of their blessedness. The Holy Church throughout all the world, founded by their toils and watered with their blood—that Holy Catholic Church to which we by God's goodness belong—see how she exalts and magnifies this priceless treasure which has been entrusted her of the Body and Blood of her Divine Lord! It is the one centre of her whole system, that which gives meaning to all her services and ceremonial; that which is the end of all her other Sacraments, the great Sun in her heavens, around which all her other devotions circulate, shedding light and warmth and life on all. As the ages go on, and as heresies abound, she clings all the closer to her heavenly gift, and bids a holy defiance to an unbelieving world, and multiplies everywhere her altars and her sacrifices, her processions and benedictions; and if the world believe not, she raises Him on high, and fearlessly exposes Him to the hard gaze of incredulity, and leaves it to Him to convert the world.

But it is not, my dear brethren, your faith in this blessed mystery that I would seek to strengthen, so much as your devotion to our sacramental King. Your faith, thank God, is doubtless firm and strong, so firm and strong that I believe there is not one among you who would not choose to die rather than to deny it. But your very familiarity with this mystery, the very ease with which, as the faith-gifted children of the Church, you believe in it, will, if that belief be not accompanied by frequent acts of love and communion, beget in you a spirit of carelessness and indevotion towards this heavenly mystery.

Consider then, and make it a habit frequently to meditate on, the wonderful goodness and compassion of our Blessed Lord in bestowing on us so divine a gift. When He was upon the mountain of Galilee, His Sacred Heart was touched with sympathy at the sight of that famishing multitude who for three days together had been listening to His discourses. The food they had brought with them was all consumed; hunger made itself felt, and they were far from home. "I have compassion," He said, "on the multitude, for they have now been with Me three days, and have nothing to eat, and if I send them away fasting to their homes, they will faint on the way." But what was this compassion which He felt for them in their temporal necessity, but a shadow of that deep yearning compassion which He feels for us in our far greater spiritual necessities? For we too, my brethren, have in ourselves, and of ourselves, nothing; nothing but wants and miseries and cravings and famine of soul. We, too, are far from our Home, far from that land where they hunger no more, nor thirst, where the possession of God fills up every want of the soul with His own joy and blessedness. He Who made us alone knows how needy we are in this pilgrimage of life, how tempted by the world and the flesh, how haunted by evil, how beset by subtle and malicious foes. Truly, our Home is afar off, and the way thither is crowded with perils. He knows it, He compassionates us,—and see what He has done; He has spread a table in the wilderness. He has rained down upon us the heavenly manna, the Bread of angels, containing in itself all sweetness and delight. He has given us His own Divine Body and Blood to be our very food, our solace, and our strength,—the support of our pilgrimage, the joy and refreshment of our weary souls. Are we tempted by the world and its false promises and glitter? Then here is One Who will open our eyes to its illusions, and disenchant us of its vain shows, and awaken within us a *new* world of secret hopes and joys which neither deceive nor fade away. Are we tempted by the flesh, and weary of contending against its importunities? Then here is One Who, received into the soul, will allay its concupiscence, and calm its passions, and kindle in it the fire of that Divine Love which burns not to destroy and consume. Are we assaulted by the ever-shifting attacks of Satan, by pride, or covetousness, or presumption, or despair, or by the deadly drowsiness of spiritual indifference? Then here is One Who is stronger than our enemy, and Who will give us His own strength to overcome him, Who for pride will give us humility, for covetousness liberality, for presumption diffidence, and for despair hope, and for the spirit of sloth the spirit of wakefulness and earnestness.

And, lastly, are we amidst all these dangers and trials, far from home, anxious for the future, fearful lest we should faint by the way, and lose ourselves for ever? Then there is One here, hidden beneath these sacramental species, Who if we but keep by Him and live by Him, will every step of the way be our guide, our companion, and our secret strength—Who will uphold our trembling steps, and raise us from our falls, and empower us to persevere to death, and Who then, even at that hour when flesh and heart are failing, will give Himself to us as the Viaticum of that last dread journey, as the strength of our failing heart, and as our portion for ever.

Truly then, we may say that of all the miracles of that adorable Sacrament, the greatest of all is the miracle of love and divine pity which prompted its institution. Ah! then, dear brethren, let us not be cold and indifferent to such goodness and grace. Love is the only return you can make for such love, and frequent devout communion is the best way in which you can show your love. Remember that it is He Who will be our Judge Who now shrouds His Majesty beneath these sacramental veils, and offers

Himself as the daily food of our souls. How shall we appear before Him then? what plea, what excuse, shall we then be able to urge, if here we have treated this amazing condescension and goodness with neglect and indifference? Strive, then, to make reparation to His Sacred Heart for past coldness by the increased fervour and frequency of your communions. You cannot, I know, communicate sacramentally every day; but at least let no day pass by without a fervent act of *spiritual* communion, without a heartfelt desire of uniting yourself with Him. For He deigns to value and to reward the slightest act of love and desire made to Him in this special sacrament of love. He rewards it by increasing that desire; and as He enlarges the desire of the soul, He enlarges its capacity, and gives Himself to it with greater fulness and greater fruit, changing us thereby ever more and more into Himself, living within us ever more and more, as the strength of the life of grace, and as the pledge of the future life of glory.

XXI.

ON THE CHOICE OF ST PETER.

"Blessed art thou, Simon Bar-jona: because flesh and blood hath not revealed it to thee, but My Father Who is in heaven."
—S. Matt. xvi. 17.

THE character of St Peter comes out so vividly in the many incidents the Gospels relate of him, that we seem to have a fuller and more intimate knowledge of him than of the rest of the Apostles. And no doubt it was so designed by God—he was to succeed his Divine Master as Vicar and representative, he was to be the pattern of all future popes in the exercise of that supreme authority; and so the details of his life, its strength and its weakness, its poverty in worldly gifts, its wealth in the order of grace, are set before us, and we learn the secret of that excellence for which infinite wisdom chose him out and set him in the foremost place.

What strikes us, perhaps, first of all in reflecting on the character and office of St Peter, is the exclusion of so many who to us would seem to have been far more fitted to occupy his place. He was to deal with the intellectual errors of the world. Would not then an intellectual man, such as Nicodemus, with a social position to sustain him, or one like Gamaliel, learned in the law, be naturally looked for as the fitting instrument for such a work? For the Law in such men's hands would have made manifest that Christ was indeed the Messias foretold; their station and their mental gifts would have secured them a hearing which the fisherman from Galilee could scarcely hope to gain, while their rule and authority among the convert disciples might surely be expected to outweigh any that such a one could pretend to. We know, in fact, that the character of St Peter and most of his companions was the very argument with some of the Pagan writers, the sufficient ground, as they conceived, for rejecting and despising Christianity.

Then again, besides St Peter's ignorance, he was impulsive, unreflecting, ready to walk upon the waters or to strike with the sword; but ready, too, to desert his Master in Gethsemane and deny Him in the courtyard of Caiphas.

What then is the connection between Peter so humanly weak, and Peter so mightily exalted by his Divine Master? I think we shall find a clue to it in considering how things stood in the world when the Church of the new law began.

Before doing so we may remind ourselves that God had, of course, no need of cultivated human intellect to work out His designs. Knowledge is His creation and His gift, a natural and a necessary instrument in the hands of His creatures by which to work out human ends, but not with Him. He can give or withhold it, make use of it in those who have it, or dispense with it at His will. In founding His Church He chose to do without it, speaking comparatively and of human knowledge; and passing over the wise and learned men of the time, He chose for His instruments men who were, most of them, strikingly devoid of what is called education.

Thus Infinite Wisdom fitted the means to the end. The end was the world's reformation, and the world which had gone astray in the pride of its intellect and the evil desires of its heart, was to be brought back by the preaching of a fisherman and the ignominy of a cross.

It was the world of which St Paul declares to the Romans (i. 21), "that when they had known God they did not glorify Him as God, nor gave thanks, but became vain in their thoughts, and their foolish heart was darkened: for professing themselves to be wise, they became fools. . . . Wherefore (he adds) God gave them up to the desires of their hearts, to uncleanness."

Surely then, even to our poor human wisdom, the means were well fitted to the end. To humble the world's pride by subjecting its intellect to the teaching of His messengers, to subdue its passions by binding them with the fetters of His law, would be the completest overthrow of the kingdom of Satan, the plainest manifestation of divine power and goodness. And this is what He did; and His instruments in the work were so chosen as to shew beyond dispute, that it *was His* work, above and beyond all human calculation; and that the way of salvation to which He called the world, was open to the lowliest, that none could be too poor, none too ignorant, to find and follow it.

How clearly all this comes out in the after teaching of these messengers of His! Take, for instance, those words of St Paul to the Corinthians (1. Ep. i. 21), where he tells them, "seeing that, in the wisdom of God, the world by wisdom (that is, its own false learning) knew not God, it pleased God by the foolishness of preaching to save them that believe. For the Jews," he says, "require signs, and the Greeks seek after wisdom. But we preach Christ crucified; to the Jews a stumbling-block, and to the Gentiles foolishness." And so the world was brought face to face with the Church, which was sent to save it by the destruction of its false wisdom.

Still, what had St Peter to commend him as the leader in this mighty undertaking? Certainly not learning, nor power, nor riches. Something, however, he had which was better than all these, that simple, upright, honest heart, that unselfish goodwill which was all the Divine Master required in him.

Whatever knowledge might be requisite, He would supply in His own time. And so while learned Pharisees came and went with supercilious questionings, refusing the baptism of John and sneering at the doctrine of Christ, He said (St Matt. xi. 25), " I give thanks to Thee, O Father, Lord of heaven and earth, because Thou hast hid these things from the wise and prudent, and hast revealed them to little ones;" that is, the supreme knowledge which these men of the world missed in the blindness of their pride, He gave to others who, like Peter, beholding His miracles, had recognised His claim and sought His teaching with a humble heart. In that teaching Peter knew and confessed the Divinity of his Master, and was blessed because he had found that truth which *men* could not teach him, but only God. "Blessed art thou, Simon Bar-jona, because flesh and blood hath not revealed it to thee, but My Father Who is in heaven" (St Matt. xvi. 17).

Now in this "flesh and blood" our Lord speaks of, we shall find another indication of our Lord's design in choosing Peter for His vicar. The expression, as we know from other places in Scripture, signifies *mere* human nature—man as apart from God and His grace, working out his natural aims by merely natural powers, and in accordance with his natural appetites and desires.

To such as these God is not revealed, nor can they make Him known to others. Theirs is the "wisdom of the flesh" which, full of self trust, seeking no light from God, pushes recklessly out into the deep waters of the unknown, and tries every question by the light of its own feeble reason. These are they who discover the error of all who have gone before them, and drifting for awhile over a sea of human opinion, founder at last in their own conceit.

Our times are not without melancholy instances of miseries like these: they are *our* warning. For with the spirit of the world like an atmosphere surrounding us, who is safe from temptation? It is not that our enemy will suggest to us an open defection from the faith. He is far too crafty. But he will tell us that in these enlightened times we must open our mind and ears to what the world has to say and judge for ourselves; that we must not be held back by a reverence for antiquated prejudices; that the learning of our times is exploding much of the ancient teaching, &c. He will even hint that the Church is perhaps a trifle behind the times. And all this flatters our vanity. For it makes us judges between the world and the Church, supposes us competent to pronounce on all questions, even the most difficult, and bids us rest in our judgment with a faith which is itself truly marvellous when we consider what we are and what our opinion is worth.

Now let us recognise all this as the work of an ancient enemy, ever the same in all his varied forms of deceit. "You shall be as gods" (Gen. iii. 5), he had said to Eve. "Despise the cross and exalt human nature," he said to the pagan philosopher. "Follow your private judgment and reject the authority of the Church," he whispers to men of now-a-days. It is the first and fundamental lesson of that false wisdom, which St Paul (1 Cor. iii. 18) had met with no doubt amongst his disciples of Cornith, and which he deals with so summarily. "If any man amongst you seem to be wise in this world, let him become a *fool* that he may *be* wise."

Do we then reject knowledge? No; but we hate

intellectual conceit, the knowledge without humility "which puffs up" (1 Cor. xiii. 1), full of self-assertion, of pity for the ignorance of the past, and of the placid conviction of its own competence to judge all things. *This* we condemn and despise in God's name. If such folly tempt us to judge for ourselves what we shall believe, let us answer it, "I believe in all the teaching of that Church to which Christ said (St Luke x. 16), 'He that heareth you, heareth Me.' I believe in Peter, to whom God revealed what flesh and blood can neither know nor teach, and I believe in the successor of Peter, of whom St Ambrose witnessing to the ancient faith declared, 'Ubi Petrus, ibi Ecclesia.'"

XXII.

THE POPE.

"Thou art Peter, and upon this rock I will build My Church."
S. Matt. xvi. 18.

TO-DAY, brethren, our thoughts naturally turn to our Holy Father, the Pope. It is in some sense, indeed, his own special feast, for it is the feast of the foundation of that glorious Pontiff line of which he is the representative; and therefore it is fitting we think of him to-day, and congratulate ourselves that he is still spared to us, and thankfully rejoice at the worthy manner in which he watches over our Lord's interests on earth. And we pray God to continue to preserve a life so precious to His Church, and still further to enlighten and strengthen him, and to comfort and console him for the sorrows and the wrongs he is forced to endure.

The attitude of an ordinarily good Catholic towards the Pope seems to be a thing of mystery to those outside the Church. Why, they say, should we take such an interest in, and manifest so deep an affection and love for an old man living hundreds or thousands of miles away; an old man whom most of us have never seen and can never hope to see, and in whose welfare we are in no wise personally concerned? Why should it be matter of rejoicing to us here in England, that an aged priest in Rome has lived as long as he has lived, or matter of moment that he should live a year or two longer?

Brethren, do people who talk in this way understand anything of the depth of gratitude, and devotedness, and love, and manly, noble-hearted pride, with which a son looks upon the grey hairs of a father who never caused his youth a blush of confusion, or brought a pang of grief to his manhood? Do they know anything of the joy with which he will look forward to his father's special feast-days as they recur, and with what intense gratification he will lay before him some little token of a love which is so tender and so reverent? If such filial affection be not absolutely strange to them, then they ought to understand somewhat of our feelings on a day like the present. For Pius IX. is the father of each one of us, and each one of us is proud of being his child, and we honour ourselves when we call him our father—our Holy Father.

But, brethren, the secret of our rejoicing is deeper and holier than any revealed by earthly ties, however strong and sacred they may be. We regard indeed the Pope with feelings akin to those with which a son looks upon the face of the father that begot him; but there is far more than this. There is somewhat of the reverence and affection,—I had almost said, the supernatural devotion with which we regard our Lord Himself. "He that heareth you heareth Me; and he that despiseth you despiseth Me," are words true of the Pope in a far higher sense than they are of any one else; for he above all others is the representative—the visible presence, as it were—of our Lord upon the earth. We therefore strive to listen to his words with somewhat of the reverence and devotion with which the Apostles heard the sound of their Master's voice; we submit our judgment to his infallible decision; we follow out the line of action he traces, and obey his commands as the commands of God Himself. For us Catholics, the Pope is as the cloud by day, and the pillar of fire by night; he represents God's authority among men, and is the means by which God governs and directs His people. We regard him therefore not only as children who look upon the face of a loved and venerated father, but we reverently bow down before him, and hearken to his voice, and treasure up his words, and are loyal and loving to him as our divinely-appointed Ruler, and Teacher, and Guide. He is no stranger, therefore, to any one of us. For just as length of years has not diminished the intimate personal love which Christians entertain for our Lord, so distance of place cannot cool the affection or lessen the reverence we feel for His Vicar. To-day our Lord is loved with the same strength and tenderness as He was eighteen hundred years ago, by those who had the happiness of standing in His sacred presence: and His Vicar here, in far-away

P

England, is loved, and revered, and obeyed with all the earnestness and fervour and truth of those who are privileged to be the eye-witnesses of his virtues and his wrongs.

This then, brethren, is the explanation of our enthusiasm on a day like the present. It is the enthusiasm of the great Catholic family rejoicing on the feast of their father; the enthusiasm of the disciples of Christ glorying in the glory of their divinely-appointed Master; the enthusiasm, in a word, of Christians honouring Christ Himself in the person of His visible representative. No wonder that to the mere earthly-minded it is all a scandal and a folly; for, brethren, its secret comes from heaven. And might we picture to ourselves that eternal court, we might see in it the model of our own weak rejoicings, as well as their reason and account. For surely as the angels of God look down from their thrones of light upon the faithful, long-suffering, holy old man, who occupies here below the place of their Master in heaven, surely the spectacle fills their hearts with overflowing joy; joy that that old man has fought so long and so well against the enemies of their Lord; joy that we, their brethren afar off, honour his worth, and grieve over his sorrows, and glory in his triumphs. And as they look at the years of that great Pope; as with their angelic intelligence they take in at a glance the period of his unsullied boyhood, and see him lay the freshness of his youth as an offering at the feet of the afflicted and the ignorant; as they watch him devote the strength of his manhood to the salvation of the heathen in distant lands; as they accompany him back to the home of his childhood, and see the episcopal unction but increase his zeal for God's glory and his love for God's poor; as, above all, they saw him (as they often did) without even the necessaries of life, because the greatness of his charity would not allow him to retain a single coin for his own use as long as there was a hand outstretched in want to receive it; as they saw all this, and much more of which earth was not a witness, surely they must have felt that his was the pure life, and large heart, and unselfish soul, and forgiving nature, ay, and clear sight, and firm hand, and undaunted bravery, that was destined to guide the bark of Peter safely and surely through gloom and storm and danger.

Well-nigh thirty years have passed away since God called him to that post of awful responsibility. And what a history those years have written to those who can read it in all its fulness! Even we ourselves have seen the Church exposed to so many and such severe trials, to opposition so well organised, to enmity so bitter and so unrelenting, as to frighten us into thanking God Who has so far brought her safely, even triumphantly through it all. Perhaps no other equal period was ever fraught with such peril to the dearest interests of Christianity. When, since the days of Herod, did the rulers of the earth ever show themselves so jealous of our Lord's influence? When before did they ever perpetrate so much injustice, and exert such malign cunning in order to render His Church powerless in the world which she has to save? And surely never before did so-called science and learning so strive to discredit her mission among men, so systematically strive to clothe her in the purple garment of ridicule and scorn! And saddest, perhaps, of all, the people themselves who had always found in her their truest friend and strongest protector, against the extortion of the rich and the tyranny of the great, they who had heretofore been faithful among the faithless, even they would war against her, because under the profaned names of popular liberty and popular rights, she refuses to sanction injustice and sinful rebellion. And against all this, and more, has Pius had to contend, and has contended, thank God, as became a great Pope called to rule the Church in times of great danger. And as though his courage and constancy were to be proved in fire, he has gone through the trial which formed the chief glory of many who have gone before him. Personal wrong, and insult, and persecution, and exile—that too has been added to the grandeurs of his reign.

These things, brethren, as I have said, we ourselves may see; but how much there is of those thirty years which is known only to God and His angels. Who can tell the secret sorrow and anguish which must have so often deluged that great soul? Sorrow and anguish all the bitterer too because at times it was caused by those who ought to have been his consolation and his stay, and who like him were sworn to defend the interests of God's Church. So true it is, that a man's chiefest trials come from those of his own household. Surely as the angels gaze upon that long life, not the least part to them of its sorrows, and its sufferings, and its merit will be from those weak-minded, craven-hearted men, who preferred the applause of the great ones of the world, or their own petty private interests, to the honour and dignity of manfully standing by their father and their chief in the face of kingly displeasure and popular disfavour.

And yet, despite it all, Pius has never, for one moment, even seemed to waver in the intrepidity with which he has defended the cause of his Master. Well, then, may the angels rejoice at the spectacle which earth presents of the just man whom nothing has been able to turn aside. And well too may we believe that on a day like this, there is an increase of joy in the heart of that Virgin Mother, whom Pius has so truly loved. Surely out of heaven she looks down affectionately and gratefully on that venerable Pontiff, who has ever had her honour at heart, and who in these later days has been privileged to add the glory of the Immaculate Conception to the hitherto incomplete golden chain of dogmas which proclaim her greatness and her grace. And Joseph, too, her most chaste and holy spouse, will not his heart also join in the joy with which we celebrate our father's feast? For he cannot forget that just as of old God chose him to be the protector of what the earth held most precious, so Pius has committed to his guardianship what there is now on earth which speaks most of heaven. And our Lord Himself, I cannot but believe that He looks down with complacency on that faithful steward of His, so trusted, and so tried, and always so true, His Vicar so like Him in his sorrow and his sufferings, and so like Him, too, in his meekness and forgiveness; so like Him in his indulgent tenderness to those who weakly err, and so like Him in his bold, outspoken denunciation of error. Yes, brethren, we may well believe that our Lord feels His Church is in safe keeping while her honour and her rights are guarded by Pius IX.

And, therefore, it is, brethren, that we may understand that our own rejoicings are but feeblest imitations of the joy with which heaven is filled, and that our prayers are poor and cold, compared with those which the saints and angels and the Queen of Angels present before the throne of God, that He would be pleased to pour forth, without stint or measure, His choicest blessings on the head of His Vicar. It is heaven and earth uniting to extol God's goodness and beg God's mercy on the world. For it is not merely that we pray for length of years for Pius, nor even that he would be gladdened by the consolation of seeing, ere his own days are done, the victorious end of the struggle in which he is engaged. Nor are our prayers merely intended to obtain for him an increase of light, and grace, and strength. Our prayers mean all this indeed, but they mean far more. Their aim is really the extension of God's kingdom on earth, and its deliverance from the wiles and the power of evil; the reign of truth and justice, instead of the lying and robbery which now usurp their place.

And, brethren, let us be mindful also of those other duties we owe our Holy Father. Chief among them, let us reckon a complete and thorough obedience. Here, less impossible than elsewhere, let there not be the shadow of a compromise, for the sake of any apparent advantage, social, political, or otherwise, however great. Let us, above all, be jealous of that great truth which, in these latter times, the Holy Spirit has been pleased to place beyond the reach of doubt or denial—the truth that God has here on earth now, as He always has had, a living representative, who proclaims His law to men without the possibility of misleading them. To the infallible voice as it issues forth from the successor of Peter, let it be our joy and our glory to yield an assent that shall be complete, and hearty, and thankful, and loyal. Let us be ever faithful, and loving, and true to Him, our Holy Father, the Representative of God, the Vicar of Christ, and the Infallible Teacher of the Church.

XXIII.

FEAST OF THE SACRED HEART.

"This man receiveth sinners, and eateth with them."—S. LUKE xv. 2.

A GOOD and pious practice has grown up amongst the faithful, under the sanction of the Church, of setting apart certain months of the year in honour and for the encouragement of particular devotions which have justly gained the love and veneration of all sincere and earnest Catholics; and we know and feel by experience how beneficial are the results of such a practice. Surely we all can say that the month of prayer for the holy souls seems to bring us into closer relationship with those suffering fellow-members who have gone before us through the gates of death; and who that has tried to enter into the true spirit of the devotions for the month of May, has not felt within his heart a more tender love for his Mother Mary? Indeed, true and solid devotions are at all times good; for they are, so to speak, the fresh bloom, the bright flowers of a lively faith.

We do not wonder, then, to find this month of

June specially dedicated to the Sacred Heart of Jesus; rather should we be filled with surprise, if in these days of love for the Sacred Heart, some particular time were *not* set apart for this beautiful devotion. This month's devotion is, of course, centred in the feast of to-day: that feast may be justly styled the Feast of the Love of Jesus for men; it is the record of the Church's appreciation of that love of our God Incarnate; it is destined by Holy Church to be a means for the propagation of a devotion which tends so much to arouse the slothful and to inflame the tepid; and truly, in these days of indifference and unbelief, we do need something to impart the warmth of charity to our cold hearts, and to keep alive our faith and piety. God grant that during this month our thoughts may often dwell upon the love of the Sacred Heart of Jesus! They will do so with much profit to our souls.

In order to assist you in the devotion of this month, I propose to point out to you the manner in which we ought to regard, and the dispositions with which we ought to approach, the Sacred Heart of our Saviour. Think not, however, that mere human words have power to unfold the wondrous thoughts which the mystery of the Sacred Heart suggests. Around that mystery are centred the most sublime dogmas of our holy faith; dogmas in which you are well instructed, and of the depth and incomprehensibility of which I need hardly remind you. But my object to-day is, not so much to explain what the Catholic Church tells us of devotion to the

Sacred Heart, as to seek to lead you to regard this mystery with more tender feelings of love and piety. This lesson is suggested by the gospel that is read on this Sunday. That gospel speaks to us of the compassion of the Sacred Heart of Jesus ; it reminds us of what we should never forget,—that the Son of God made man had a human heart like ourselves; a heart moved by tender feelings and emotions, similar in kind to those which our human hearts are wont to experience. Surely there is much consolation in this thought ; it seems to bring God nearer to us, and so to bring us nearer to Him, teaching us to approach to Jesus with more tender love and childlike confidence. And these human feelings are ennobled and supernaturalised by faith, which tells of that hypostatic union which has so strangely deified the human actions of our Lord. We know how to love and admire a gentle and compassionate heart when we meet with it in one of our fellow-creatures ; how worthy of our love and admiration is not the compassion of the Sacred Heart of Jesus—of Him, of Whom we say that He is our God! Ought it not, then, to be our joy and delight to dwell upon those external evidences of the inward feelings of His Sacred Heart, which Christ has deigned to set before us in His mortal life? For this reason do I wish to direct your attention to the gospel of to-day ; without doubt, it is a most touching record of the tenderness and compassion of our Saviour Jesus Christ, shewing us by His acts, as well as by His words, how gentle, how loving, how compassionate is that Sacred Heart which burns with an undying love for men.

We read: "The publicans and sinners drew near unto Him to hear Him." Even these simple words must suggest much to a thoughtful mind. Ordinarily speaking, publicans and sinners would not have ventured to draw near to Him Who was regarded as the Messias, or at least as one of the greatest of the prophets, and Whose whole life was so great a reproach to their wicked excesses. True, the glory of the Divinity was concealed, and men saw not adoring angels hovering around His Sacred Person; but still we know well how worldliness and wickedness always shun the presence of all that breathes of spirituality and holiness. And yet the publicans and sinners seem to have had no fear, or even hesitation, in drawing near to the Person of our Lord. Does not this fact tell us as plainly as any words, that the whole manner and bearing of our Lord bespoke a welcome to such men? Does it not assure us of the kindness and gentleness with which they were received, notwithstanding their misery and sinfulness? Indeed, we read that the scribes and Pharisees murmured against our Lord, saying, "This man receiveth sinners, and eateth with them." Oh, they would not have murmured, had they known the love and tenderness which were ever welling forth from the Sacred Heart of Jesus! It was not indeed a new thing that He should receive sinners; He had always done so, for they had always been the special objects of His loving care and solicitude;

but these proud men could not understand the feelings which prompted our Lord's conduct. Surely I may say that such is not our case ; for we do know and admire the gentleness and compassion of our dear Saviour, and to us such knowledge brings unbounded consolation. May God in His mercy increase this knowledge within us !

Our Blessed Lord had come to seek and to save those that were lost. You have heard in the gospel of to-day, how He speaks of Himself as the Good Shepherd going in search of the lost sheep, and carrying it home upon His shoulders with much joy; and again, He compares Himself to a woman searching diligently for a lost piece of money, as though, forsooth, He would tell us that the lost sinner is a treasure in God's sight, a treasure which He must regain at any cost, with any sacrifice. And, as if to complete this most consoling teaching, the very chapter from which these parables are taken, concludes with the narration of that most touching of all parables, the parable of the Prodigal Son. Truly, with such heavenly teaching before us, it is not hard to realise in our poor degree the wondrous compassion of the Sacred Heart. What the Pharisees said of Jesus was true : He did receive sinners, and He was accustomed to take meat with them; and we love Him for that very thing which they condemned in Him. He went about amongst sinners, in order to make Himself known to them; He spoke to them, and conversed with them ; He performed miracles in their presence; He even became their guest; and all this He did solely to win their love, and so to win their souls.

Turn to the gospel narrative with which you are so familiar, and you cannot fail to find abundant proofs of this gentleness and compassion of our Blessed Saviour towards all poor sinners. What more touching than the history of Mary Magdalen! She was a public sinner; her crimes had made her notorious throughout the city; yet she ventured to draw near to Jesus. He was seated at table in the house of one of the Pharisees, and Magdalen the sinner was drawn to Him, as it were by some irresistible attraction; nay, she did more than draw near, she cast herself at His feet, she washed those sacred feet with her tears, she wiped them with her hair, and kissed them again and again, and anointed them with precious spikenard. Where was her fear? She could not fear in the presence of Jesus. And how did Jesus receive this poor sinner? The proud Pharisee, indeed, condemned our Lord in his own mind, saying: "This man, if He were a prophet, would know surely who and what manner of woman this is that toucheth Him, that she is a sinner" (St Luke vii. 39). Without doubt this man needed to learn a lesson from the Sacred Heart. That heart felt boundless pity and compassion for the unhappy Magdalen; Jesus could not reject the sinner prostrate at His feet; He would have pardoned her, had she been a thousandfold more guilty. May we not say that Magdalen owes it to the love of the Sacred Heart that she is now a glorious saint in the kingdom of Christ?

Again, behold our Lord at the well of Samaria conversing with another sinner. We read that the Apostles wondered that He talked with this strange woman; for even they had not yet learnt to understand the ardent longings of His Sacred Heart after all poor sinners. But our Lord heeded them not; He wished to gain another soul, and so, even at the risk of misunderstanding and of misrepresentation on the part of His Apostles, He took compassion on this poor sinner, and opened her eyes that she might know Him to be the Messias, and so might believe.

Once more, represent to yourselves the woman taken in adultery standing before our Lord in the Temple. See how the scribes and Pharisees press forward, earnestly accusing her, and declaring that she must be stoned to death: they feel no pity for the sinner, although they are sinners themselves. How opposite the conduct of our Lord! He confounded the woman's accusers, bidding him who was without sin first to cast a stone at her. And when all had departed filled with shame and confusion, Jesus turned to the woman, and said: "Woman, where are they that accused thee? hath no man condemned thee? Who said: No man, Lord. And Jesus said: Neither will I condemn thee: go, and now sin no more" (St John viii. 10, 11). Where will you seek a clearer proof of the compassion of the heart of Jesus? How true it was: "This man receiveth sinners." Yes, He had a welcome for all who came to Him; He rejected none—not even Judas when he came to give the traitor's kiss. Even for him He had a gentle word of reproof, saying: "Friend, whereto art thou come?" (St Matt. xxvi. 50). Yes, He even called the traitor *friend*, as though He would seek by this endearing word to soften his hard heart.

My brethren, these are not solitary or exceptional instances of the infinite compassion of the Sacred Heart. The whole history of our Lord's life presents a similar picture of goodness and gentleness and mercy. Throughout that life the splendour of the Divinity was deeply veiled; Mount Thabor seems to stand out as a solitary proof of His glory. On that mount, and then only for an instant, did the dark clouds part and the bright light of heaven burst full upon the prostrate Apostles. But at every turn, on almost every occasion, the tenderness of Christ's human heart made itself known and felt. It was said of Him: "Who went about doing good" (Acts x. 38), and what words could more beautifully or more truly express the goodness of His heart? He seemed to live for others, not for Himself: He forgot Himself in His longing desire to do good to others; all day long He preached, and healed the sick, and spread comfort and consolation on every side; and at night He had nowhere to lay His head—in fact He sought not rest; He would spend His nights in prayer for sinful, erring man.

Can you wonder, my dear brethren, that you are asked to love and worship that Sacred Heart which has thus poured forth its love for you? To you I need hardly say that it would be indeed strange if you did not love the Sacred Heart of Jesus. You do love it, and you honour it by your holy Confraternity. One thing only remains: to urge you to still greater love. Remember that the Sacred Heart never changes; with God there is no change or shadow of alteration. And so that Sacred Heart beats now with love for us, even as it beat with love for all poor sinners in the days of Christ's earthly life. It has the same feelings, the same emotions, the same pity for sinners, the same love for all, the same compassion for man's infirmities, the same desire to assist him in his needs.

How many beautiful lessons suggest themselves to us on such a feast as this? We feel that, if we have our trials and our difficulties, at any rate there is One Who has suffered for us; One, Whose compassion is boundless as the ocean. We gaze upon the Sacred Heart of Jesus, and we gain fresh strength to bear our lot of earthly pain and sorrow. Or, if we have sinned and guilt lies heavy on our souls, we come like Magdalen to the feet of Jesus; we are not afraid to draw near to Him, for we have often learnt how great mercy and compassion lie hidden in the recesses of the Sacred Heart. And, having poured forth our tale of woe, we rise refreshed with hope and confidence. Nor is it hard for us to repent of sin, for indeed we are overwhelmed with shame and grief at the thought that we could have dared to sin against such unparalleled love and goodness. As the Church reminds us in the beautiful hymn for the Matins of this feast:—

> "Turpe est redire ad crimina
> Quæ cor beatum lacerant."

Learn to know the compassion of the Sacred Heart, and you will daily grow in love for Jesus. Let this be your aim during this month. Daily repeat that sweet ejaculation :—

> "O Sacred Heart of Jesus, I implore
> That I may ever love Thee more and more."

The noblest thing that can be said of devotion to the Sacred Heart is, that it cannot fail to teach us the fulfilment of that first and greatest of the commandments: "Thou shalt love the Lord thy God with thy whole heart, and with thy whole soul, and with thy whole mind" (St Matt. xxii. 37).

XXIV.

FEAST OF THE PRECIOUS BLOOD.

"Jesus Christ hath loved us, and washed us from our sins in His own Blood."—APOCALYPSE i. 5.

OUR Blessed Lord in one of His parables compares the Church, the ministers of His Word and Sacraments, "to a man that is an householder, who bringeth forth out of his treasure new things and old." And this comparison seems to foreshadow and to justify that peculiar feature in the Church's history, which to her children is so full of interest and beauty, but to strangers so incomprehensible; I mean the additions and variations which are made from time to time in some of her devotions and other practices. Strangers cannot understand this; they would fain require of the Church a rigid uniformity, the unalterable sameness of a picture or statue which stands year after year always looking one way, with the same smile on the face, the same attitude of the foot or hand, under all circumstances and throughout all ages, so long as it lasts; whereas over the countenance of the real and living truth there pass a thousand various expressions which the emotions of the hour call forth, as she turns on her children that speaking, loving face, which yet in all its variations is ever one and the same. Truth is indeed the same yesterday and for ever; but it looks this way or that, wears this or that outward form and expression, according to the needs of to-day and tomorrow.

These thoughts are naturally suggested to us by the festival which we celebrate to-day, the Feast of the Precious Blood. In its present form, it is one of the latest additions to the Calendar, in its substance, it is as old as Christianity itself. The feast was instituted by our present Holy Father, Pope Pius IX., in thanksgiving for his return to Rome, and the restoration of his temporal power after his exile in Gaeta; but the devotion had been felt and practised a thousand years before, and more. How could it be otherwise, since it is nothing else, in fact, than a concentration of devotion to Jesus Christ as our Redeemer? The Precious Blood was the precise instrument of our redemption, for the Blood is the Life; so that we say *all* when we say that Christ shed His Blood for us; and hence St Paul seems to have had nothing dearer to his heart than to repeat this phrase again and again with grateful love in all his epistles: "In Him we have redemption through His Blood;" "He made peace through the Blood of His Cross;" "He hath purchased the Church with His own Blood" (Eph. i. 7; Col. i. 14–20; Acts xx. 28).

The Blood of Christ—that is, of God—of God

made man! These words set before us the most simple and fundamental, yet at the same time the most sublime and startling, mystery of our holy religion. It is not enough, however, that we should give a cold assent to the truth they contain as a theological dogma; the Church desires to make our faith the parent of charity, and so she singles out from time to time the most precious jewels of her treasury, one by one, for our separate contemplation, that so we may attain to a more perfect knowledge and a deeper love. In this way, besides the verbal profession that we are saved by the Blood of Christ, she presents that Blood to us to-day as a special object of veneration, and encourages us in the practice of a peculiar oblation of it to God, knowing that by that which purchased our redemption we can scarcely fail to purchase all we need. How then shall we best enter into the mind of the Church to-day? What is the peculiar spirit or temper, so to speak, of devotion to the Precious Blood?

All devotions have their peculiar spirit; some persons are led to one and some to another, according to the natural bias of their minds, or the guidance of God's Spirit in their regard. They do not exclusively receive this or that, rejecting others; but there are some trains of thought and modes of feeling on which their souls specially delight to dwell as in a pleasant pasture. It is like the peculiarities of great painters, or musicians, or writers. Some favourite grouping, some strain of singular harmony, some words or phrases, are being ever repeated, which reveal to us the hidden secret of their author's soul. In heaven it will not be so; for there will be the perfect vision; but here, each one catches a different glimpse, and one is captivated by the brightness of the beryl, another of the onyx, and another of the sardine stone.

To gain the spirit of a devotion, we place ourselves in sympathy with its object. Have we a special devotion to some particular saint? immediately we try to enter into his feelings, to think his thoughts and pray with his desires. Even so, if we would enter into the spirit of devotion to the Precious Blood, we must go stand before our crucifix, gaze upon those five fountains whence it flowed, and try to realise to ourselves the mind, the thoughts, the intentions of Jesus, as He hung between heaven and earth, thus pouring out His Blood for the world. This thought at once sets before us the especial feature of devotion to the Precious Blood which I wish to speak of to-day —I mean its largeness. It has no other limits than those of the open arms of Christ. The Dominican Tauler, one of the great mystic writers of the fourteenth century, has left us a striking passage with reference to this subject, which it will be worth while to set before you. He is speaking in the style so popular in his day of the allegorical significance of the four arms of the cross, and he says, "The upper part signifies the restoration of the angels, and the lower, the release of the fathers in limbo; the right hand was to protect and bless His friends, and the left to draw to Himself and to convert His enemies and all sinners. Above, the restoration of heaven, and below, the destruction of hell; on the right hand the diffusion of grace, and on the left the remission of sins." We see at once, then, that if we are to unite our intentions with those of Jesus on the cross, we must enlarge our hearts; we must no longer confine our prayers to a single grace or virtue, the prevention of some one mortal sin, or the salvation of some chosen soul; we must stretch our hearts and our prayers far wider. There is one prayer, and one only, large enough for our own to be modelled upon. It is the prayer of Jesus the night before His Passion, a prayer for the universal Church. Any one who tries to cast his thoughts into the channel I am speaking of, will find that they are insensibly led on from self to others, and from others individually, to the whole Church, and from the Church militant on earth to the Church suffering in purgatory; and ever and anon his mind will shape itself to those words, "And not for these only do I pray," "that they all may be one," "that they may be made perfect in one," until when He thinks of sinners and of the precious Blood that was shed for them, he cannot be content with less than the words so familiar to many saintly lips, when they cried out in a transport of holy zeal, "No more sin, O God, no more sin!"

And, as a matter of fact, this forgetfulness of self and self's petty wants, this largeness of intercession for others, this lively zeal for God's Church, and remembrance of it in all its branches, is the peculiar feature in the character of those saints who have been most devoted to the Precious Blood. I will name only one, St Catharine of Siena. It was of St Bonaventure that St Francis of Sales said that he seemed in his writings to use no other ink than the Blood of Christ; but the expression might be applied with still more singular propriety to the writings of St Catharine of Siena. She never began a letter without these words, "I write to you in the Precious Blood." It was the one object ever visible to the eye of her soul; its name was never absent from her lips; the one subject of her continual exhortations was that men should forget themselves and think only of it; she used to call it "the key," because it unlocked both to the whole world the treasure-house of divine grace, and to her own soul the knowledge of divine truths. She seemed to recognise all the attributes of God, as it were, mirrored in the sea of the adorable Blood. "I know thee now, Abyss of Charity," she exclaims, "O high eternal Trinity; now hast Thou manifested to me Thy truth and Thine inestimable charity in the Blood of Thy Son. It is there we see Thy power which was able to wash away our sins in that Blood, and Thy wisdom whereby Thou didst find a way to cover our humanity with the cloak of Thy Divinity, and so take away the lordship of the devil over us, and Thy love and charity also, whereby Thou didst purchase us with that Blood, having no need at all of us." Passages like this might be gathered without number from the prayers and meditations of St Catharine; and together with this continual remembrance of the Blood of Christ, I need not say how remarkably we find in this saint that spirit of large intercession and self-forgetfulness of which we have spoken. For she is known even in history as pre-eminently the saint *of the Church;* her labour on earth was for its Pontiff; her last prayers were for him and for all bishops; two words contain the abiding thought of her life, God's honour, and the salvation of souls. "It is time to forget ourselves," she writes to her confessor, "and to think only of God's honour in the salvation of souls. Wherefore take these poor dead souls on to the table of the Holy Cross, and feed on them bathed in His dear Blood." And the following passage from one of her prayers has in it the character which runs through all her writings, as if she had caught in rapture the very echo of the prayer of Christ. "O God!" she exclaims, "give health to the weak, and life to the dead, and give us a voice whereby we may cry to Thee as with Thine own dear voice of mercy, for the world and for the reformation of Thy Holy Church; yea, hear Thine own voice whereby we cry to Thee. And if I pray for all the world, above all do I pray for Thy Vicar, and for those who are its columns, and for all whom Thou hast given me and whom I love with so singular a love. Although I am sick, yet would I see them strong, and though I am imperfect, yet would I see them perfect, and though I am dead, yet I desire to see them alive in Thy grace." There is no need to quote any more; no one who has any acquaintance with the writings of this saint can fail to have observed the close connection which is to be seen in all of them, between her devotion to the

Blood of her Lord and her constant and pre-eminent habit of intercession for the Church and its visible Head. When therefore the present Pontiff had been driven from his throne into exile, and the similarity of the circumstances to those of St Catharine's own day had vividly recalled her to the memory and veneration of the faithful, and many prayers had been offered through the intercession of her who, in her life, had brought back a former Pontiff to his own people, it was not without a peculiar fitness that, on his return to Rome, the first feast instituted by Pius IX. in token of gratitude, should be in honour of the Precious Blood; and since that date he has ranked St Catharine herself among the saintly Patrons of the Eternal City.

Such then, my brethren, is the history of this festival, such the peculiar temper or spirit of this devotion; and do not say within yourselves that we are wandering this morning far beyond the narrow circle of your duties, or powers, or privileges; that we are speaking of a devotion that belongs only to the saints, and that is connected only with visions and raptures and ecstasies. Far otherwise, be assured of it; this largeness of prayer is a kind of devotion which the Church specially recommends; nay, under certain circumstances, enjoins on every one of us, as I will presently show you. Look into any authorised Prayer-book, and you will find there the "Conditions for gaining a Plenary Indulgence." They are various, but none is more common than this, "prayer for the Pope's intentions." Now St Catharine was wont most familiarly to write and speak of the sovereign Pontiff (as the poor faithful Catholics of Italy do at this day) as the Christ on earth. She saw nothing in him but the representative, the Vicar of his Lord. See, then, what is meant by his intentions; they are sometimes explained as being the peace of all Christendom, the exaltation of our holy mother the Church, the welfare of all Catholic kings and princes, and the extirpation of all sin and heresy: in a word, we are enjoined to pray for the glory of God, and the peace and freedom of the Church; these are the Pope's intentions, this is "the mind of Christ" (1 Cor. ii. 16); and this is the tribute which the Church demands of those to whom she unlocks the treasury of her indulgences. Again, the Church has laid upon us the obligation of hearing Mass, and of learning *how* to hear it. And what are the intentions for which we are to hear Mass? Nothing small, or narrow, or selfish. They are, first, the supreme worship of God; secondly, as a thanksgiving for all His benefits, not to ourselves only, but to the human nature of Christ, to our Blessed Lady, to the saints and to all mankind; thirdly, as a propitiation for our sins, and for the sins of the living and the dead; and, fourthly, to obtain whatever graces we desire for ourselves or others. He who hears Mass in this way will find at the end of the half hour so spent, that he has wandered far beyond himself. He has placed not himself alone, but all men and all things, in that chalice of Blood which is offered to God. According to a beautiful expression of St Catharine, he has been *annihilated* in the Blood of Christ. O happy annihilation of self! Even as sinners fly to intoxication or the delirious excitement of vain pleasure, or the lethargy of sleep, that they may forget themselves; and, waking back to consciousness, feel how painful it is to recover the sense of that identity which is to them a gloomy and sorrowful prison, so does the Christian look back upon that half hour spent in hearing the daily Mass, as a refuge from thoughts of self, when, in the presence of God sacrificed for man, his heart has been put into sympathy (if I may so speak) with God, and for a while God and the soul have had all things in common. Self has been forgotten, lost, by reason of its intimate union with others and with God. He has been in communion with the angels and saints, and has joined with the seraphim and cherubim in offering those wondrous hymns of praise and thanksgiving, the Gloria in Excelsis and the Sanctus. He has been honouring the memory of the Blessed Virgin and of all the saints, and congratulating with them on the eternity of their bliss and glory; his thoughts have been busy with the living and the dead; he has been praying for himself, indeed, but for himself only in communion with all around him, with the whole congregation, with his bishop, with all Catholic bishops and the flocks committed to their charge, with the Pope, in a word, with the whole Catholic Church throughout the world. All sin and suffering he has placed under the Cross, that the drops of the Precious Blood falling upon them may cleanse and heal them all; all deeds and words and thoughts, all hopes and fears, all joys and sorrows, all plans and disappointments of himself and of all other faithful souls he has laid on the same Altar, that they too may receive the sprinkling of the same ruby drops, and by that touch may be truly consecrated, marvellously transmuted into an oblation pure and holy, acceptable to God. And perhaps when the blessing has been given and the last gospel recited, and the worshipper awakens again to his own self-consciousness and the round of his daily duties, he sighs and wishes that life were one perpetual Mass. This is precisely what the Church would have it to be, and what devotion to the Precious Blood enables it to be.

This thought suggests to us another characteristic of this devotion, on which it may be well to say a few words. Holy Scripture and the Church teach us that we have not only to ask God for what we want, but also continually to give Him something ourselves. Our worship of Him does not consist merely in petitions; we are called upon to "offer sacrifices to God," "to pay our vows to the Most High," and in many other ways to make oblations to Him. This duty is of course perfectly fulfilled in the holy sacrifice of the Mass. We can give God nothing of our own; but in the Mass we offer Him a gift of infinite value, for it is the very Body and Blood of His own Son. As often then as this sacrifice is offered, an infinite act of worship is rendered to God, an infinite satisfaction, an infinite thanksgiving. But this is not enough.

The spirit of oblation must be continual; it must enter into all our prayers and our whole life; and the Precious Blood has been given to us as "the treasure of the Church," as St Catharine calls it, which we may offer again and again all day long both for ourselves and others; as we read in the life of St Mary Magdalen of Pazzi, that when in a state of rapture she was heard making this oblation to God for every state and condition of men; for priests and holy virgins, for seculars, for poor sinners and infidels, for the dying and the souls in purgatory, and lastly, against all sin; and she used to reproach the sisters of her community for not renewing this oblation with sufficient frequency, saying, "We shall have to give an account to God for many souls now burning in hell, for had you and I been more fervent in prayer and in offering the Blood of Jesus for them, perhaps He would have been appeased, and they would not have been in those flames."

But even this is not all. The Precious Blood is a gift which has the power of making other things, worthless in themselves, fit to be offered to God also. These worthless things are our own actions; our good works, done by the grace of God working in us, dyed in the Blood of Redemption, clothed with that "garment of charity which is the Blood," and so offered to God. If I might venture to use a familiar comparison on so sacred a subject, I would remind you of those petrifying wells which some of you, I doubt not, have seen up and down the country, whose waters have the power of encrusting the objects over which they fall with a covering as of stone. Men place all kinds of common things, leaves and straws and shells and coins, under these dripping waters, till the substances themselves are hidden and covered over, or (as the phrase is) turned into stone. Even so we too are privileged to place all our actions or sufferings, our pains and pleasures, under the cross of Christ, and the falling Blood annihilates their human worthlessness and clothes them with its own Divinity. The Blood of Christ is, as it were, on the doorposts of our houses, making our most ordinary and familiar duties a perpetual oblation to God. We pray and work, speak and are silent, do and suffer all things through Him. Sacraments and indulgences and means of grace are not merely Divine ordinances, they are fountains of the Precious Blood; so that the saints do not hesitate to speak of going to receive the Blood of Christ in the Sacrament of Penance.

It has been said that more souls have been saved, and more petitions granted, through the oblation of the Precious Blood, than through any other kind of prayer; so that, even in this view, as being a devotion which yields such abundant fruit, I desire earnestly to commend it to your use. But there is something better even than getting all we want, and that is the advancement of God's glory. We in our day may surely repeat with St Catharine, " Turn where we will, we see nothing but sins, and the Blood of Christ crucified, persecuted and despised." What are we to do? Were we to spend our life before the Tabernacle, we could not of ourselves give God the honour which would atone for one mortal sin. But the price of the infinite Atonement is in our hands, and can never be exhausted; by means of it each one of our actions is capable of receiving an infinite value and an infinite power of prayer. Let us not neglect so precious a treasure; let us apply ourselves at once and continually to the practice of this most excellent devotion; it is the devotion of unselfishness, not of examination of our own consciences, and regret and repentance for past shortcomings and deprecation of future punishment, but of habitual intercession, of unceasing prayer for the Church; of the worship of Christ, pleading His merits and making a generous hearty oblation of ourselves to His service in and through Himself.

XXV.

HOW TO SAY THE ROSARY.

"I will pray with the spirit, I will pray also with the understanding."
1 Cor. xiii. 15.

MY DEAR BRETHREN, I think we most of us say our Rosary, if not daily, yet at least often enough to recite the whole of it every week; it will be worth our while then to-day, Rosary Sunday, or the Feast of the Most Holy Rosary, to inquire *how* we perform this part of our devotions, what fruit we derive from an act of religion so frequently repeated, and whether this fruit be not capable of much further increase by the use of a little more care and diligence on our part.

A story is told of one of the Saints—I think it was St Camillus de Lellis, who founded a religious order for ministering to the sick in the sixteenth century—that one day as he was looking on at the building of a new church for his congregation, watching the progress of the work, one of the men employed came up to him and said, Father, I hear everybody saying that you are a great Saint; I wish you would give me your secret, and tell me how I may become a

Saint too. St Camillus answered, "Are you in earnest in what you ask?" "Never more so in my life," was the reply. "Very well then," said the Saint, "I will give you an infallible recipe for becoming a Saint, if only you will persevere in using it. Read a certain portion of the Life of Christ every day, then think upon it, turn it over in your mind, digest it, and then in the course of the day as often as you are going to do anything, and especially if you are in any doubt or difficulty, say to yourself, How would Jesus Christ have acted if He had been in my place; and be sure that you act accordingly." The story goes on to say that three months later this poor man met with an accident in the building and was killed, and that St Camillus said it had been revealed to him that he was already in heaven, and that God would some day glorify his name by wonderful favours granted at his tomb. Now the daily or weekly recitation of the Rosary involves the weekly rehearsal of all the principal mysteries of our Lord's life. It would seem, then, that the Rosary sets before us, puts into our hands, as it were, the very means of grace which St Camillus considered to be an infallible recipe for becoming a Saint, *i.e.*, if only we go on and make the *practical* use of it which he recommended. If our frequent recitation of the Rosary has no tendency in this direction, has no practical influence on our life and conversation, it is clear that we are not getting half the good out of it that we ought to get, and this through our own fault, for want of *meditating* on the mysteries set before us.

And do not let anybody, however young or however thoughtless among you, take fright at this word meditation, as though we were speaking of an exercise fit only for the learned or the perfect. Meditation is not a thing above the skies, that a man must take wings in order to attain to it, neither is it beyond the seas that he must take ship to reach it, but it is a thing within ourselves, nothing else than the exercise of the three powers of the soul, which we all have, which we learnt about in our Catechism, which we are so incessantly using on other matters. It is the making use of our memory, our understanding and our will, on spiritual matters, in the same manner as we make use of them in human and temporal concerns. For just as when a man sets himself to reflect upon some business which concerns him greatly, he first brings before his memory that business and all its circumstances; next, he discourses with his understanding, weighs all the reasons for or against such a way of handling the business, and then proceeds to take a third step, which is to make a resolution, a firm purpose in his will, to adopt or to reject this or that scheme of action which he has been considering; just so, precisely the same course is followed in meditation, though on a different subject. The first thing is to present to the memory the point of the history on which we are going to reflect, for example, one of the mysteries, as we call them, of the Rosary. The second is to discourse with the understanding on that point, weighing the circumstances contained in it, and marking any bearing they may have on our own conduct, any example or encouragement to this or that special virtue, or warning against vice. And then the third, which is the outcome, the end and fruit of the whole, viz., the good resolution made by the will, and which is afterwards to be carried into effect in the practice of virtuous actions.

And all this may be done, whilst with our lips we are reciting the Ten Hail Marys and the Our Father of each decade of the Rosary. Indeed, something of this kind *must* be done if we would gain the many and great indulgences attached to the saying of the Rosary. It is one of the conditions attached by the Holy Father to these indulgences that we should meditate somewhat on the mystery whilst we repeat the vocal prayers. Of course the mere recitation of the vocal prayers with intelligence and reverence is an act of religion, which will not be left without its reward. It is better to do this than to do nothing. It is at least an act of homage to God and our Blessed Lady; it is giving so much of our time and thoughts to Jesus and His Holy Mother. But we shall not gain the indulgences, nor derive half as much spiritual profit from the Rosary as we ought, unless we meditate on the mysteries as well as recite the prayers; and meditation includes all that I have said.

If we content ourselves with merely recalling the historical scene of the mystery by an effort of memory, and do not ruminate on it at all, it is simply like looking at a holy picture or reading a spiritual book, —good and pious in itself, but probably without any lasting benefit. Or if our exercise closes with the use of the understanding, considering the circumstances of the event and the lessons they teach, but without any personal application of them to ourselves, it is mere study and speculation, useful indeed as far as it goes, but not deserving the name of prayer. But if we exercise our will and affections upon the truths which our understanding has set before us, if our consideration of the mystery moves us to form good desires and resolutions, then indeed the recitation of the Rosary becomes real prayer, and prayer of a very excellent kind, and it is capable of doing great things. It has power to turn men away from an evil life, or to rouse them from the torpor of a sluggish one; it has power to strengthen and encourage beginners in the path of virtue, to help them to overcome their faults, and to make progress in holiness, whilst to the more advanced, it sets before them the most perfect example, and is a most powerful incentive to Divine love. Hence the great Apostle of the Gentiles said that he knew nothing but Christ crucified; to his mind this one mystery comprehended everything. St Bonaventure said that the crucifix was his only book, the book whence he drew all his spiritual knowledge and his burning eloquence; and many others of the Saints have used similar language, wholly giving themselves up to the contemplation of this mystery, and spending their whole lives in drawing forth some of the treasures of wisdom that are hidden in it.

It is easy to see how this can be. Let us suppose, for example, that the first sorrowful mystery is proposed to us, the Agony in the Garden. First, our memory recalls the circumstances of the history, and we picture to ourselves in the imagination a garden of a certain size and form, with eight of the Apostles remaining at a spot somewhere near the entrance; then, at another spot further on, the three more highly privileged, whom our Lord took aside with Him; and lastly, further on still, withdrawn from them as it were a stone's throw, our Blessed Lord Himself, prostrate upon the ground, praying with most intense agony, and His sweat becoming as drops of blood trickling down upon the ground. You have all seen pictures of this mystery, and it is the mere work of a moment therefore to recall and set it before your eyes as soon as you hear the mystery announced. Then, whilst our lips almost mechanically repeat the words of the prayers, our understanding breaks up the scene, so to speak, into several parts, and turning them over on one side and another, it seizes hold of some one particular point that strikes us more than another. This will not always be the same; but at one time this, at another that, lest the soul should be wearied by always eating of the same food; and according to the difference in the point chosen, there will follow a corresponding difference in the affections aroused in our hearts, and the practical resolutions suggested by them, and adopted by the will. Thus, sometimes we may be attracted by the intensity of the Divine love for man, exhibited in these sufferings, and we shall feel moved to desire and pray for grace to make some less unworthy return of love for love. Sometimes we may stop short in the mere contemplation of the greatness of the sufferings themselves, which naturally predisposes us for the reception of the gift of compassion. At another time, we shall be lost in admiration of His patience, His obedience and conformity to the Divine will as manifested in the prayer He uttered on this occasion, and from the contemplation of this will naturally spring a desire to imitate Him in these virtues. Or again, fervour in prayer, hatred of sin as the cause of all Christ's suffering, fear of the Divine justice which exacts so severe a punishment as its penalty, these and other great truths are one and all contained in this one mystery, the Agony in the Garden, are naturally suggested by it, and each has its own proper fruit for the soul, to be derived from it.

You see then, my brethren, how profitable an exercise the recitation of the Rosary may be made, if only we will use our faculties, as the Church requires of us, in meditation. And this is why the Rosary is a devotion so popular and useful for all classes and conditions of men, for the learned or the ignorant, the saint or the sinner. It is so easy yet so profitable; so simple and yet so varied; so short yet so pregnant with results; within the reach of all, yet incapable of being exhausted by any. The fifteen mysteries comprehend the whole of our Lord's life. Every mystery contains many and different parts; each part might be divided into several points, and every point has tender considerations of its own, and may be looked at in various ways at various times. There is none of us so ignorant or so helpless but that he can lay hold of one or other of these points and use it. We can all see how the mystery of the Annunciation, for example, teaches us humility; and the Visitation, charity; how the carriage of the Cross inspires patience, and the Crucifixion, self-sacrifice; how the Resurrection is the foundation of faith, and the Ascension, of hope; and so of all the mysteries, each in its turn; and how all together, steadily and perseveringly meditated upon, month by month and year by year, cannot fail to produce in us some faint shadows at least of those virtues which in them we contemplate in perfection.

St Teresa does not hesitate to say of the soul that perseveres in prayer of this kind, that in spite of temptations and sins, and relapses into sin, brought about in a thousand ways by Satan, our Blessed Lord will bring that soul at last to the harbour of salvation. She says emphatically, "*I am certain of it;*" and therefore (she continues), let him who has once begun it never cease from it, though he should have the misery of falling into sin and leading a wicked life; for prayer is the way to amend it, and without such prayer amendment will be much more difficult. And as to him who has not begun to pray in this way, "I implore him," she says, "by the love of our Lord not to deprive himself of so great a good. If once he begin, even without any real desire of perfection, yet, if he persevere, little by little he cannot fail to attain to the knowledge of the road which leads to heaven. For prayer of this kind is nothing else than courting the friendship of God : it is frequently to converse with One Who (we know) loves us with an everlasting love. Now, true love and familiar converse require certain similarities of disposition : those of our Lord are absolutely perfect; our own are vicious, sensual, earthly; yet, if we often hold this intimate converse with Him, we shall insensibly grow like Him. It cannot be otherwise, excepting through our own fault. If we put honey into our mouth and do not taste its sweetness, or fire into our bosom and do not feel its heat, we know that our taste and our bodily frame must be in a very disordered state." Just so, if our soul reaps no effects from the spiritual good provided for it by the Rosary, this can proceed only from a want of disposition on our part. But to those who use the Rosary aright, the little beads become the very seed of everlasting life. They enkindle holy thoughts, which, nourished in the depths of the heart, and ripened therein by the strong heat of meditation, bring forth in due time under the influence of Divine grace, and through the intercession of Mary, the flowers of good affections, desires, and resolutions, to be followed by the fruits of holy habits and perfect virtues.

Do not forget, then, the story which I have told you of St Camillus' recipe for making a Saint ; remember that the use of that recipe is brought within your use daily by the recitation of the Rosary, and resolve henceforth to make the best use of your opportunities.

XXVI.

GUARDIAN ANGELS.

"There shall no evil come to thee, nor shall the scourge come near to thy dwelling; for He hath given His angels charge over thee, to keep thee in all thy ways."—PSALM xc. 10, 11.

THE belief of Catholics as to the ministry of angels is sometimes spoken of as a mere superstition, which can be entertained only by the weak-minded or the ignorant; or sometimes it is regarded as, to some extent at least, the product of a pious imagination working upon a basis of revealed truth. The infidel wants proof of the existence of angels at all. And the Protestant, though he cannot deny that the Scripture teaches there are angels, and that they have certain offices or relations toward men, yet agrees with the scoffer in looking upon the belief of his Catholic neighbour as a fancy, touching it may be and beautiful, but still a fancy. The idea of a guardian angel watching over every individual of our race, seems to him more akin to the dream of the poet, than the reasoned belief of the Christian, and he regards it as adding rather to the luxuriance of religious literature than to the dignity of religion itself.

Possibly too some Catholics, did they question themselves, would find that they are not altogether disinclined to sympathise with views of this sort. Of course they would not for a moment dream of questioning any express doctrinal decision of the Church on this, or any other subject of Christian belief or practice. As becomes Catholics—as is, in fact, an essential element in the very idea of a Catholic— they are prepared to submit their own judgment to that of the Church, whenever she expresses her judgment as an article of faith, to be accepted by all her children under pain of heresy. So far, then, the persons to whom I am alluding are not heretics. But though they are within the letter of the Church's definitive teaching, they are far from being in harmony with her mind and spirit and action, and are therefore in a position at once undutiful to her, and dangerous to themselves. Such persons would readily recognise the appropriateness of speaking of the guardian angel of a child. There is so much freshness, and beauty, and grace, and innocence about a little child, that it almost seems a meet companion for an angel. And then the touching helplessness of infancy would appear to call for the fostering care of some protecting spirit. And as new capacities for virtue and goodness make themselves felt, and especially as new possibilities of evil are revealed, and as the opening mind comes to question itself about the mysteries around it, and the deeper mysteries which are within it — what more fitting than that a guardian spirit should hover around the timid, untried steps of the youthful wayfarer in a land so new to him, and so strange, and so full of danger? But is not the case somewhat altered when it is question of the grown-up man who is gradually being seasoned to the struggles and dangers of life—the man who is already marked with the scars of many rough encounters and discreditable wounds, who has known sin, and tasted of the fruit that seemed so fair, until, perhaps, very satiety had made it unpleasant? To give such an one as this an angel for his companion would, it is thought, seem incongruous, if not absurd. And this erroneous view is encouraged, although unconsciously, by religious artists and poets who depict angels with children's faces, or write hymns to them whose language and sentiment are in great measure applicable only to children; until, at length from being unusual, it comes to sound strange, to associate angel-guardians with any other period of life than infancy and early youth.

The Catholic belief, on the contrary, is, that the companionship and protection of our guardian angel never ceases, and is never interrupted, from the first breath we draw, until we have entered into the possession of our eternal lot. So far from his attaching himself to us only during the peace and innocence of childhood, his friendship becomes closer and more intimate as passion grows stronger, and the battle of life fiercer. Even sin, though it makes us so unlike him, does not cool his affection, or slacken his zeal for our welfare. He mourns our fall indeed, and his love is filled with sorrow, but it is thereby all the more intense, and ought to be all the more endearing, like the strong, yearning, pitying love of a father for his erring child. To the grey-haired old man his angel-guardian is as fitting a companion as in the days of his youth, for after all the greatest age, and the largest experience, are but as infancy and childish ignorance compared to the years he has known and the wisdom he possesses. And of the two, surely that is the more beautiful in heaven's sight, the strong man in the prime of his manhood and the consciousness of his power, taking loving counsel with, and seeking loving aid from, his heavenly guide, rather than the timid child holding by his angel's hand to support his tottering steps. To human ears the clear, fresh voices of children, singing the praises of their guardian angels may be more sweet, but surely the coarse husky broken voice of declining years has a beauty of its own in the harmony of heaven.

Nor is our angel's protection less needed as life advances. Rather we require it all the more. For in proportion as we lose the vigour and elasticity of youth, with its uncalculating faith in those around it, and its unsuspiciousness of evil, and its unlimited trust in the future—in proportion as the high hopes with which we set out, and generous resolves, and ardent aspirations, are dashed by disappointment and failure—in proportion as the enthusiasm wanes of the young undefeated spirit—that enthusiasm which by its very impetuosity carried us so far in the way of virtue, and so easily over the dangerous allurements that beset our path—in proportion as all this comes to be exchanged for the wisdom that is begotten of bitter experience, and the knowledge that is linked with care, and the weariness of soul that comes of unavailing efforts — in proportion as the heart tends to lose its freshness, and the mind its hopefulness, ah! then, surely more than ever we need the presence by our side of that bright joyous spirit, who is the untiring enemy of sadness, and mistrust, and gloomy foreboding.

And let it not be said that all this is an unreal fancy with which the undisciplined mind seeks to gild the commonplace dulness of life. Was it a fancy that led Lot from the doomed cities of the Plain, or stayed the arm of Abraham, raised to sacrifice his son, or consoled the outcast Agar, or delivered St Peter from his prison, or wrought those other marvels of loving protection we read of in the Holy Scriptures? And does not God expressly promise by the mouth of the Psalmist to send His holy angel to protect those that fear Him, and further, that He has given His angels charge over us to keep us in all our ways, so that evil shall not come to us nor the scourge to our dwelling? Was it not the realisation of this truth that led the aged Jacob, one of the most practical of men, to invoke on the heads of his grand-children the blessing of his angel, who, as he expressed it, had delivered him from all evils? And surely nothing can be more impressive than the way in which our Lord Himself denounces against those who induce others to commit sin, the vengeance of the angels of those who are thus led astray. "See that you despise not one of these little ones,"—little, whether in age or in the power to resist sinful allurements—" See that you despise not one of these little ones, so as to be to them an occasion of sin; for I say to you that their angels in heaven always see the face of my Father Who is in heaven" (Matt. xvii. 10). Here is Scripture warranty enough for our faith in angel-guardians. It is a sufficient answer to a Protestant, and more than a sufficient answer to a Catholic who has any hesitation in accepting to the full the belief of the faithful on the subject; for he ought to know that the fact of such belief, though unaccompanied by the Church's formal definition, is clear evidence of its truth.

Rationalists, indeed, who do not really accept the authority of the Sacred Scriptures, and profess to reject everything which does not approve itself to their own individual way of thinking—such people seem to see in this belief in angel-guardians something hardly respectful to Almighty God, as though we thought Him obliged to employ the ministry of angels in the aids and inspirations He gives us. Why, they ask, should He not be supposed to do these things directly and immediately Himself? Rather, we ask, why should He? Why should we believe that His action in this matter is an exception to the general scheme of His providence as it elsewhere reveals itself; for do not all the blessings we receive from His bounty in the temporal order come to us through the agency and instrumentality of others? And is not society itself, one grand scheme of assistance, by which the weak, and ignorant, and the miserable are helped by their stronger, and wiser, and happier brethren? And in a higher sense still, do we not owe much of what is true and good in us to the instruction, and example, and encouragement of the friends whom God has given us? Angel-guardians! We have had such, and we have them, here on earth, men and women like ourselves, who in various ways have aided us in our struggles with sin and kept our steps aright. Thank God for it! The lives of every one of us, if we think them over, is but a history of such timely helps, none the less efficient, because perhaps they were unconsciously given and received. From various persons they came to us, only some of whom we have known and prized; and in lovingly mysterious ways too; though in our ignorance we but deemed them the ordinary occurrences of life. And why should not God for like purposes employ the agency of higher beings? The object is the salvation of our souls, and that is surely important enough in His sight, seeing that He died to secure it. It is no dishonour to Him, but to us it is unspeakable honour, that He should send the very princes of His heavenly court to be our companions and our guides. And it is an honour to them to be sent even to such as we are; for the instrument which God selects to work out His wonders of mercy, cannot but be unutterably dignified by the choice. No, no; our belief is not unworthy of Him. Rather, it serves to give us truer and higher notions of His power and goodness, that can and does bestow on mere creatures a share in His own greatness, by making them instrumental in producing results, which only infinite love could conceive and omnipotence effect.

Let then, brethren, the only effect of the carping scoffing criticisms we may have heard or read, be to deepen and intensify our belief in a truth so beautiful and so consoling. Let us, as the years go on, cherish more and more, and more vividly seek to realise, our faith in the presence of our guardian angel. Let it not be regarded merely as a fitting adornment for childhood and youth, but rather look upon it as one of the great mainstays appointed by God Himself for our manhood and our old age. Invoke him frequently. School yourselves by constant practice into an abiding recognition of his presence, so that you will come to turn to him easily and naturally, and, as it were, instinctively, and without an effort. Remember that how many friends soever you may have had, and how loyal soever they may have been to you, he is your oldest and most faithful friend, most tried by you and most true to you. One day, with God's help, you will be able to read the complete history of his loving solicitude—all along the journey of life, through childhood's dangers, and amidst the wayward rebellion of youth, and the more deliberate sins of later years—in the terrible perils of the last hour—how throughout it all his love never grew weary, and his care never slackened. O Angel of God! my Angel! may I, even before life's close, repay you somewhat for the deeper and truer than human love you have lavished upon your unheeding and ungrateful charge. Praise to the mercy of God Who has given to our loneliest hours the sense and reality of most intimate endearing companionship, an almost sensibly felt protection in every trial and difficulty, an ever-present friend utterly devoted to us, whose counsel is never wanting and whose aid never fails.

Brethren, do we think of this as we ought? Or rather, have we not to accuse our folly of almost entirely neglecting to avail ourselves of this great source of strength and consolation that God has placed by our side. A dry, formal, soulless, heartless acknowledgment and petition to our angel-guardian, night and morning, if even so much, is a poor, poor return for all his love, and is a stupid disregard of our own truest interests. Our conduct surely, when we come to think it over, is a mystery even to ourselves—hardly a throb of affection for him whose love for us is stronger and tenderer than a mother's— hardly a feeling of gratitude for services so urgently and critically important, that perhaps on this side the grave we could not bear the knowledge of them —hardly a wish to avail ourselves of help that with loving importunity is almost thrust on us—perhaps even outraging the sanctity of his presence by actions which we would not that the lowest and basest among men should have witnessed. Ah! who shall say what Christian souls are lost that might have been saved, had they been less criminally indifferent to the presence of the guardian God sent them? Who shall say how much the habit of lovingly communing with their angel, has contributed to create holy men and women on earth, and people heaven with saints? At any rate, we know that just as God's servants have advanced in His love, they have acquired a deeper, and more grateful, and more reverential, and more real and more vivid sense of the presence of their angel-guardian, until at length his visible appearance was hardly a matter of surprise. Let us, brethren, imitate them, at however great a distance. Only once thoroughly awake to the fact that he is there by your side, and your feeling of need will, under God's grace, do the rest. In pain, and sorrow, and sin, you will recognise his aid and fly to it. More than all perhaps, in gloom and despondency, and when harassed by thoughts you would be rid of, you will come to acknowledge his power and his love—the power and love of a bright radiant spirit, whose very nature is heavenly light and sunshine, and whose desire it is to reflect some portion of his own joyousness on the soul whom God has entrusted to his care. Let us be affectionately and gratefully mindful of him during life, and when earth is fading from our view he will soothe the pain of parting, and whisper words of strength and comfort; and when the end has come, and we stand before the Judge, he will be then our advocate, and our friend, and our guide to our eternal home.

XXVII.

THE FEAST OF OUR LADY'S PATRONAGE.

"We fly to thy Patronage, O Holy Mother of God."

ONE grand and beautiful, yet simple and impressive element reveals itself, my brethren, throughout the history of the Church, in all times, and under all circumstances. It is that inter-communion which exists between all its members who form one body, having Jesus Christ, our Divine Lord, as its head, and though the action and working of this body be partly visible and partly invisible, yet we all believe that the faithful of Christ's Church can and do assist each other, by their prayers and good works, whether struggling along the world's thorny and dangerous road, or suffering in the fire that purgeth yet killeth not, or happy for ever in the enjoyment of God's unending peace and love. Heaven, purgatory, and earth, though so very distinct, are yet inseparably united by this mutual assistance they give to each other. We who are still wandering, still under trial, feel keenly the weakness of our nature, and hence have recourse to the Saints in heaven for help, since we know and believe in the efficacy of their intercession. Hence then, we are under an obligation at times to use their influence and power with Almighty God; for it is a means within the reach of every one that must be used when the occasion requires it. The peculiar circumstances in which one may live, the various occasions of sin to which one may be exposed, the necessity of overcoming an evil habit of long standing, or of acquiring some particular virtue, all these tend to increase the obligation. To reject the means of obtaining grace implies that one has little or no care about obtaining the end. Every one, who has at heart the salvation of his soul, must know that it can only be secured by God's way, and not his own way. It is without a doubt a part of our duty, not only to invoke the assistance of our own special Patron Saint, the Saint of our baptism, to whom we owe many a grace, but also to impetrate God's blessings on others through the same mediation.

To-day then, we will consider the very special duty that attaches to each one here, whatsoever his position, of prayer to God through the mediation of Mary's powerful patronage, both for this College and its welfare, as well as for ourselves who constitute it. To appreciate and realise its necessity and importance, we have only to recall to mind the history of our College, its singular mission, and the graces it has received to accomplish the object of its establishment; for, my brethren, we, as well as those who have preceded us, or will come after us, will be one day judged according to our use or abuse of those self-same graces.

It was towards the end of the last century, when this country was most Protestant, that some few of the clergy and laity conceived the plan of establishing a place of education for the Catholic youth of England. It was a bold, and at first sight, a rash speculation; for the deeply-rooted bigotry and prejudice of almost 300 years were against them; it was a penal offence—an offence not condoned even by fines and confiscations; but, my brethren, God's ways are not man's ways. Though the very name of Catholic was hated with all the unjust animosity of an Englishman; though our religion was practised in out-of-the-way places, our clergy persecuted, and our laymen avoided and suspected; even though the terrible penal laws were yet the spirit and the letter of English justice; yet, in spite of all these difficulties, spite of fine, confiscation, and death, these good men, worthy alike of our veneration and gratitude, at last succeeded in carrying out their plan, and you now, at this moment, are reaping the fruits of their labour: their work has helped very effectually to crush intolerance and bigotry, and you, my brethren, enjoy the privilege of being educated in the walls of this College.

But they were even yet more venturesome, more rash; they dared to place their labour of love under the powerful patronage of Mary; and that name, so offensive to Protestant ears, so hated by our countrymen, was again openly invoked: and this, our own College, claims the great honour of being the first, since the Reformation, dedicated to Mary's name, and placed under her loving care. Such is the history of its foundation and its name.

Every one of our Catholic colleges and institutions has its history, and each has had its part in the restoration of the old religion throughout the length and breadth of this land, helped by its own Patron Saint; but ours was destined to have a special mission, since it had the Mother of God, the queen of heaven, the greatest of God's Saints, for its protectress. And if there be a meaning in the Church's teaching of the invocation of the Saints, its verification is shown in this, as well as in its further history. If ever a mother watched her infant child with loving, anxious care through its slow development from childhood to manhood, Mary, whose aid was never asked in vain, whose solicitude for our welfare has never diminished, has been to us a true Alma Mater.

Now to-day we keep the Feast of her Patronage. We are her children; we accept her as our mother, and whilst others may call their own Patron Saints by loving terms, we can address her by the fondest and dearest of titles, mother. Have we then to-day offered her our tribute of love and gratitude for the blessings she has procured for our College and selves? Many a time and oft has she thought of us, when, alas! our minds have been far from her. When things have gone wrong with us, and difficulties have beset us, she has lent unseen a helping hand, and assuaged our sorrows. We will reflect on our privileges, on the treasures of our history, and stimulated by past favours, we will at her feet pour forth our gratitude, and implore her further protection.

One thing, my brethren, seems pretty clear; viz., that from its central position in this country, from its close proximity to one of our largest towns, from the particular time of its foundation, from the zeal and virtues of its founders, and the important positions they held in the Church, our College was destined to be one of the chief causes of effecting a change in the religion of this country. It brought Protestants into contact with their fellow Catholic countrymen, and helped greatly to remove that hostility they had felt against us, that was so unreasonable and unjust. Our beautiful services, carried out with all the rich and impressive ceremonial of the Church, attracted many to our chapel, doubtless at first out of curiosity, but who were at length forced to examine, and judge for themselves, as to the truth or falsehood of the statements brought against us. And in this way, silently and unostentatiously, did the great work of England's conversion begin. This has clearly been our mission, and God has wonderfully blessed us. For it has been by no mere accident or chance circumstance that this was our privilege, for not in this way does God distribute His graces; but it has been the invocation of Mary's sweet name, the sound of her Angelus bell, the chant of her Litanies, her oft-repeated Rosary, that has brought to us our rich store of blessings, and to others the grace of conversion to our faith. She has indeed done great things for us, and holy is her name.

And again, when the first streak of light betokened the dawn of England's conversion, hither came many a soul, who, having strayed to pastures that yielded no support, at length made his submission to the truth, and recruited his lost strength in the one fold of the one shepherd. And here also it was that the idea of one grand, universal prayer for England's return was conceived by that good and holy man, Father Ignatius Spencer, who, but a few years ago, was called to his reward, dying like his Divine Master alone and abandoned; for such had ever been his prayer. This work of England's conversion was begun by him here amongst us, and he made it the great object of his life to propagate this devotion. Our Holy Father gave it his special blessing, and enriched it with indulgences. It has been, so far as human opinion can judge, a great success. It began under Mary's name, and the prayer selected was her "Ave Maria." Now in co-operating with this grace, you have reason to be thankful; for those who say each evening the Rosary, at the same time say the Ave Maria for England's conversion. It is a custom of long standing; and though it seems but little for the object intended, it is most acceptable to God and pleasing to Mary; and if, loving your patroness and protectress, you give up a few minutes of your own time every day to say her Rosary, and pray for the return of those who know her not, you will receive many a grace, and perhaps obtain many a conversion. Shew, then, your gratitude to-night, and honour her feast by this tribute of your love.

And again, later still, we keep an event, the most memorable perhaps since England's great fall at the Reformation. Within these walls, under Mary's name, assembled in their first synod our new hierarchy. Here, for the first time for three centuries, met together in perfect security her mitred bishops, her many religious orders, each with its own distinctive badge, her secular clergy, among whom may be seen many who have kept the faith alive, undaunted and fearless, and some who once were persecutors, but now, like another St Paul, have sheathed their swords, and themselves become preachers of the true Gospel of that One, Holy, Catholic, Apostolic Church, that is to subsist till the end of time.

Thus, my brethren, has this College seen the gradual redevelopment of our religion through its three great successive stages, and been itself the active co-operator in them, namely, when its establishment prepared the way by removing prejudice, bigotry, and ignorance; again, when it received so many new members, illustrious by their talents, by their position, by their generous sacrifice; and lastly, when it witnessed a new life, a second spring, on the day it gathered under its shelter its new Episcopate. Oscott's name is thus to be perpetuated, and to have a place in the annals of England's conversion.

And yet more, my brethren. In the vale below, where stands what once was the germ of this institution, there was established, by the illustrious Bishop

Milner, an association in honour of the Sacred Heart of Jesus, and the Altar of the College chapel was the first dedicated in England to this devotion. This was dear to Mary, for the Sacred Heart was formed of her pure flesh and blood; in her virginal womb it first throbbed; she witnessed its last struggle for life on the wood of the cross. It is, without doubt, one of the most popular of our devotions. We have but to listen to Our Lord's own words to one of His chosen servants, and we shall at once be urged to be more faithful and more regular in practising it. "My Heart," He says, "shall dilate itself, and shall pour profusely the gifts of Divine love on all such as shall devote themselves to Me by this special service." We have our Altar and our statue of the Sacred Heart to remind us of Mary's first gift to us. Let us thank her then to-day for all these privileges and graces, and pray that having received the word of God, we may keep it as she did.

And now, my brethren, does not all this very deeply concern us? We must keep her feast to-day; and our thoughts must be of her, and of the work begun, and still going on under her name and protection. We know not, nor can we tell, how far our own conduct and lives may have to influence others; but if we would perpetuate in its integrity and lustre the history of our College and its devotion to Mary, as we are bound to do, we must tell her to-day our gratitude and love. We must ask through her God's blessing on this house, that it may carry out the purpose God intended in its foundation. It has done indeed a great work. It has spread Catholicity throughout every part of the world, and sent her students far away to distant lands to edify by their example those with whom they are to associate; and whether they have been called upon to rule and govern the Church, chosen by God, as Aaron was, to minister unto Him, or required to shed their blood in their country's cause, or fill their allotted place in the world's society, they have been equally doing God's work, and fulfilling the end for which they were sent here. It is for you, my brethren, to say whether it is to complete its work. If you venerate its traditions and its history, if you respect its discipline by a life subordinate to its rule, if you edify others by your religious duties, by your zeal for Mary's honour, and your earnestness in invoking her intercession, then you are completing that great work; and if you persevere in doing so, your College will be the greatest of our Catholic institutions, because it is under Mary's name, and has her special help.

Each morning and each evening, our first and last prayer in common is to Mary. In the Litany which we say together before our daily mass, we address her with those terms of endearment the loving child delights to give to a still more loving mother. We ask her to be the guardian of our purity, our consoler in afflictions, our help in trouble, our last blessing in life, the crown of our faithfulness. In the hymn we sing in the evening, we ask her to protect us in our sleep during the night, and more especially in the last and long sleep of death.

Go, then, to her statue to-day. It is consecrated by the blessing of the Church. There she, with her Holy Child, awaits you. Let us, then, my Reverend brethren in Jesus Christ, who are permitted to touch that sweet Babe, go to her with confidence, and pray that we, in our work, may have her blessing and help, that our labours may be successful, not for our own honour, but for her Son's, to Whom alone belong all honour and glory. Do you also, my dearest brethren, who step by step are advancing to our great privilege, pray to her to-day that you may not fail; that the world's influence and charms may never wile away your affections from your holy calling. Your studies will be successful under her teaching; under her guidance you will complete them, and obtain the end you long for. And you, my dear brethren, who form the burden of our responsibility, whom we have to educate and train, do you go to her feet, and ask her that as you advance in age you may also increase in grace and wisdom, before God and man, as did her Holy Child. Do you who are in trouble go to her, and she, your comforter in this vale of tears, will pity your sorrows, will calm your fears, and soothe with hope your misery. Do you go to her, who are tossed about on life's dangerous surge; you can claim her care; she will save you from peril and from woe. Do you go to her, and she, who is the spotless, chaste, and gentle Maid, will preserve your lives unstained, will quell your foolish affections and lustful passions, and make you pure and chaste. O guide of the wanderer! O hope of the pilgrim! be to us what thou hast ever been; in the dark night, across the bleak wilderness, guide us on to Jesus, guide us home.

APPENDIX.

TWO FUNERAL SERMONS.

In Memoriam.

MAURICE NOEL WELMAN was born December 7th, 1847.

He was sent to Oscott when he was very young, and remained till the autumn of 1859. His studies were then interrupted for awhile, as he went abroad with the rest of his family. He returned to college after the summer vacations of 1861, and from that time, till the completion of his course in July 1866, he always carried off the first prize in his class. He also gained the first silver examination medal in 1863, and in the two following years, the prizes for Latin and English Composition. In 1865 and 1866, he was *Præstantissimus* in Religious Instruction; and on leaving the College, he divided with another student the Oscotian Society's prize for Philosophy, and received the silver medal "for undeviating good conduct throughout the whole educational course, awarded by the suffrages of all the superiors."

In August 1866, he took lodgings in London to read with a private tutor for the Indian Civil Service Examination in the following spring; but on the 15th of January 1867, whilst skating in Regent's Park a few hours before the fearful accident of that day, he strained himself severely in trying to avoid a fall. From the ice he went to the lecture-room, and caught a chill. This, combined with the previous accident, brought on a congestion of the kidneys, rheumatic fever, and inflammation of the spine and brain, of which he died on Wednesday, the 30th of January, after a fortnight of very acute suffering and almost constant delirium.

His body was brought back to the College, and the following discourse was delivered at the Requiem Mass of the funeral, which was celebrated on Sunday, February 3rd.

A FUNERAL SERMON.

I AM sure that you will not expect a mere sermon from me on the present occasion: when the heart is fullest, it does not always find the most ready utterance in words. Nor is it necessary for me to preach, for well I know, here is that which pleads more eloquently in behalf of a virtuous life than any sermon which I could utter. But I have been desired to speak to you, my friends, and I must not shrink from the task. I wish now, if ever, to speak, not merely to your ears, not merely to your minds, but to your hearts, about this visitation of the Hand of God in the death of that dear friend whose funeral rites we are now celebrating. I will speak of the fact itself and of its lesson for us.

What, then, is the meaning of this—I cannot say melancholy—event? O my friends, let us divest ourselves of human notions (of human feelings we cannot divest ourselves) on the subject of death—and such a death as *his!* God forbid we should "sorrow like others who have no hope!" The Christian religion brought into the world a new estimate of life: it also brought into the world a new estimate of death. "Here," one might say, speaking as the world speaks, "is indeed a melancholy spectacle, to be deplored with the deepest grief! A youth just entering into the world, after having most especially distinguished himself at college,—in the very ripeness of youthful energy, flushed with the anticipations of youthful hope, with every bright prospect, and every good wish and prayer of others, *cut off.*"—No, my friends, this is what I wish most especially to impress upon your minds, that he was not "cut off." Our dear friend came to us from God, and God took him home,—when we had little expected it; but he was not cut off. That would imply that he did not fulfil himself in life, that he did not finish the work which his Heavenly Father had given him to do; but he *did:* and not till he had finished it, did God take him home.

A simple flower is born in the morning, and withers in the evening; but, before it withers, it has attained its full growth, it has unfolded its beauty, it has gladdened the heart, and refreshed the senses, and taught the lesson of its Maker's goodness; and then—for its purpose is accomplished—it withers and dies. And, as with such a flower, so with the life of man, if indeed he live to God. He is sent into this world with a purpose: he fulfils that purpose, and then, not before, does the dust return unto its earth from whence it was, and the spirit return unto God Who gave it. This is what man was really sent into this world for—to accomplish the will of God in his life; and, if indeed he make this the main object of his life, it matters very little whether his life were long or short. The longest life is indeed short, if this object be not attained; and, if it be obtained, the shortest life is equal with the longest.

God may have many designs in the lives of each one which are hidden from us; but one purpose is clear and plain, and ought to serve as a rule to all our lives—to do the will of God in that sphere of life and labour in which He Himself has called us. "My meat is to do the will of Him that sent Me, that I may perfect His work," says our Blessed Lord. And, as with the Master, so with the disciple. And this, which ought to be the characteristic of every Christian life, was especially the characteristic of the life of our dear friend. Not only in religious matters, not only in matters of college duty, but in the minutest detail of daily life, he was thoroughly conscientious. His whole character might be summed up in that one word; and it is sufficient, for it comprehends everything. It was this feeling of the thorough conscientiousness of his life that made him to be not only beloved but reverenced by every one who had to do with him. And when I say that he was "reverenced," I speak it advisedly; that feeling of reverence I felt towards him myself. As his director, it is true, I was intimate with his very soul, and knew the springs of his conduct and actions; but I should not have used the word of him, unless I had found him just the same in his everyday life as he was in his religious life, and were I not fully persuaded, that that very same feeling of reverence which I entertained for him myself was shared by every one of you. This thorough-going conscientiousness, this perfect simplicity of intention, was the great charm of his character. It made him what he was—modest, unselfish, unassuming, unobtrusive, gentle, refined, courteous, candid, sincere, earnest. In a word, he was perfect—so far as it is human to be perfect: to be faultless is not human. "Be ye perfect," says our Blessed Saviour, "as your heavenly Father is perfect." And to perfect himself in his moral and religious character, in his mental character and acquirements, and in the everyday relations of life, was the conscientious aim of his being, and, by Divine grace and the co-operation of a good natural disposition, perfection was the result. But this charm of perfection was especially enhanced in him by the simple, modest unconsciousness of his own worth. Need I say more? You know—this was MAURICE WELMAN.

And what he was in his life, such was he also in his death, the account of which, as written by his mother, I am now going to read to you, instead of giving it in my own words, because I wish to be exact, and because, in recording his last sayings, I wish to give, not merely the substance of what he said, but the very words in which he said it:—

"The evening I arrived I found Maurice had already sent for Father Davis, and made his confession—and he added, 'I have been so happy to-day, oh, you don't know how happy.' All through the night his soul was longing for Holy Communion. He was very wandering in mind, and constantly distressed by fearing that he could not receive because he could not go to church, and because he was not fasting; and I had over and over again to comfort him by explaining that our Lord was coming to him, and as Viaticum. Once I heard him say to himself, 'The King of Heaven is coming to me, and I cannot receive Him;' once he stretched out his hands, raising himself in bed and with his head thrown back and mouth open, seemed waiting; then after a time, he sunk back saying mournfully, 'I have received nothing.' His attitude made one think of the picture of St Philip Neri at Rome; his arms and hands were in just the same attitude. Seeing his anxiety, I wrote to hurry Father Davis, but when he came, Maurice was too wandering and unconscious. He returned two hours later, and was able to give him Holy Communion; soon after I went to his bedside, and he gave me a look of perfect satisfied peace, and said, 'that was all right.' At intervals during that first night, he talked a good deal to me; said he had been learning a great deal during his illness—felt we were sent into the world for very different purposes from what the generality of people thought; spoke of the vanity of learning, influence, conversation, position, &c., &c., and that all he wished was to be a 'plain Catholic, a plain, true, pure Catholic, a Roman Catholic,'—nothing else for him. And these words he kept repeating. [In his very last letter to me he had said, 'I am going to give up the *Saturday Review;* it is so sceptical and bigoted.'] Also there was something that I could not catch, as if he spoke of a change of plans, and it ended by his saying twice, 'The precious jewel of the Priesthood—the precious jewel of the Priesthood.' Once when beginning to wander, he said suddenly, 'What were we born into this world for?' I said, 'To know Him.' He caught it up and eagerly said, 'To know Him, to love Him, and to serve Him in this world, and to be happy with Him for ever in the next.' Several times he said, 'Oh my life has been so useless—what good have I ever done to any one in the world?'

"He often spoke of Oscott, and said, 'I have never forgotten my Oscott principles—that I know—and I never will.'

"Most of the time he was in wild delirium; or in a sort of semi-conscious state, when he knew everything but could not express himself rightly. The perfectly lucid intervals were the exceptions; but all of these were full of beauty and comfort. In all his delirium there was never *one word* painful to hear. He raved chiefly about his studies, talking in all languages, quoting all authors, or about that terrible accident in Regent's Park which had taken great hold on his mind, or about his own family; often saying he was dying, and bidding every one good-bye. He was full of thought for others during his illness, and only the day before he died, he begged us to go out of the room, and then he explained to Mr S—— how unhappy he was at our discomfort and fatigues, wanting to know whether it was not possible to make some change of arrangements for us. [There was only one small room in the house in which he was lodging, that we could occupy.]

"Two days before his death, when I thought him much worse, he repeated the invocations after me, before the priest came, though I had thought him unconscious when I began; and then of his own accord he added, 'May the adorable will,' but could not finish it. Twice he said, 'This is not bravery, this is not bearing illness with courage.' 'But you *wish and intend* to bear it lovingly and with courage.' 'Yes! yes!' and then he made the acts of resignation, &c.

"He appeared unconscious when Extreme Unction was given; but later when Father Davis visited him, though his eyes were shut, he knew his voice. 'Maurice, do you know me?' 'Yes!' 'Who am I?' 'The priest who attended me.' He could not say his name, but remembered he came from Ogle Street. 'Do you wish to say anything to me—do you wish to speak to me alone?' 'No.' 'You know you are very dangerously ill—do you remember my giving you Extreme Unction?' 'Yes, I remember that.'

"He made no sign when the last blessing was given; but when he caught sight of the Crucifix, his face became radiant with love; he kissed it and pressed it to him, laying his face on it, and saying, 'O dear darling Lord, you have suffered so much for me, and I suffer so little for you.' No one who saw it could ever forget that scene. The evening before his death, he suddenly began to pray aloud—I could not catch all—'that the Church may be built up in Him. Come, Divine Spirit, fill our hearts, for God will shew His goodness to His children—that which in my infirmity I have done amiss, do Thou in Thy pity forgive,' &c. I caught those sentences. Very shortly before he ceased to speak to us, he suddenly raised himself, stretched his arms wide out in the form of a cross, and said vehemently and in a loud voice, 'O Jesus, Mary, Jesus, Mary, I love you—oh, I love you—I have always loved you,' and some more which we did not catch. After that he seemed only to see the Crucifix—and even when he could not see it, it was thought from his expression that he heard the slight clink which the ring on the top of it made when it was moved—and he breathed out his soul just as the last words were finished of the prayers for a departing spirit."

Since such he was in his life as in his death, you will readily understand, my friends, why I refuse to think or say of him, however premature his death may appear to us, that he was cut off. Had it been the case of one who was so very young that it could not possibly be conjectured of him whether he would have gone to the right hand or to the left, one might have said: "He was taken away, lest wickedness should alter his understanding, or deceit beguile his soul:" but of our dear friend, who with all his heart and soul had taken God's side, who had solemnly protested that he would never forsake his Oscott principles—those Christian principles, that is to say, which he learned at Oscott, I would rather say, "Being made perfect, in a short space he fulfilled a long time." "For venerable old age," says the wise man, "is not that of long time; neither is it counted by the number of years: but the understanding of a man is grey hairs, and a spotless life is old age." Why, then, should his life be prolonged, when the great purpose of his life was accomplished — his perfection, and our example. And if it seem a hard case, and it does, never more to see that dear face till we meet him in Heaven; yet remember that sooner or later, we must all of us bid each other farewell, and be gathered into the same Home! And who is there, who considers what that Home is, and what a crown he has gone to obtain, would wish him back? Who is there that, could he bid that dust live again by raising a finger, would wish to raise it? No! No! A death-bed such as his makes one understand that saying of Holy Scripture, that "better is the house of mourning than the house of feasting." They are sweet tears, I know, which will be shed over his grave.

And you, my friends, — you will not forget the lesson of that life which you witnessed here; you will not forget the lesson of that death, the account of which I have just read to you? You will know how to cherish those Oscott Christian principles which he cherished? It is (as it were) to impress the more forcibly upon your mind this lesson, that he is come to be buried here.

Lastly, there remains towards him a duty of gratitude and friendship which it is scarcely necessary to mention: — I *know* that you will most fervently pray for him.

In Memoriam.

OSMUND CHARLES DE LISLE was born November 6, 1847.

He came to St Mary's College, Oscott, on the 15th August 1857, and remained there until July 1866, when he received at the same time with Maurice Welman the silver medal " for undeviating good conduct throughout the whole educational course, awarded by the suffrages of all the superiors."

At first, he intended to have accompanied a younger brother to one of the colonies; when this brother was otherwise provided for, he determined (at the end of a Retreat at St Mary's) on devoting himself to the service of the Church as a Papal Zouave. But before the time came that had been fixed upon for the carrying out of this resolution, he was convinced (not without reason) that his health would not stand the hardships of a military life, and he finally determined on qualifying himself for the general management of his father's property. For this purpose he became a student at the Royal Agricultural College, near Cirencester, going there about the middle of August 1869. On Monday the 4th of October, after a few premonitory symptoms which had not been specially noticed, he became suddenly insensible, and remained so for about twenty-four hours. On the second day he rallied, and for a short time there was great hope of his recovery. But at the close of the week there was a relapse, and he died on the evening of the 17th October, the Feast of the Purity of our Blessed Lady. Extreme Unction had been administered to him at an early stage of his illness, and he made his confession and received the last blessing on the Friday before his death, but he was not able to receive the Holy Viaticum. His remains were brought to Grace Dieu Manor, and deposited in the family vault, on Friday the 22d inst., on which occasion the following sermon was preached.

A FUNERAL SERMON.

MY DEAR BRETHREN IN JESUS CHRIST,—I have need to crave your kindest indulgence in the few words I am going to say to you this morning. Bear with me, if I speak more familiarly than is usual in this sacred place; but we are assembled here as one family, mourning a common loss, and the Church which has called us around this bier will allow us to soften and hallow our sorrow as we may. Excuse me too, if I seem sometimes to speak abruptly, perhaps even coldly and without feeling; for I fear this will be the only way in which I shall be able to speak to you at all. For there are times when the very force and fulness of our feelings prove the greatest bar to their utterance, and such a time is this to me. Certainly, I would not willingly have been absent from this place to-day, to pay a last tribute of love and reverence to one whom I have loved and reverenced so long; but I would rather have been here as a silent mourner than as a speaker. Those, however, whose slightest wish at such a moment has all the force of a command, have willed it otherwise; they said it would be some comfort to them; and who then could refuse? But what shall I say? How shall I begin? A heathen orator complained, two thousand years ago, of the extreme difficulty, or even impossibility, of speaking well, and in a fitting manner, about the dead. He said—what certainly I feel to-day to be most true—that you are in danger either of saying too little, and so falling short of the truth, and disappointing the just expectations of surviving relatives, or of saying too much, because you say more than your hearers feel to be within their own power, or at least within the range of their own practice, and so your words gain no credence.

Let us, however, boldly utter a word which will take us at once to the very heart of our subject, and raise us to a higher sphere of thought, the only one which seems to me really befitting this occasion. It is a word which I know has escaped the lips of many during the last few days, whilst he whom we are here to bury lay between life and death. Many have felt and said that Osmund de Lisle was *a saint*. Now *saint* is a word in the Catholic Church of very high and solemn import; it may not be lightly handled. Generally, indeed, we associate it in our minds with the idea of heroic deeds or heroic sufferings; our thoughts recur as soon as we hear it, to great apostles and doctors of the Church, to martyrs or holy virgins, or famous penitents, whom the Church has canonised; and of course these are saints of the highest order, and in the highest sense of the word.

But I think we do a wrong to truth and an injury

to ourselves, if we confine the word within such narrow limits. We do a wrong to truth, because, just as in the material world God's power and wisdom are as present and as manifest in the tiniest insect that crawls upon the ground, and in the very grass with which the earth is clothed, as in the cedar of Libanus, or the mightiest beast of the forest, so in the spiritual world the operations of His grace are as beautiful and as wonderful in those whose lives are perfected amid the quiet seclusion of ordinary life, as in those whose histories are full of dangers and difficulties; illustrated, as it were, by torrents of light or of blood. We do also an injury to ourselves; for after contemplating the heroic deeds or sufferings of canonised saints, we take the measure of our own weakness, and decide that, because such heights are beyond our strength, therefore we are not called to sanctity. Yet St Paul, in his Epistles to the various Christian Churches, addresses those to whom he writes either as "saints" or as men "called to be saints." Let us briefly, then, consider what sanctity is, in its simplest and most essential form, and then let us apply the test to the life of our dear friend.

If you open the works of the prince of theologians, St Thomas, you will find him declaring that sanctity is "a *general* virtue, whereby the acts of all the other virtues are ordered and directed towards the supreme good, God;" and when he comes to analyse it, he says that it seems to rest upon two special foundations, to consist of two special elements, which he calls purity and firmness, or constancy. He does not here use the word purity in its narrower and more restricted sense, as opposed to that foul vice, the mere mention of which would here be out of place; but he uses it in a far higher and more perfect sense, such as the Church meant when she celebrated last Sunday the Feast of the Purity of our Blessed Lady, viz., perfect detachment from the things of this world, so that God can take full possession of the soul, and the soul can attach itself with the energy of an undivided affection to God. We are so constituted by nature, that the goods of this world in some shape or other—"the creature," as St Paul speaks—are for ever soliciting and attracting our souls and making demands upon our affections; and in proportion as we give heed to these solicitations, even if we stop short of what is sinful, the soul contracts a certain stain, sufficient to dim its brightness and render it incapable of reflecting with integrity all the rays of Divine light which fall upon it. Those chosen ones, then, whom God has called to the heights of perfection, are ever most watchful against this danger; they keep close guard upon their bodily senses, those gates whereby chiefly the temptations of the outer world gain access to the soul, and even set a bridle upon those affections of the heart which have a tendency to withdraw them from God; knowing that thus only they can keep their souls in virginal integrity. This is the purity of which St Thomas speaks as one of the essential conditions and fundamental elements of sanctity. And I dare to ask you who knew *him* best who lies there in the midst of us, whether you do not recognise in this description one of his striking characteristics. His own parents have sometimes wonderingly said to one another, that "Osmund seemed to have no passions." His brothers and sisters, and college friends, seeing his complete indifference to the world, have laughingly told him that surely it was his vocation to be a priest and a monk. Yet he never seems to have drawn such a conclusion himself: he saw no reason why he should not continue to live in the world without therefore being of it. He fulfilled the apostolic precept with admirable simplicity— "rejoicing, as if he rejoiced not; buying, as though he possessed not; using this world, as if he used it not" (1 Cor. vii. 31). He had a keen relish for the manliest and most healthy sports and amusements belonging to his age and position in society; but at the slightest call of duty, they were as freely abandoned as if he had been wholly indifferent to them. Without a moment's hesitation, and with a cheerful grace and readiness which made the sacrifice doubly precious in the sight of God, whilst it served almost wholly to hide it from the eyes of men, he would give up a day's pleasure just when the cup was at his lips, if he saw that he could thereby render any service to his parents, or do any good to his neighbour. And in this respect he was always the same; his schoolfellows, as well as others, testify that he always seemed to have his will under perfect control, even on every emergency—never forgetting himself, never losing his temper, though often tried. Surely these, my brethren, are indications of no common degree of purity of soul, of detachment from the creature, and such habitual obedience to the law of God, that "the law in the members" (Rom. vii. 23) seemed almost to have lost its strength. The doctor who attended him in his last illness said, "He had never seen such an instance of habitual obedience in all his practice."

Let us next look at that other condition of sanctity whereof we spoke: firmness or constancy, whereby all the powers of a man's whole being, body and soul, head and heart, will, memory, and understanding, as well as the affections, are brought into subjection to the one ruling principle, and directed to a supernatural end; and this continuously, perseveringly, without ever losing sight of that end, or turning aside from it, except by those indeliberate and (we may almost say) unavoidable movements which spring from the weakness and corruption of our nature. This firm, immovable purpose, to live not for self, but for God, was, so far as we can judge, most deeply marked on the life of Osmund de Lisle; and no man can tell the day or hour when first it was formed. "I never, from his cradle," says one who has a right to speak, "heard him utter an angry word, nor can I remember to have seen in him the commission of any deliberate sin." Such is the testimony borne to his blameless childhood; but this period of his life, spent beneath the shelter of a peaceful and pious home, did not last long. At the early age of nine he lost an elder brother, his favourite companion and playfellow, who was killed by a fall upon the ice; and Osmund seemed to feel the loss so keenly, that it was thought better to send him at önce to school, where he might form other friendships, and have his mind diverted to other interests. I need not remind you of the great importance of this change in the outward circumstances of a boy's life. A large school is a miniature world; and however carefully its superiors may hedge it round about with wise laws of discipline, and administer those laws with prudence, vigilance, and charity, it is impossible but that, sooner or later, in a greater or less degree, some evil should creep in and try the temper and principles of all its inmates. The world, the flesh, and the devil will insinuate their poison, and ply their arts of seduction, without fail, in any place of education where a considerable number of boys are gathered together, in the course of a long term of years. Our dear young friend, then, was sent into such a world, when he was not yet ten years old, and he remained there for nine years. Surely here was time and opportunity for testing the firmness of his principles, and learning the true strength of his character. And how did it stand the test? What is the testimony of his superiors, and of his companions, during this long and important portion of his life? The venerable President who received him into St Mary's College, Oscott, has long since entered into his rest; but his written records survive, testifying to the gentleness and docility, yet independent and energetic character, of his young charge. After Osmund had been there for two years, I succeeded to the responsible office of President; and during the six or seven years that I knew him, I protest that I cannot remember ever to have had a single occasion, I will not say to rebuke him, but even to entertain for a moment so much as a passing thought of blame of him. I cannot question the able priest who for four or five years had special charge of the discipline of the house, governing the boys in their hours of recreation, and so seeing them at their most unguarded moments, for he too has gone to his last home; but I well remember the value he set upon Osmund's example and influence, and the use he made of it, on more than one occasion, for the good of others; and the friendship which continued between them, even after he had left the College, and so long as he lived, is a sufficient proof of the estimate he had formed of our friend's character. I have asked his successor in the important office of the Prefectship, whose duties, as I have already explained, give such special opportunities for learning the true character of a boy, and his answer is briefly this, "I never had an occasion to reprimand him; and when his whole class incurred punishment, I was obliged to make him an exception." I questioned another of his masters, who knew him well, and he said, "I may mention a circumstance which, though connected with a fault he once committed, gave me a very high opinion of his sincerity. He had failed to present his composition at the proper time; and I asked him, 'What excuse he had to give for the omission?' 'No excuse at all, sir; sheer idleness,' was the reply." And a very similar anecdote is told by another master. How blameless must that life have been, in which the keen eyes and retentive memories of superiors either fail to testify to any fault at all, or only to faults redeemed by such noble sincerity as this. Yet I have not been able to find a trace of anything more serious than this. I called for the testimony of those of his classfellows who were within my reach,—they are only two, both studying for the priesthood; and this is what they write:—" Osmund always got up, went to bed, and performed all his other duties with clockwork punctuality. He always *knelt* during the whole of meditation-time, not availing himself of any of the ordinary indulgences, but uniformly observing a straight, motionless posture. At meals he invariably took the same quantity, and always chose the plainest fare upon the table. He was in every particular zealous for the rules of the College, both in time of study and recreation. Thus, in the wintertime he would not read in the common room of his class, where there was a comfortable fire, for fear he should be tempted into conversation with his companions, but always withdrew to his own room, and read with open window in the severest weather. He observed most exactly the most minute regulations, even where some perhaps had been allowed practically to fall into abeyance though they still remained as the written letter of the law. As head of the games, he was as zealous for the boys' rules as for those of his superiors, but was never boisterous in enforcing them, He ruled by example and force of character, not by words. He never *shouted* his injunctions, as boys generally do, but if any one were in fault, spoke to him with the same quiet manner, sweet smile, and subdued voice, which were habitual to him. He always reminded us of the saying, *Suaviter in modo, fortiter in re.* All his spare recreation time was devoted to the common public good. He would work for the junior boys, splicing their bats or otherwise helping them; always occupied, and always at everybody's service. He could not bear to see any waste in the public property, and spent much time in sewing up cricket-gloves and other apparatus, so as to keep everything in a serviceable condition, as long as possible. In conversation, he was never known to utter a word against anybody; nor would he ever hear any one say a word against his neighbour, or against superiors, or against the College regulations, so that boys learned to know better than to grumble or speak unkindly before him. One who had been somewhat annoyed at a rebuke he had received, once complained to him that "he never seemed able to see anything bad in any one." It was noticed that he always defended the weaker side. His manner impressed us with the idea that he was always engaged in subduing himself. He used to make light of what he called his *stoicism*, alluding to the severities which he practised on himself, as though he adopted that manner of life as a whim, and to please himself. But no one was or could have been ignorant of the real motive, to acquire the perfect mastery over himself, so as to conform his life in all things to the will of God, as dictated in his conscience." "To one who did not know him," adds another, "he might have appeared reserved; but when spoken to, he was always singularly open and cheerful in his conversation. He would anticipate a superior's or a companion's wishes, if he could. A wish expressed in his presence, even though not really meant, was enough to secure its fulfilment, if it was at all within his power to accomplish it. His ruling principle, founded on the instruction so often given us in Retreat, was this: 'Play well in playtime, pray well in prayer-time, and study well in study-time.' Hence he made it a rule always to study the subject-matter of the lesson during the whole time appointed for that lesson, but on the same principle he did not study *out of* study-time. In consequence of this, he failed on one occasion to pass in an examination, to prepare for which all his class-fellows had stayed up beyond the hour allotted for going to bed. Once, when he did not see the meaning of the subject given for composition, he inquired it of a companion, but ultimately thought it his duty not to use the knowledge so acquired. In a word, he did everything as conscientiously, as unselfishly, and as perfectly as it could be done."

Such was the life and character of this dear youth, as appreciated by those amongst whom he lived for so many years, and on the closest terms of schoolboy intimacy. Of his life at home during the last three years *you* have been witnesses, and I have not; but I boldly appeal to all who hear me, whether there has been anything in it out of harmony with what went before; or whether, on the contrary, it has not been simply a continuation and consistent development of the same habits, the same beautiful graces and virtues which had been admired in him elsewhere. His parents testify to the same regularity, the same absence of self-indulgence, even in trifling matters, and the same kindness and consideration for others. He never missed the family-prayers in the morning, read a chapter or two of the Gospels or other portions of Holy Scripture after breakfast, recited a third part of the Rosary daily, and paid a visit to the Blessed Sacrament before going to bed at night. Every Sunday for the last two years, as you know, he has never failed to go to a neighbouring village to teach a class of young men and boys. He received Holy Communion once a fortnight, and often went weekly to Confession. He occupied himself all day, either in his workshop, or going wherever his father might wish to send him on any business. As for dutiful respect and affection to his parents, and to all whom he regarded as superiors, it was evident that he saw God in them in a most wonderful way: and the perfection of his conduct towards his equals and inferiors, is sufficiently attested by their sorrow at his loss, and the touching way in which they have expressed that sorrow. Everybody had the most perfect confidence both in his justice and his kindness; and hence he had a special talent for reconciling differences, and he often exercised it. He had a quiet, patient way of listening to the tales of each, and then gave his judgment with so much gentleness and moderation, that no one could be offended at it. If at any time conversation was begun in his presence which he could not approve, he would either keep silence or quietly change the subject; or even, if the age and circumstances of the speakers allowed him to do so, he would administer a gentle reproof, yet always with such a sweet simplicity and unaffected humility, that no one was ever heard to say a word against him. Thoughtful observers could detect a certain gravity about him even when joining in the amusements of others, a certain not unpleasant reticence, and a moderation both in words and deeds beyond his years. Nevertheless, his unassuming manners, his obliging attentions, his genuine kindness, which seemed always to come from the heart, so endeared him to everybody, that whole families, strangers to him in blood, have expressed themselves as feeling as if they had lost a near and dear relation, when they heard that he was gone.

My brethren, I have said all that I have to say about the life of our dear friend, for it was short and simple, and had nothing in it that the world would call extraordinary. Yet we need not hesitate to say, that "he was made perfect in a short space, and fulfilled a long time;" "He pleased God and was beloved." Does it seem to you so very far removed from sanctity, because of the absence of any of those marvels which delight our imagination and gratify our love of the wonderful in the lives of those who are canonised? Or does any one suspect that such a life as this might have been the mere accidental product of a singularly happy nature, nurtured amid exceptional privileges and safeguards, and ripened by a rare combination of specially favourable circumstances? In a word, does any one doubt whether all this that we have been describing was the fruit of nature or of grace? The doubt is not altogether unreasonable, for it cannot be denied that nature does sometimes counterfeit grace, so as even to be mistaken for it; and the reason of this is because "the difference between them is in a great measure an inward, and therefore a secret one." "Outward gravity of deportment," it has been truly said, "is no warrant that there is not within an habitual indulgence of evil thoughts and secret offences odious to Almighty God." Listen then, my brethren, yet another moment, whilst I say a few words about this young man's last sickness and death. For death sets the seal upon a man's life, and is, moreover, a great revealer of secrets. I shall not detain you, then, by describing any of the outward features of his sickness as it affected the body; I shall say nothing of the alternations of hope and fear to which its changing symptoms gave occasion in the hearts of his afflicted parents. I only wish to speak of it so far as it sheds a light upon his previous life, and reveals to us anything of the past history and condition of his soul. It pleased God that during by far the larger portion of his short illness, he should remain in a state of only partial consciousness; with his senses apparently already dead to the world around him; without either the will or the power of communicating his thoughts and feelings to those who were so tenderly watching him; without even the knowledge of their presence. Yet, during all this time, he still retained the power of speech, and often used it; but only in one way, and that continually, to speak to God in prayer. This condition of body is by no means uncommon in dying persons—*i.e*, the power of speech is retained, but that power no longer under the absolute control of the will; and some of you may have seen, doubtless you have all heard or read, what painful scenes, what frightful revelations are sometimes occasioned by it. Even in the case of persons of apparently blameless lives, it sometimes seems as though the devil had received the power of bringing back to the memory, or of suggesting to the imagination, at that supreme moment of death, words and deeds of evil which we hardly thought the dying man could ever have heard of, which we refuse to believe that he can have ever loved, or which we are at least quite certain, that if only he had the full use of his senses now, he would turn away from, with the utmost horror and disgust. Yet there they are; inflicting deep wounds of sharpest pain in the hearts of all that hear, even though we may firmly believe that they do no harm to the soul, of him that utters them. They reveal a past stain, or a past temptation, without creating a new one. The first circumstance, then, which I would name, of Osmund's dying moments, though the least important in itself, is certainly not without its significance, nor without consolation to us. Never, in all those weary days and nights of watching, did he utter a single word which it could pain his own mother to hear. Nay more, I have not heard that he ever spoke a word, or showed that his thoughts were for a moment occupied, even on the innocent pleasures and business of this world. No; his words were always as of one whose whole soul was occupied with the things of eternity; and whether this was now a merely mechanical act, the result of long habit, or whether it was the fruit of a present act of consciousness, it matters not here to inquire. In either case, "out of the abundance of the heart the mouth speaketh;" and Osmund's mouth was opened only to utter prayer.

But, secondly, we have every reason to believe that these prayers were no mere outward act of the lips, but came straight from the heart. Again and again would he sign himself with a large sign of the cross, clasp his hands together, and pour forth his prayers with such touching earnestness as to move bystanders to tears. He often began to recite the Rosary, but generally fell asleep before he could finish it. He was continually invoking the holy Names of Jesus, Mary, and Joseph, in those pious ejaculations with which good Catholics are so careful to arm themselves during life, that they may be ready with them at the hour of death. Of these, one which he used with special frequency was, "Sweet Jesus, have mercy on me; be Thou not my Judge, but my Saviour." Another of his favourite prayers was that which you know under the name of the Universal Prayer, and which he repeated so frequently and so distinctly, that, spite of its great length, his attendants, who had never heard of it before, came at last almost to know it by heart. Another prayer, not so long, but which he used quite as often,—it immediately precedes the Universal Prayer in some of our prayer-books, and doubtless he had been in the habit of using them both together during life,—I will read to you in full, because it seems to reveal to us the very secret of his life, a secret which nothing but his death would ever have brought to light. The prayer is one of those to the use of which the Church has attached an indulgence, and it is generally known under the name of " Petitions for Graces." It begins in this wise :—" O Father, O Son, O Holy Ghost ! O most Holy Trinity ! O Jesus ! O Mary ! Ye blessed angels, and all ye saints of Paradise, obtain for me these graces, which I ask through the merits of the most Precious Blood of Jesus Christ." And then it goes on to enumerate nine several graces to be prayed for, and I beg your very special attention to these, because (as I have said) they do seem to furnish us with the very key we wanted to the due reading of the life we have been considering ; the life seems to be the very living reflected image of the prayer ; living, yet reflected, for it derives all its life and strength and supernatural virtue from the prayer to which it was an answer. The nine graces asked for are—

1. Always to do the will of God.
2. To be always in union with God.
3. To think only of God.
4. To love God alone.
5. To do everything for God.

6. To seek only the glory of God.
7. To make myself a saint for God's sake alone.
8. To know my own nothingness.
9. To know more clearly the will of God.

Then the tenth space is left vacant in our printed books, and we are told to supply here whatever grace we specially desire. Osmund's special desire,—we learn it for the first time, but from his own lips, unconscious that he was revealing one of the secrets of his soul,—Osmund's special desire was the "grace of holy purity"—and then the prayer concludes, and Osmund repeated it to the end :—"O most Holy Mary, offer to the Eternal Father the most Precious Blood of Jesus Christ for my soul, for the holy souls in Purgatory, for the needs of Holy Church, for the conversion of sinners, and for the whole world."

Now, I would ask you, my dear brethren, to try to picture to yourselves a life and character that should be perfectly moulded upon this prayer; and unless the partiality of affection greatly blind my judgment, I believe that the picture, when you have drawn it, will be found to bear a striking resemblance to the life of Osmund de Lisle, as you have yourselves seen and known it. There would be in it the same outward show of calm simplicity; the same unflinching integrity; the same active, open-hearted, yet unobtrusive kindness; the same utter unselfishness, forgetfulness, and almost unconsciousness of self; the same sweetness, candour, innocence, patience, humility, and obedience; and above all, the same quiet, unalterable perseverance in the exercise of these virtues, which so won our love and admiration in him. The modest grace of his appearance, the virginal reserve of his whole bearing and carriage, the sincerity, yet gentle pleasantness of his words, and the ever-willing readiness of his charity, were such fruits as seemed to betoken a soul deeply rooted in grace,— such fruits as might naturally have been looked for in one who aimed at living only for God ; and therefore we have felt and said that " his lot is among the saints." In the vineyard of the Church, which Christ purchased with His Precious Blood, and which He never ceases to water with the abundant showers of His graces, there are reared from time to time rare and wonderful plants, of such extraordinary size and beauty, as almost to awe and dazzle us by their splendour and magnificence ; but there are also others, more lowly but not less lovely, which attract us by the delicacy of their hue or form, and by the sweet odour which they exhale, " as the flower of roses in the days of the spring, and as the lilies that are on the brink of the water, and as the sweet-smelling frankincense in the time of summer " (Ecclus. l. 8) ; and such an one, it seems to us, was our dear friend here. At a time of life when other plants of the same age, and apparently not less sheltered from wind and storm, nor less favoured by sun and soil, have scarcely raised themselves above the level of the earth, or gained strength to stand without support, this chosen plant was already covered with bright flowers, ready to be transplanted into the garden of the heavenly Jerusalem, already laden with rich, ripe fruit, ready to be gathered into the everlasting garners. "His soul pleased God; therefore He hasteneth to bring him out of iniquities;" "He was beloved of God and men; his memory is in benediction;" "His memory shall be sweet as honey in every mouth, and as music at a banquet of wine" (Wisdom iv. 14; Ecclus. xlv. 1, xlix. 2).

And now what remains but that we should complete the holy sacrifice that has been begun, recite the psalms and prayers for the dead which this discourse has interrupted, and consign his dear remains to their last resting-place in the grave? But this thought reminds me that there may seem at first sight to be some inconsistency between what I have been saying and what we are doing; and I must say one word to remove it. I have been speaking of him whom we have lost as a saint, whereas we pray and offer the holy sacrifice for sinners. God forbid that anything I have said should stay the course of your prayers and sacrifices for the deceased. An attitude of prayer is the only one that becomes us all by the tombs of our best and dearest friends; and I shall have been guilty, if not of impiety towards God, yet certainly of great cruelty towards him whom I love and would fain benefit, if I have so praised him as to have created an impression on your minds that he stands in no need of your prayers. But I remember to have seen in the Roman catacombs, those oldest burial-places of the ancient Christians, several inscriptions on the grave-stones, in which the survivors first called upon Jesus to have mercy on the soul of him whose body they had laid there, and then (in the very same breath, as it were) begged that same departed one to pray for the husband or wife, father or mother, brothers and sisters, whom he had left sorrowing behind him. I will not stop to inquire whether there was in this double prayer any inconsistency, logical or theological; but at least I will dare to say that there is no inconsistency with the best and truest feelings of the human heart. On the contrary, these inscriptions have always seemed to me a beautifully natural, unstudied expression of the most intimate thoughts of sorrowing survivors, in the first moments of such a bereavement as this which we are mourning over to-day. Thinking of him whom they have lost in the light of the severity of God's judgments, before Whom they know that he has now gone—God, "Whose eyes are too pure to behold evil, and Who cannot look on iniquity" (Hab. i. 13)—a strong cry for mercy is the only prayer that rises up from their hearts; they call upon the Lord Jesus to "remember their dear child." Yet again, when they think of God's mercy, and of what His power and goodness has wrought in the soul of the deceased,—when they call to mind his many gifts and graces, and the fidelity with which he laboured to do God's will on earth, they cannot doubt that God will receive him into heaven; and so they ask him whose struggle is now over, and his crown won, to intercede before the throne of grace for themselves, the battle of whose life is yet undetermined. In the same way, and under the influence of the same mixed feelings, I commend him whom we are now to bury, at once to your prayers and to your imitation.

I have spoken, not for the flattery of the dead, but for the consolation and instruction of the living, whom nature forces to sorrow, yet whom faith bids to rejoice; you, his father and mother, brothers and sisters, in whom, as in so many living reliquaries, there will ever be retained, I know, a most sweet memory of him whom you have lost, and, if I may so express myself, a certain *cultus* of love and veneration, and—which is so much more important—of imitation. I have set these things before you as the titles of that assurance which a loving God has allowed you to have of the eternal happiness of your brother and your son. I have spoken also for our own edification and improvement, on whom the example of such goodness ought not to be thrown away. It is a talent, for the use of which both you and I shall one day be called to account, that we should have had the opportunity of knowing and seeing so touching an example of holy wisdom matured in one so young, of such angelic purity perfected in the midst of us. And, lastly, I have spoken also for the honour and glory of God, Who is always admirable in all His saints, and not less so in those in whose souls He has worked most silently and most immediately, not deranging (so to speak) any of the outward conditions and circumstances of their lives, but only using them to build up in their inmost souls a perfect model of sanctity. Let us thank, praise, and bless God for His goodness to this His chosen servant, now taken away from our sight, and entered into his everlasting rest,—who, while he lived, was a striking witness of the power of the Catholic faith over the errors and passions of youth, and the memory of whose virtues, so long as we retain it, will ever serve as a protest against two of the special sins of our age, the spirit of softness and self-indulgence of the body, on the one hand, and of intellectual pride and independence, on the other. Let us diligently follow him with our prayers and sacrifices, for his sake and for the love that we bore him whilst on earth; let us also do our best to imitate him in our lives and conversation, for our own sake, and that we may the more surely rejoin him in heaven; and let us pray God that, when our turn comes, it may find us as well prepared as he was, and that our last end may be like his.

THE END.

www.ingramcontent.com/pod-product-compliance
Lightning Source LLC
Chambersburg PA
CBHW021200230426
43667CB00006B/486